The easy Guide to Your First Walt Disney World Visit 2014

Dave Shute & Josh Humphrey

Theme Park Press

Theme Park Press publishes its books in a variety of print and electronic formats. Some content that appears in one format may not appear in another.

Editor: Bob McLain
Layout: Artisanal Text
Cover Design: Emily White

ISBN 978-1-941500-06-4
10 9 8 7 6 5 4 3 2 1
Printed in the United States of America

Theme Park Press | **www.ThemeParkPress.com**
Address queries to bob@themeparkpress.com

To my mom and dad, for introducing me to Disneyland, Disney World...and everything else —Dave

To my mom, dad, brother, and friend(s)—without your help and guidance this would probably be a prison memoir rather than a Walt Disney World guidebook —Josh

Contents

Introduction

Congratulations. You are about to embark on a trip filled with magic and memories to one of the world's most popular vacation destinations. But with a Walt Disney World trip comes hundreds of decisions, from when to go to where to stay to what to eat to which attractions to experience. Walt Disney World spans more than 39 square miles and includes four major theme parks, two water parks, an expansive shopping and dining district, a 24-screen movie theater, more than 20 Disney-operated resorts, dozens of restaurants, hundreds of attractions, and a whole lot more.

That's where we come in. This book will prepare you and your family to make the best choices, eat at the restaurants that provide the most value, make sure you experience the best Disney has to offer, eliminate as much time waiting in line as possible, and guarantee that your experience at Walt Disney World is magical and stress-free.

This guide is written specifically for the first time visitor, with the idea that this may be your only opportunity to visit Walt Disney World. Whether that's due to budget constraints, finite vacation time, or concern that dad isn't going to don those Mickey Ears without a fight, the reality is that many people are planning that "once-in-a-lifetime" vacation. (Just to be safe, though, we suggest you budget for "The easy Guide to Your Second Walt Disney World Vacation". You're not going to be the first family that's already planning the next trip by lunch. And you won't be the last.)

Why this book in particular, you ask? Dave and Josh share thousands of theme park visits, hundreds of hotel rooms stays, and far more theme park meals than either of them would probably like to remember. Their experience culminates in this carefully crafted guidebook designed to be the framework for every step of your vacation planning. Both are firm believers that a little planning goes a long way. By spending time mulling the many options now, you'll set yourself up for the best vacation possible.

Sit back, relax, and enjoy the planning!

How to Use This Book

This chapter has two purposes: introducing the topics of the rest of the book and boiling down our recommendations into an easy-to-digest list. The chapters that follow it offer detailed information on the whys and hows behind our recommendations. For example, you may be interested only in eating at one or two sit-down restaurants. Instead of forcing you to read through a hundred reviews, we've listed the best values and the most immersive experiences here in an effort to speed up and simplify the planning process. And you never know, as you read the later reviews of our favorite restaurants, something else might catch your eye.

While you can skip around the book, we do suggest consuming the full text from beginning to end—perhaps a chapter per night with the help of a glass of wine and a roasty, toasty fire. The chapters build on each other, with decisions made during Chapters 2 and 3 affecting the choices you make in Chapters 4 and following. Chapters 8 and 9 come full circle and serve as the road map for your entire trip.

Changes, corrections, updates, links to larger color versions of key charts, and such, can be found at YOURFIRSTVISIT.NET/EASY-GUIDE-2014-CHANGES or at EASYWDW.COM/EASY-GUIDE.

Why Age and Height Matter [Chapter 2]

Children of all ages enjoy wonderful visits to Walt Disney World every single day of the year. However, if this may be your kids' only childhood visit, consider going when your youngest child is at least 8 or 9, and your shortest child at least 48 inches tall.

Many of Walt Disney World's best and most popular attractions require riders to be 48" tall, and kids around the third-grade-age are mature enough to appreciate the layers and nuances of each Disney experience. Those already planning to return may want to start earlier, when the kids are younger and all aspects of the Disney magic are open to them. While toddlers and younger kids are charmed and enamored with the Disney princesses, older kids may be less enthusiastic about a sit-down meal with Belle and Cinderella. Starting young offers an opportunity to enjoy many varied trips as the kids get older. But starting too young and too short on a once-in-a-lifetime trip means passing on several of Disney World's best rides. Chapter 2 describes how easy it is to design an itinerary with kids (or adults) of any age.

How Long to Stay [Chapter 3]

Wonderful Walt Disney World vacations come in all shapes and sizes, with guests enjoying trips that last anywhere from just one day to as long as several weeks. However, for a once in a lifetime trip, we recommend spending nine days in Orlando.

Guests planning to return enjoy the ability to ease into visiting the theme parks with shorter trips of four or so days, knowing they can catch missed attractions and experiences in the future. Those planning once-in-a-lifetime style vacations are best served pushing their stay to eight or nine days. This affords the opportunity to enjoy most of the best of Walt Disney World, and also allows a mixture of longer days in the theme parks tempered by more relaxing downtime back at the resort. While a longer trip will be more expensive than a shorter one, fixed travel costs and the way Disney prices tickets make the per-day costs of a longer trip significantly lower.

Shorter stays are often rewarding and enjoyable for everyone involved, but the limited time necessitates skipping key experiences and often requires a more ambitious schedule with fewer opportunities to relax.

When to Go [Chapter 4]

If you can, visit Disney World at some point between the day after the Martin Luther King Day holiday in January until the Thursday before President's Day in February, or the two weeks beginning the Sunday after Thanksgiving.

In picking dates, it's important to consider crowd levels, pricing, weather, possible refurbishments, and special events. Our specialty is honing in on the less crowded times to visit, when wait times are lower at attractions, lines are shorter at stores and dining venues, and there's less congestion inside the parks. Lower crowds mean being able to do more in a less stressful environment. From there, we typically prioritize lower resort pricing, followed by weather, refurbishments, and special events.

Based on these factors—but especially low crowds and lower prices—we recommend the following weeks:

- From the day after the Martin Luther King Day holiday in January until the Thursday before President's Day in February
- The last week of February through the first week of March
- The week that begins the Sunday after Easter until mid-May
- From the day after Labor Day through the rest of September
- The last two weeks of October
- November after Veterans Day until the Saturday before Thanksgiving
- The two weeks beginning the Sunday after Thanksgiving

Among these, Josh especially recommends the late January and early February dates, with the lowest prices, comfortable daytime temperatures, and some of the lowest crowds of the year. Dave prefers the two weeks after Thanksgiving, which marry below average-crowds and prices with Disney World's astonishing Christmas displays and offerings like the Osborne Lights, Holidays Around the World, and Mickey's Very Merry Christmas Party.

Those embarking on a possible once-in-a-lifetime trip should note that the peak of the hurricane season ends in early October, and that a few rides are almost invariably closed for refurbishments in January and early February.

If these dates won't work, Chapter 4 offers a blow-by-blow overview of everything to expect all year long.

Where to Stay [Chapter 5]

Stay at Disney's Art of Animation, Pop Century, Port Orleans French Quarter, Port Orleans Riverside, Grand Floridian, Wilderness Lodge, or Contemporary Resort.

We suggest that you stay in a Disney-owned resort hotel. While more expensive than hotels operated by third parties, they are also typically:

- Much more fun
- Much more convenient
- Much more "Disney"

The Disney-owned hotels also offer unique perks. The most advantageous perks include:

- Free airport transport to and from your hotel via Disney's Magical Express.
- Free and frequent transport from your hotel to the parks, water-parks, and Downtown Disney.
- Free parking at both your hotel and the parks.
- The right to book dining ten days further out than non-Disney guests, which can be critical for high-demand meals like dinner at Be Our Guest Restaurant.
- The right to book FastPass+ reservations for key attractions beginning 60 days in advance of arrival. At press-time, non-Disney guests can only book these 30 days in advance.
- Access to the various Disney Dining Plans, which are a convenient budgeting tool even if they often don't present much actual savings.

Perhaps even more important than any of these quantifiable perks is the comfort and safety of staying inside the "Disney bubble", far removed from the hustle, bustle, and worry of the outside world. Staying on property is the easiest way to forget about life's problems and truly enjoy an immersive experience together. While a vacation staying off-site is generally less expensive at first blush, consider additional expenses like resort fees, car rental, and the price of your time. There is no more convenient way to experience Walt Disney World for the first time than staying at one of their resorts. There is a reason Disney commands premium prices and why so many return visitors stay on property over and over again. Strongly consider the additional cost of an on-property stay and find out for yourself.

Specifically, we recommend, depending on budget:

VALUE RESORTS

Art of Animation, Pop Century

These resorts are among the least expensive on property, offer dedicated bus service, have great food courts, and newer rooms. Art of Animation is the newest Disney resort on property, and Pop Century is a short walk away.

MODERATE RESORTS

Port Orleans French Quarter, Port Orleans Riverside

French Quarter enjoys the smallest footprint of the moderate-level resorts and all rooms are just a few minutes away from the resort's amenities, including the bus stop, food court, boat dock, and resort concierge. Riverside is much larger, but offers better amenities, including a table service restaurant, a more robust feature pool, several quiet pools, and prettier surroundings.

DELUXE RESORTS

Grand Floridian, Wilderness Lodge, Contemporary

The Grand Floridian is Disney's flagship resort and its most opulent, providing several of its nicest restaurants, beautiful pool and garden areas, and a convenient location to Magic Kingdom. Its rooms were refurbished in early 2014. Wilderness Lodge is considerably less expensive and its woodsy atmosphere and stunning lobby may be more appealing to some guests, but its rooms are smaller and it's a bit less convenient across Bay Lake from Magic Kingdom. We love its lush public areas and variety of restaurants. The Contemporary is a magical space and just a short walk away from Magic Kingdom. Theme park view rooms in the tower look over Cinderella Castle and the monorail zooms through the center of the resort all day.

Note: The Polynesian will join this list after construction is completed in early 2015.

Chapter 5 includes in-depth reviews of every Disney-owned hotel.

How to Spend Your Time [Chapter 6]

Set daily plans from the example itineraries and "cheat sheets" we provide.

Planning your time at Walt Disney World can be easily broken down into three parts:

- Dividing your days among the parks
- Picking the best parks for each day
- Setting your plan for each park day

There are two different easy ways to use this book to plan your time at Walt Disney World, each designed around Disney's new FastPass+ program:

- For those who can use them as a starting point, we provide sample 9-day, Saturday-arrival itineraries, and
- For everybody else, we provide "cheat sheets" for designing your visits that work for both younger and older kids, and for longer and shorter trips.

Here's an excerpt from one of the example itineraries:

Meals:	Wednesday	Thursday
Breakfast	*Hotel Room**	*Hotel Room**
Lunch	Chef Mickey's 11a	Hotel Counter
Dinner	Magic Kingdom or Hotel Counter	Hollywood Studios Counter
Parks, Etc:		
Early Morning	Off	Off
Late Morning	Off	Off
Early Afternoon	At Magic Kingdom by noon	At Hollywood Studios by noon
Late Afternoon	Magic Kingdom	Hollywood Studios
Evening	Magic Kingdom	Hollywood Studios
Late Evening		
Notes:		
Parade	Afternoon Parade	
Fireworks	Wishes	Fantasmic
Park-Open Target	n/a	n/a
FastPass+ Target	Space Mountain	Toy Story Midway Mania

And here's an example from one of the Cheat Sheets:

Late Arrival Touring at the Animal Kingdom (with 6pm or Later Close and Fastpass+)

1. Arrive between 10:30am and 11am. Schedule FP+ at Expedition Everest (12:30pm–1:30pm), Adventurers Outpost Mickey and Minnie Meet (1:30pm–2:30pm), and Kali River Rapids (2:30pm–3:30pm).
2. Visit Oasis Exhibits until 11:15am.
3. See It's Tough to be a Bug: 11:15am–11:30am.
4. See Finding Nemo the Musical: 12pm–12:45pm.
5. Ride Expedition Everest with FastPass+: 12:50pm–1:05pm.
6. Have lunch. Yak & Yeti and Flame Tree Barbecue are closest.
7. Meet Mickey and Minnie at Adventurers Outpost with Fast-Pass+: 2pm–2:15pm.
8. Walk Maharajah Jungle Trek: 2:20pm–2:45pm.
9. Ride Kali River Rapids with FastPass+: 2:50pm–3:10pm.
10. Ride Kilimanjaro Safaris: 3:20pm–3:50pm.

Chapter 6 includes in-depth reviews of all the theme park attractions and explains theme park touring strategy in detail.

Where to Eat [Chapter 7]

Target your dining venues based on our recommendations, our reviews, or simply where you are when you're hungry!

First-time family visitors to Walt Disney World need to know three things about dining:

1. Several dining venues are among the most memorable and delightful experiences Walt Disney Word has to offer.
2. Table service reservations open 180 days in advance, and availability at the most sought-after restaurants is gobbled up almost immediately.
3. Disney World dining is expensive. Expect to pay 25 to 40% more on-property than you would for comparable meals off-property. For most (but not all) visitors, the Disney Dining Plan won't save any money.

For families, we recommend:

- The Princess meals: **Cinderella's Royal Table** at the Magic Kingdom and **Akershus Royal Banquet Hall** at Epcot. The first has the better setting, the second is much less expensive.
- Dining with Tigger, Pooh, and friends at the **Crystal Palace** in the Magic Kingdom.
- Dining with Mickey and friends at **Chef Mickey's** at Disney's Contemporary Resort and **'Ohana** breakfast at Disney's Polynesian Resort.
- Dining in the Beast's Castle at **Be Our Guest Restaurant** in Magic Kingdom.
- Various degrees of wait-staff induced silliness at **50's Prime Time Café** at Disney's Hollywood Studios and **Whispering Canyon** at Disney's Wilderness Lodge.
- **The Hoop-Dee-Doo Musical Revue**, a silly, energetic dinner show with interactive elements and plenty of audience participation at Disney's Fort Wilderness Resort.
- Exotic settings in the local versions of national chain restaurants like the **Rainforest Café**, in both Disney's Animal Kingdom and Downtown Disney, and **T-Rex** in Downtown Disney.

For couples looking for the most romantic atmosphere and the best food, we suggest:

- **California Grill**—located on the 15th floor of the Contemporary Resort, it offers breathtaking views of Magic Kingdom during the evening fireworks, in addition to a great menu focused on fresh ingredients, sushi, and contemporary cocktails.
- **Artist Point**—nestled inside Wilderness Lodge, it is themed to the restaurants found in the great National Park lodges of the Northwest. Buffalo, salmon, and a terrific mushroom soup and berry cobbler are menu mainstays.
- **Victoria & Albert's**—offering impeccable service and astonishing attention to detail, dinner at this Grand Floridian restaurant is a truly memorable experience.

Chapter 7 includes advice on the Disney Dining Plan and in-depth reviews of all the major Disney World dining options, plus suggestions on the best quick service options.

Which Tickets to Buy and How Much to Budget [Chapter 8]

Big budgets allow for more extravagances, but a vacation can be tailored to just about any budget. Realistically, a family of four is looking at spending more than $4,000.

"What should we budget?" is the hardest simple question for this book to answer. This is because smaller families, families whose kids are younger, families staying at a less expensive hotel, families going during a less expensive week, and families on shorter trips will pay less. Larger families, families where everyone is over nine, families staying at a more expensive hotel, families going during a more expensive week, and families on longer trips will pay more.

- A parent and one younger child with three days of tickets and three nights in a value resort during one of the less expensive price seasons could spend as little as $1,300 in Orlando.
- Add another parent and another younger child and this trip jumps to $2,100.
- Stretch the visit out to the 8 nights we recommend for "only visits" and the in-Orlando price exceeds $4,000.
- Stay this long in one of the more expensive deluxe resorts instead, and the price is more than $7,500.
- Shift to the most expensive times to visit at this deluxe resort and add $1,700 more.

(All the figures are before transportation costs and souvenirs.)

The good news is that budgeting for a specific trip is relatively straightforward, once you've made the key decisions that are outlined over the course of this book.

How to Set Everything Up and Get Everything Done [Chapter 9]

Your plans should be firm at least 181 days before your arrival date. Then see the To-Do List for exactly what to do, and when, to prepare for your trip.

There are three key dates to consider:

- Restaurant reservations open for booking 180 days before a potential dining date

- For those staying at a Disney-owned resort, FastPass+ reservations can be booked beginning 60 days before their arrival date

- For everyone else, FastPass+ reservations can be booked beginning 30 days before planned use

Building a To-Do List is keyed to these three dates because booking as early as possibly will result in the widest selection of experiences being available. Chapter 9 covers exactly how and when to make these decisions.

Disney World planning may feel like a daunting task. Don't worry. You're in good hands. The following chapters are a step-by-step walkthrough of the entire planning process, offering just the right amount of detail so you can make informed decisions. When everything goes according to plan and the group asks, "How did you make this trip so wonderful?" you can respond with a smile, "It was pretty easy, actually."

Why Age and Height Matter

Children of all ages enjoy Walt Disney World in their own ways, whether it be meeting the characters, riding the thrill rides, or blending both roller coasters and princess breakfasts into an overall itinerary. When deciding whether it's time to book a trip, consider the ages and heights of the kid(s) and what they can and will be able to experience once they arrive. If one or more of the kids are under 48 inches tall, they will run into attractions they aren't able to experience due to height restrictions. If they don't have the intellectual and emotional maturity of the typical eight year old, other rides for which they are tall enough may be too frightening, or just a little too sophisticated for them to fully enjoy.

If your kids aren't eight or older and over 48" tall, and this is a once-in-a-lifetime trip, you need to decide whether you should wait until they are tall enough and mature enough to enjoy everything Walt Disney World offers. Even with height restrictions and the possibility that the content of an attraction like Ellen's Energy Adventure will fly over their heads, younger and shorter kids typically have as much fun as their older counterparts. With a little planning, it's easy to design an itinerary around the unique needs of kids of any age.

This chapter first discusses trips with kids of various ages. It then covers handling a single visit with kids of wildly different ages.

Visits by Age and Height

PRESCHOOLERS

Preschool age children especially delight in the magic of meeting the Disney characters. They are young enough that they still believe they are meeting *the* Cinderella and *the* Winnie the Pooh. Pictures of the kids entranced with characters like Snow White and the Seven Dwarfs will turn into memories that last a lifetime. Some kids remain shy or apprehensive about meeting the characters. Mickey is, after all, an alarming five-feet tall. Goofy, with his oversize top hat, stretches over six feet. With apprehensive and shy kids, run a search on YouTube for "Disney World characters" and watch some interactions leading up to the trip. This will familiarize the kids with what to expect and reduce many of the first-time jitters and the tears that accompany them. While preschoolers will be too short or young for many of the premier attractions, there's still plenty for them to experience, especially at Magic Kingdom.

But they shouldn't try everything. Some attractions are simply too scary or intense for preschoolers. To help you figure out what is what, we have sorted every attraction based on how well kids of varying ages are likely to enjoy them.

Comprehensive Guide to Rides

Key: E= Epcot AK= Animal Kingdom HS= Hollywood Studios MK= Magic Kingdom
Underline: Particular favorite of older kids; *italic: particularly skippable for older kids*

FOR PRE-SCHOOL KIDS

	Skippable	Mixed Reactions	Favorites
Avoid	E: Captain EO, *Gran Fiesta Tour (Mexico)*, Innovations, *Journey Into Imagination With Figment* HS: Magic of Disney Animation MK: Carousel of Progress, The Hall of Presidents	E: Impressions de France, O Canada!, Reflections of China, Agent P's World Showcase Adventure MK: Stitch's Great Escape	E: The American Adventure, Mission: Space, Soarin, Test Track AK: Dinosaur, Expedition Everest HS: Fantasmic, Rock n Roller Coaster, The Tower of Terror MK: The Haunted Mansion, Space Mountain, Splash Mountain
Mixed Reactions	E: *The Circle of Life*, Living With the Land, *Norway Film (Norway)* AK: *Conservation Station*, Primeval Whirl, *Wildlife Express Train* MK: Country Bear Jamboree, *Enchanted Tiki Room*	E: Ellen's Energy Adventure, The Seas with Nemo and Friends AK: Pangani Forest Exploration Trail HS: Studios Backlot Tour, Lights Motors Action Stunt Show, American Idol Experience MK: The Barnstormer, Seven Dwarfs Mine Train, Swiss Family Treehouse	E: Spaceship Earth AK: It's Tough to be a Bug, Maharaja Jungle Trek Jones Epic Stunt Spectacular, Walt Disney: One Man's Dream MK: Big Thunder Mountain Railroad, Pirates of the Caribbean
Best-Loved	AK: *The Boneyard*, Dinorama, Triceratops Spin HS: *Honey I Shrunk the Kids Movie Set*, Disney Junior: Live on Stage MK: Astro Orbiter, Prince Charming Regal Carousel, Dumbo the Flying Elephant, The Magic Carpets of Aladdin, Mad Tea Party, Tomorrowland Speedway, Tomorrowland Transit Authority PeopleMover, Tom Sawyer Island, WDW Railroad	E: Maelstrom AK: Afternoon Parade, Finding Nemo the Musical, Flights of Wonder HS: Voyage of the Little Mermaid MK: It's a Small World, Liberty Belle Riverboat, The Many Adventures of Winnie the Pooh, Monsters Inc. Laugh Floor, Under the Sea: Journey of the Little Mermaid	E: Illuminations, Turtle Talk with Crush AK: Festival of the Lion King, Kali River Rapids, Kilimanjaro Safaris HS: Beauty and the Beast, Muppet Vision 3-D, Star Tours, Toy Story Mania MK: Afternoon Parade, Buzz Lightyear, Enchanted Tales with Belle, Evening Parade, Jungle Cruise, Mickey's Philharmagic, Peter Pan, Wishes Fireworks
	Skippable	**Mixed Reactions**	**Favorites**

FOR THIRD GRADERS AND UP

For example, in the bottom left box we have The Boneyard, which is a richly themed playground at Disney's Animal Kingdom. Younger kids love to play there, but most older kids will find it juvenile. The upper right box contains several of Disney's best attractions, many of which aren't suitable for younger children due to height restrictions or scary content. Most older kids (and their parents) love these attractions, which is why they fall into "favorites" for third graders and up, and into "avoid" for preschoolers.

With preschoolers, try to match their interests, stamina, and routines with what the family plans to accomplish...or you'll have the joy of experiencing the same tantrums every other parent is enjoying come 3pm.

When the meltdowns begin, it's not uncommon for Josh to turn to Dave and say, "It must be 3 o'clock." Indeed, even more common than Mickey bars and WDW t-shirts are the afternoon hissy fits. Be realistic about how long the kids are going to be able to go. While Disney World might be a magical place, pixie dust does not seem to increase kids' stamina or reduce their inclination to break down when they're overstimulated and ready for a nap. Plan a daily afternoon break for when crowds, wait times, and heat peak. This will rejuvenate the kids and their parents and prepare them for a fun and relaxing evening back in the parks.

YOUNGER SCHOOL-AGE KIDS

Kids between the ages of five and eight are young enough that they still enjoy most character meets and some of the other sillier entertainment that older kids may have lost interest in. They are also beginning to approach the height required to enjoy Disney's more thrilling major attractions.

Disney World Rides Excluded by Height

Children less than 38" tall can't ride:	Children less than 40" tall can't ride:	Children less than 44" tall can't ride:	Children less than 48" tall can't ride:	Height Requirement/ Comments
Rock 'n' Roller Coaster	Rock 'n' Roller Coaster	Rock 'n' Roller Coaster	Rock 'n' Roller Coaster	48" One of three most popular rides at Studios
Primeval Whirl	Primeval Whirl	Primeval Whirl	Primeval Whirl	48"
Space Mountain	Space Mountain	Space Mountain		44" One of two most popular rides at Magic Kingdom
Mission: Space	Mission: Space	Mission: Space		44"
Expedition Everest	Expedition Everest	Expedition Everest		44" One of two most popular rides at Animal Kingdom
Big Thunder Mountain	Big Thunder Mountain			40" One of two most popular rides at Magic Kingdom
Splash Mountain	Splash Mountain			40"
Stitch's Great Escape	Stitch's Great Escape			40"
Soarin	Soarin			40" One of two most popular rides at Epcot
Test Track	Test Track			40" One of two most popular rides at Epcot
Star Tours	Star Tours			40"
Tower of Terror	Tower of Terror			40" One of three most popular rides at Studios
Dinosaur	Dinosaur			40"
Kali River Rapids				38"
Seven Dwarfs Mine Train				38"

The chart illustrates which attractions shorter kids are disqualified from riding. Unfortunately, this chart could double as a list of Disney World's best and most popular attractions (with the exception of Stitch's Great Escape), including the headliners at each park. With a single trip on the horizon, if you can't wait until the kids are 48" tall, consider waiting until they are at least 44" tall. They'll then be eligible for every ride on property but two. And the two they aren't eligible for aren't necessarily deal break-ers. Primeval Whirl is an off-the-shelf carnival ride at Animal Kingdom. Rock 'n' Roller Coaster is located inside a relatively nondescript building at the end of a long road on Sunset Boulevard at Hollywood Studios. Simply avoid it and the kids won't feel like they're missing anything.

Keep in mind that "tall enough for" doesn't necessarily translate into "ready for". Moreover, many of Disney World's best attractions are like a Pixar movie in that there are layers of substance and humor that guests of all ages enjoy for different reasons. Kids between 5 and 8 understand and enjoy the attractions on a basic level, but nuances and deeper meanings are often lost.

KIDS BETWEEN 8 AND 88

Kids who are eight or older are tall enough, old enough, and mature enough to enjoy all of Disney World's rides and entertainment. Unfortunately, they may be getting too old to be swept up in the magic of breakfast with Cinderella inside the Castle. Most remain happy to participate, if for no other reason than it makes mom happy.

With just one planned trip, consider waiting until the kids are around this age. Returning guests that begin visiting when their kids are younger enjoy the widest range of experiences over many years. Cherish the memories of their first visit with Mickey Mouse and look forward to pretending you're not afraid when junior first starts begging to ride Expedition Everest.

Trips with Children of Very Different Ages

There are several ways to cope with and plan trips around kids of wildly different ages and maturity levels. The underlying problem, as illustrated in the previous chart, is that kids of varying ages enjoy different things. This is not unique to Walt Disney World. At home, young kids may still enjoy playing with Legos, while older kids have moved on to Xbox Ones and Playstation 4s. At Disney World, kids may occasionally want to or need to split up in order to enjoy and experience certain attractions. Fortunately, Disney has made this relatively easy by building play-grounds and diversions aimed at younger kids in close proximity to the thrillers. Here are a few other ideas:

Take advantage of Rider Switch. Commonly referred to as "Child Swap", Rider Switch allows those eligible and willing to experience an attraction with a height requirement to ride, while others either wait alongside them in line or do something else. Most attractions require the group to approach the attraction's entrance and present the child too short or too leery to board the ride. The Cast Member will hand the group a Rider Switch pass that looks similar to legacy paper FASTPASSes. The members of the group experiencing the attraction wait in line. Members not experiencing the attraction may wait at the same time or head elsewhere. Once the group has experienced the attraction, up to three people can use the Rider Switch pass to enter the FastPass+ line, eliminating much of the wait. This can include a member or two of the original group. For example, let's say a family of four wants to experience Test Track, but one child is too short. Parent 1 and the older child wait in line and ride, while Parent 2 and the younger child head off to Innoventions to play. Once Parent 1 and the older child are off Test Track, up to three members of the family may use the Rider Switch at the FastPass+ line. That means the older child that previously rode Test Track can ride again alongside Parent 2. Parent 1 can then take the younger child elsewhere—perhaps to the interactive play area at Mission: SPACE's exit.

Have part of the family focus on rides for older kids, and the rest on attractions designed for the youngest. Split the family up, with older kids and a parent on one set of rides, and the littler ones on another age-appropriate set. This works particularly well if one parent has little interest in the thrill rides and coasters anyway. You can build completely different itineraries and FastPass+ selections for the two groups, or have some experiences in common and some different.

Consider childcare services. Disney vets use an independent in-room babysitting service called "Kid's Nite Out" for kids between six months and twelve years old. Rates start at $16 per hour for one child and go up to $24 an hour for four children (four hour minimum). There's a $2/hour surcharge after 9pm and a one-time transportation fee of $10. Babysitters arrive armed with age-appropriate games, crafts, and books.

In addition, Children's Activity Centers are available for potty-trained kids between 4 and 12 at select resorts:

- Simba's Cubhouse at Disney's Animal Kingdom Lodge
- Never Land Club at Disney's Polynesian Resort (re-opening as Club Disney in June 2014)
- Cub's Den at Disney's Wilderness Lodge
- Sandcastle Club at Disney's Yacht Club and Disney Beach Club Resort
- Camp Dolphin at Walt Disney World Dolphin and Walt Disney World Swan

Rates are $11/hour with a two-hour minimum. Call 407-939-3463 for more information or to reserve. These services are available to all guests, but are most convenient for those staying nearby or for families that want to drop off a youngster before heading to some of Disney's finer dining choices.

Families visiting with kids of any and all ages thoroughly enjoy their Walt Disney World vacations, but keep in mind that the experience will be quite different depending on who it is you're taking. Groups consisting of families with kids of varying ages will need to make some compromises, but the good news is that the vast majority of your time can and will be spent together as a family.

How Long to Stay

This chapter addresses the decision-making process for how long to stay at Walt Disney World. Guests planning to return enjoy the ability to ease into visiting the theme parks with shorter trips of four or so days, knowing they can catch missed attractions and experiences in the future. Those planning once-in-a-lifetime style vacations are best served pushing their length of stay to eight or nine days. This affords the opportunity to enjoy much of the best of Walt Disney World, and also allows a mixture of longer days in the theme parks tempered by more relaxing downtime back at the resort. Shorter stays are often rewarding and enjoyable for everyone involved, but the limited time necessitates skipping key experiences and requires a more ambitious schedule with fewer opportunities to relax.

We'll first cover the basics: budgets, time, and the ages of the kids. Then, in the next section, we'll address the importance of taking time away from the parks to relax, followed by a section about allocating time for an "only" trip.

How Long to Stay: Budgets, Time Available, and Ages of the Kids

Most prospective guests will choose a length of stay based on three primary factors: budget, time constraints, and kids' ages. Mom might only be able to get a Monday through Wednesday off work, necessitating a shorter five-day trip that begins with travel early Saturday and ends with travel late Wednesday. A budget might be stretched too thin for a seven-night stay at a moderate resort, but work with fewer nights at a value (Chapter 5 explains the difference between "moderates" and "values"). A family with very young kids may find that a delightful trip lasts only three or four days.

The good news is that guests with a wide range of budgets and trip lengths can thoroughly enjoy their visits. The bad news is that, like most things, (within reason) more is better.

A longer trip means more relaxing, more theme park visits, more Mickey ice cream bars, and, ultimately, more flexibility. Longer trips also have lower per-day costs. Most travel costs are fixed regardless of how many days you spend in Orlando. If airfare and related costs are $1500, the per-day travel cost on a five-day vacation is $300. On a ten-day trip, the per-day travel cost drops in half, to only $150 per day. Second, adding the fifth to tenth day on your Disney World theme park ticket is only an additional $10.65 (including tax) per day. A four-day child base ticket costs $291 with tax. That's $73 per day. An eight-day child base ticket costs $334 with tax. That's just $42 per day. Of course, days five through eight come with other costs like dining, souvenirs, and lodging, but one long stay is often much less expensive than two shorter stays.

If this is a once-in-a-lifetime visit, we recommend trying to stretch your vacation dollars to eight nights and nine days. This allows for the equivalent of a full day at Animal Kingdom and Hollywood Studios, in addition to two days at Epcot and two or three full days at Magic Kingdom. The longer trip length also offers flexibility in late arrivals and early departures. You may elect to leave Epcot one afternoon at 3pm to head off to the Grand Floridian Resort & Spa for afternoon tea with Alice from *Alice in Wonderland*. With an eight-night stay, there's plenty of time to return to Epcot without fear of missing anything. On a four-night trip, there's more pressure to stay in the park and tour until the last member of the family drops. It's either that or potentially miss out on key attractions that could be made up with a longer stay.

If time and budget don't allow, a shorter trip can be perfectly enjoyable, particularly if you're already planning a trip farther down the road. Two trips spread out over the years offer an opportunity to enjoy two potentially different experiences, while also providing more time to save for the hefty costs. (It also affords a great opportunity to purchase two of our guidebooks, which is pretty fantastic in itself.)

Deciding on a trip length that maximizes value and enjoyment varies a bit based on age:

KIDS FIVE AND YOUNGER tend to enjoy Magic Kingdom the most, where Fantasyland and most entertainment offerings cater specifically to their heights and maturity levels. Kids at that age may have no interest in visiting Downtown Disney or Animal Kingdom. In this situation, a three- or four-day trip focused on visiting Magic Kingdom offers plenty of time to visit over multiple half days, in addition to affording opportunities to head back to the resort for naps.

MOST KIDS BETWEEN FIVE AND EIGHT will still prefer Magic Kingdom over the other major theme parks, but will get more out of trips to Animal Kingdom, Epcot, and Hollywood Studios. Plan to spend at least a half day at each of these three, pushing the number of theme park days up to five or six.

MOST KIDS EIGHT AND OLDER will be tall enough to ride every major attraction, including the thrill rides at each theme park, and mature enough to enjoy them all. Still plan at least two days at Magic Kingdom, but add full days at each of the other major theme parks (and, if you can, even more at Epcot) to take care of attractions like Soarin' and Rock 'n' Roller Coaster.

The Value of Time Away from the Parks

Many first-time visitors equate time away from the theme parks as time wasted or value lost. This seems logical on the surface. After all, if theme park tickets are going to cost $350 a pop, we sure as heck better be in the theme parks waiting in line for *something*. But don't make the most common rookie mistake.

Touring the theme parks in Florida, by their very nature, is exhausting—particularly during the unrelenting summer when it's 85 degrees by 10:30am. It's a lot of standing. It's a lot of walking. If the kids are in strollers, it's a lot of pushing. In fact, it's not uncommon at all for guests to rack up ten or more miles a day walking through the theme park. Just a quick lap around Epcot's World Showcase Lagoon is 1.2 miles. And that's without doing anything!

Time spent together back at the resort hotel will likely be some of the most fun, most rewarding experiences of the trip. One of Josh's favorite memories from his first visit to Disney World is sitting on the beach at the Polynesian with his brother, mom, and dad holding a Mickey ice cream bar in one hand and a hot cocoa in the other. Dave has fond memories of playing on the beach at the Contemporary with his mom and sister while his dad napped back in the room. Spending time with loved ones is a big part of a vacation and spending relaxing time together with Walt Disney World as the backdrop is an integral part of the experience.

Afternoon breaks are particularly necessary with young kids (or dads) who will be bombarded with sensory overload virtually every moment they spend in the parks. A child that's spent a few hours back at the pool will be a much happier camper when it comes time to stake out a spot for IllumiNations that night. And, as an added bonus, those afternoons are also the busiest and hottest parts of the day at the theme parks. Where would you rather be? In a 25-minute-long line for a $4 Smartwater in the scorching afternoon sun, or back at the resort sipping a Mai Tai on the beach?

If It's Your Only Visit, Aim for Nine Days in Orlando

Returning visitors have the flexibility of choosing to spend less time at the theme parks and more time enjoying their resort and the other amenities Walt Disney World offers. But the four major theme parks—the Magic Kingdom, Epcot, Disney's Hollywood Studios, and Disney's Animal Kingdom—are the heart of a Walt Disney World experience. To fully appreciate the best they have to offer, you need about eight days:

- About a day each at the Animal Kingdom and Hollywood Studios
- At least a full day and an additional evening at Epcot
- Two to three days at the Magic Kingdom
- A couple of days taking it easy

Add it up and you're looking at about seven full days in Orlando with a travel day on both ends, bringing the total number of vacation days up to nine.

SHORTER "ONLY" VISITS

Shorter "only" visits are doable with some compromises:

FIVE FULL DAYS To see most of the best of Disney World, five full days in the parks are about the minimum—two in the Magic Kingdom, and one more in each of the other three parks. Working some of this park time into your arrival or departure days will give you some needed time off in the middle of your visit.

SIX FULL DAYS Adding another day lets you have more time off and more time at Epcot.

LONGER "ONLY" VISITS

If you are fortunate enough to enjoy more than nine days in Orlando, first prioritize time spent away from the parks. Time is a luxury at Walt Disney World, and more time means more sleeping in, more late park arrivals, and more time relaxing at the pool. Late arrivals are particularly advantageous with the invention of FastPass+, which offers the ability to schedule three high priority attractions for later in the day, far in advance of setting foot inside the theme park. For example, with two days of late arrivals at Epcot, you can schedule Soarin', Character Spot, and Spaceship Earth on day one, and Test Track, Mission: SPACE, and Maelstrom on day two. Show up at 11am and you'll be able to walk on six of the most popular attractions over those two days with minimal waits. Experiencing Soarin', Test Track, Mission: SPACE, Spaceship Earth, Character Spot, and Maelstrom over the course of just one day will require a very early morning, much more walking, and a carefully crafted plan. It's doable, but it requires a much longer, more intense day.

CONSIDERING ARRIVAL DAYS

If you are planning a nine-day visit, we suggest a trip that spans the nine days from Saturday to the following Sunday because it best fits the typical week off work. The sample itineraries presented in chapter six will guide you through planning such a visit.

Of course, flexible visitors may prefer to arrive another day of the week, for the sake of saving time and money. Disney World tends to be busiest on weekends as local passholders push up attendance. If possible, design your vacation to maximize the number of weekday theme park visits. As a bonus, Disney resort rates are typically higher on Friday and Saturday nights by $20 to $50. Avoiding these nights will save money and reduce waits.

Airfare is typically cheapest on Tuesdays, and there may be other travel expenses that can be reduced by traveling on certain days. Guests with flexible schedules should use services like KAYAK.COM or GOOGLE.COM/FLIGHTS to search out the cheapest or most convenient itinerary possible.

When deciding how long to stay, keep in mind that most travel costs are fixed, and the per-day cost of theme park tickets goes down as more days are added. Longer vacations allow more flexibility, in addition to providing more opportunities to experience everything Walt Disney World has to offer. Shorter Walt Disney World vacations tend to be more of a whirlwind experience. That isn't necessarily bad, but the go, go, go mentality often leaves first-time visitors thinking they need a vacation from their vacation upon returning home.

When to Go

In picking dates, it's important to consider crowd levels, pricing, weather, possible refurbishments, and special events. Our specialty is honing in on the less crowded times to visit, when wait times are lower at attractions, lines are shorter at stores and quick service venues, and there's less congestion inside the parks. Lower crowds mean being able to do more in a less stressful environment. From there, we typically prioritize resort pricing, followed by weather, refurbishments, and special events.

CROWDS Walt Disney World is the most crowded when hordes of U.S. school kids are out of school: from early June through the third week in August, Thanksgiving week, Christmas and New Year's weeks, President's Day week, the spring break month of March; and the weeks before and after Easter. Other dates see an ebb and flow of mostly low and moderate crowds, all noted in the month-by-month calendar that follows.

PRICING Disney resort pricing is constantly fluctuating, so much so that the same exact room can cost $203 one night and $259 the next night, as it does at Port Orleans Riverside from December 11-12. Picking less expensive dates may save $150 or more per night at the deluxe resorts. Disney calls periods of different prices "Price Seasons": value, regular, summer, fall, etc. Fortunately, the less crowded times are also often the least expensive.

WEATHER The main weather points that concern us are summer heat and humidity, erratic winter highs and lows, and the peak of the hurricane season from mid-August to early October. Many of the least crowded and least expensive stretches suffer from weather issues, but none are routinely as challenging as the heat and humidity of the crowded summer months.

REFURBISHMENTS Disney tends to announce refurbishments about eight weeks in advance, making it difficult to plan a vacation around an unexpected major refurbishment. Fortunately, refurbishments follow a pattern, and we've identified when they're less likely to occur. In addition, it's rare that more than one or two major attractions are closed at the same time.

SPECIAL EVENTS Certain guests, particularly those returning, may want to plan a vacation around a special event like Star Wars Weekends or the Epcot Food and Wine Festival. Our month-by-month calendar identifies these special events and offers some advice on taking advantage of them, or how best to avoid them, depending on your needs.

Based on these factors—but especially low crowds and lower prices—we recommend the following weeks throughout the year:

- From the day after the Martin Luther King Day holiday in January until the Thursday before President's Day in February
- The last week of February through the first week of March
- The week that begins the Sunday after Easter until mid-May
- September after Labor Day through the end of the month
- The last two weeks of October
- November after Veterans Day until the Saturday before Thanksgiving
- The two weeks beginning the Sunday after Thanksgiving

Among these, Josh especially recommends the late January and early February dates, with the lowest prices, comfortable day-time temperatures, and some of the lowest crowds of the year. Dave prefers the two weeks after Thanksgiving, which marry below average crowds and prices with Disney World's astonishing Christmas displays and offerings like the Osborne Lights, Holidays Around the World, and Mickey's Very Merry Christmas Party.

Those embarking on a possible once-in-a-lifetime trip should note that the peak of the hurricane season ends in early October, and that a few rides are almost invariably closed for refurbishments in January and early February.

This chapter begins with summaries of what you can expect of weekly crowds, resort prices, and weather.

Next, it presents detailed overviews of each of the months of the year, discussing prices, weather, crowds, refurbishments, special events, and recommended times to visit that month.

Finally, for first timers who may never return, it presents Dave's chart that ranks all the weeks of the year based on crowds, pricing, weather, and other essential variables.

Crowds and When to Go

When considering "low crowds", it's important to remember that Walt Disney World is comprised of four of the top ten busiest theme parks in the world, by overall attendance. Magic Kingdom averages around 46,000 guests per day. The days with the lowest attendance tend to see slightly north of 30,000 guests, while anything over 55,000 will result in much longer lines. Epcot averages about 30,000 guests per day. It's rare that the park sees fewer than 20,000 people, while anything above 35,000 will result in longer lines.

Each park suffers from bottlenecks and narrow walkways, in addition to succumbing to periodic mass exoduses from shows throughout the day. From there, certain attractions are extremely popular, with demand far outstripping supply. For example, let's take a look at Toy Story Mania at Disney's Hollywood Studios, one of the most popular rides in any theme park and often the one with the longest peak waits. The attraction moves through about 900 people an hour and the Studios' average attendance is around 27,500 people a day. On an average day with the Studios open from 9am–8pm, there are 9,900 total rides to share among 27,500 people. And it only takes 900 of those 27,500 people (or just 3.2%) in front of you to hit a 60-minute standby wait.

With exactly six rides, the headlining Studios' attractions see 40- to 70-minute peak waits even on the least crowded days. Don't be too discouraged, however. Just because everyone else waits 75 minutes in line doesn't mean you have to. Our touring tips and the cheat sheets that follow in Chapter Seven will reduce waits to virtually nothing.

In the chart on the following page, don't focus on small differences. Try to go during a lower crowd week, with a crowd ranking of four or less, and avoid higher crowd weeks, with rankings of eight or higher.

2014 Crowd Calendar

Week Beginning: Crowd Rankings

Prices and When to Go

The major prices at Walt Disney World that vary by season are hotel room costs. "Season" does not mean anything so simple as fall or winter. Disney changes prices much more frequently than that, and has a metastasizing group of invented seasonal names—e.g., not just Value Season, but also Value Season 1 and Value Season 2—to describe its price levels. Disney's price season names (excluding variants like Value Season 2 and some holiday weekends) are

- Value
- Fall
- Regular
- Summer
- Peak
- Easter
- Holiday

The first two seasons are always the lowest-priced, and the last three always the highest. Disney groups hotels into value, moderate, and deluxe resorts (more on this in the next chapter). At Disney's value resorts, Summer rates are much higher than Regular rates; at its moderates, Summer and Regular are about the same over a multi-day visit; and at deluxe resorts, Summer rates are lower than Regular rates. Moreover, deluxe seasons change according to a different calendar in the summer and fall than value and moderate seasons do.

For exact prices by day, search for "Mousesavers 2014 Disney World Room Rates" and follow the links. The chart on the following page shows the different resort prices at Walt Disney World over the year in 2014. It does not refer to the seasons themselves, as it's much more useful to show actual prices. The chart picks an example from each group, and to smooth out fluctuations that come from weekend upcharges, averages prices over an eight-night stay.

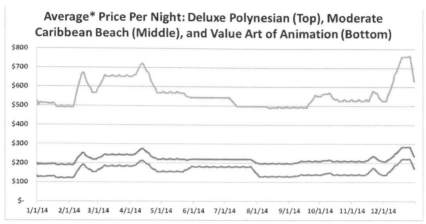

Average* Price Per Night: Deluxe Polynesian (Top), Moderate Caribbean Beach (Middle), and Value Art of Animation (Bottom)

*Average of next eight nights by arrival date; includes tax

Weather and When to Go

This chart illuminates the range of high temperatures at Disney World. The middle line is the average high. There's a 20% chance highs will be lower than the lower line, and a 20% chance that highs will be higher than the higher line. Note how large the range of temperatures is in the winter months.

Distribution of Disney World High Temperatures

Average (Middle), 20th and 80th Percentile High Temperatures

Month-by-Month Comments
On When to Go

January

COST With a few exceptions, January enjoys the least expensive resort pricing of the year. January 1, with Holiday season pricing, is among the most expensive nights of the year. The Friday-Sunday periods of Martin Luther King Jr. weekend and the WDW Marathon weekend see average pricing. (See later in this chapter for more on pricing.)

WEATHER It's the coldest month in Orlando, with erratic temperatures and an average high of 69 and an average low of 50 degrees. Historically, it rains on 22% of days.

CROWDS Many U.S. school districts continue winter break through the first week, causing some of the highest crowds of the year to persist through the first Saturday of the new year. Crowds are low the rest of the month, with two major exceptions. Marathon Weekend brings in thousands of runners and their families, but they have surprisingly little impact on theme park crowds, resulting in only average crowds. Martin Luther King Jr. weekend crowds are well above average and the highest crowd level we'll see until President's Day weekend in the middle of February. It's best avoided.

REFURBISHMENTS January usually sees the most refurbishments, including brief closures at most resort pools and typically lengthier closures at a few other attractions. Splash Mountain usually closes for at least a month beginning the second week. The vast majority of attractions remain operating.

SPECIAL EVENTS THAT MAY AFFECT CROWDS OR YOUR STAY:
- The WDW Marathon impacts transportation on the morning of the half- and full-marathons. It's best to take Disney transportation.
- Several holiday events, including the Osborne Lights at Hollywood Studios and Cinderella's Holiday Wish show at Magic Kingdom, continue through the first week in January.
- One of the water parks is typically closed through mid-March.
- Beginning in mid-January, avoid the large tour groups that become common.

BEST TIME TO VISIT January 21 on has cool weather, some of the lowest crowds of the year, and the lowest Disney hotel prices of the year.

February

COST The lowest pricing of the year continues up until the Thursday before President's Day weekend, when prices rise to the expensive Peak season. Peak pricing continues through the week following President's Day. Prices fall back to average beginning the last week of the month.

WEATHER The average high is 72 degrees and the average low 53, but temperatures are erratic and highs can get into the low 80s or dip well below 60. Precipitation is relatively low, but it does rain on about 23% of days.

CROWDS Crowds are below average to average through the Wednesday before President's Day weekend, when crowds are well above average (as well as on the week following it). Crowds return to average from the last week in February through the first week in March.

REFURBISHMENTS Most refurbishments will be completed by mid-February. A water park usually remains closed.

SPECIAL EVENTS THAT MAY AFFECT CROWDS OR YOUR STAY:

- The Princess Half Marathon is scheduled the weekend after President's Day. It affects transportation in the early morning on Sunday and keeps crowds above average until the Saturday following President's Day.
- Superbowl Sunday sees few locals visiting, reducing crowds.
- Valentine's Day makes it harder to secure dinner reservations, but does not affect attendance.
- The Atlanta Braves MLB baseball team returns to the ESPN Wide World of Sports Complex in mid-February for spring training.

BEST TIME TO VISIT A trip during the first two weeks that ends before peak season pricing goes into effect is best, with the lowest prices and some of the lowest crowds of the year.

March

COST The first week in March is Regular season with average pricing across the resorts. The rest is Peak season with some of the highest prices of the year outside of major holidays.

WEATHER Temperatures warm, but remain erratic. Expect highs anywhere from the mid-60s to the mid-80s with an average high of 77 and an average low of 57 degrees, with minimal precipitation.

CROWDS Expect average crowds the first week, followed by some of the heaviest crowds of the year the rest of the month due to spring breaks.

REFURBISHMENTS Pool closures remain common, and one water park usually remains closed until the middle of the month. Attraction closures are less common.

SPECIAL EVENTS THAT MAY AFFECT CROWDS OR YOUR STAY:

- The Epcot International Flower and Garden Festival begins the first week in March and continues through mid-May. The Festival brings millions of flowers, Disney-themed topiaries, and special activities around the Park, in addition to kiosks in World Showcase offering food and beverage samples that generally cost $2–$7 each. The Festival does not adversely affect daily crowds.

BEST TIME TO VISIT March 1–March 7 will have the lowest crowds and prices of the month.

April

COST Easter week, which comprises Easter Sunday and the week before, is one of the most expensive of the year. The week before Easter week will see Regular season pricing in years with late Easters, and peak season pricing in years with early Easters. Beginning a week after Easter, prices return to average.

WEATHER April warms up to some of the most comfortable weather of the year, with an average high of 82 degrees and an average low of 62. Precipitation remains low with chances at 18%.

CROWDS Heavy spring break crowds continue through one week after Easter Sunday. Beginning that Monday, average level crowds return through early May.

REFURBISHMENTS Pool closures are rare, and few attractions are typically closed.

SPECIAL EVENTS THAT MAY AFFECT CROWDS OR YOUR STAY:

- The Epcot International Flower and Garden Festival continues through April. See "March" for details.

BEST TIME TO VISIT Begin a trip at least one week after Easter Sunday when crowds and resort prices fall from some of the highest levels of the year to average.

May

COST Virtually all of May is Regular season, with average resort pricing. The last weekend typically moves to Summer season, when Value and

Moderate resort prices are higher than Regular, but lower than Peak. Deluxe prices during Summer season, which continues until mid-July, are actually lower than Regular season by a few dollars.

WEATHER Temperatures rise significantly in May, with an average high of 87 and an average low of 69 degrees. The weather gets wetter as you move closer to June.

CROWDS Crowds are average to slightly above average through the Thursday before Memorial Day Weekend. The earlier in May, the less crowded it will be. Memorial Day Weekend is busier than the rest of May, but not as busy as other major holidays like Easter.

REFURBISHMENTS Rare.

SPECIAL EVENTS THAT MAY AFFECT CROWDS OR YOUR STAY:

- The Expedition Everest Challenge is an after-hours race at Disney's Animal Kingdom theme park that combines obstacles, a scavenger hunt, and a 5K. It does not affect day-time crowds.

- The Epcot International Flower and Garden Festival continues through the middle of May. See "March" for details.

- Star Wars Weekends brings *Star Wars* characters for meet and greets, special celebrity autograph sessions, a parade, and nightly fireworks to Disney's Hollywood Studios. The event runs Fridays–Sundays, beginning May 16. Hollywood Studios will see some of its heaviest crowds of the year on these days. With the exception of Memorial Day Weekend, when Friday is the best day to visit, Sunday is the least crowded day at the Star Wars Weekends due to people traveling and those attending on Friday or Saturday because they can't wait until Sunday.

BEST TIME TO VISIT Any time between May 1–15 would be best, with average crowds and resort pricing, cooler and drier days than later in the month, and the Flower and Garden Festival in full swing. You also won't need to worry about the Star Wars Weekend crowds at Hollywood Studios.

June

COST All of June is Summer season. At the Values and Moderates, pricing is slightly lower than Peak Season. At the Deluxe Resorts, pricing is actually slightly lower than Regular Season and significantly less than Peak Season.

WEATHER June is hot, with an average high of 90 and an average low of

72 degrees. Precipitation inches up with a 38% chance and the highest accumulation of precipitation of the year.

CROWDS June is among the busiest months of the year as schools let out for summer and as South American tour groups drive crowds significantly upwards. Daily crowds are lower than Easter or Christmas weeks, but busier than just about any other time.

REFURBISHMENTS Rare.

SPECIAL EVENTS THAT MAY AFFECT CROWDS OR YOUR STAY:

- Star Wars Weekends continue through June 13–15. See "May" for details
- The "Sounds Like Summer" concert series is scheduled throughout June and July in Epcot outside the American Adventure Pavilion in the World Showcase. This series of cover bands doesn't make crowds any larger than they would be otherwise.
- Tour groups are common in June and July. If you see (or hear) a group of young kids walking around behind a 20-year-old carrying a flag, head in the opposite direction.

BEST TIME TO VISIT June 1–8 will have slightly lower crowds than later in the month, in addition to reduced precipitation and slightly lower temperatures.

July

COST All of July is Summer season at the Values and Moderates, with prices slightly higher than Regular Season and slightly lower than Peak Season. At the Deluxes, the first two weeks are Summer season, with pricing slightly lower than Regular season. After that, deluxe pricing is reduced further to Value season 2.

WEATHER July is among the hottest months in Orlando, with an average high of 91 and an average low of 74 degrees. Even worse than the heat is the humidity, which averages about 75%. Rain showers also increase in July, with a 49% chance of precipitation on any given day.

CROWDS Fourth of July crowds are the largest of the summer. The rest of July is the first or second busiest month overall because almost all U.S. kids are out of school. International visitation is also at its highest point of the year. Most other months have at least some portion where crowds will be smaller, but not July. It is crowded every day. Crowds are slightly lower towards the end of the month.

REFURBISHMENTS Rare.

SPECIAL EVENTS THAT MAY AFFECT CROWDS OR YOUR STAY:

- Magic Kingdom offers a special fireworks show on July 3 and 4. The July 3 show is slightly less crowded. Epcot hosts special events and meet and greets in the United States Pavilion throughout the Fourth, and offers a special IllumiNations show with several extra minutes of intense fireworks. Hollywood Studios also offers a special fireworks show. The Magic Kingdom show is the best, but Epcot and Hollywood Studios crowds are more manageable.
- The "Sounds Like Summer" concert at Epcot continues. See "June" for details.
- Tour groups remain common.

BEST TIME TO VISIT As late in July as possible is best. International visitation wanes and pricing at the Deluxes is lower.

August

COST Virtually all of August is Value season 1 or 2 with some of the least expensive resort prices of the year.

WEATHER August is one of the hottest months in Orlando, with an average high of 91 and an average low of 75 degrees. Peak hurricane season begins in the third week. Hurricanes have not directly impacted Disney World since 2004, but they and lesser storms may affect flights and bring nasty weather. Showers and thunderstorms are common in the afternoons, with a 43% chance of precipitation.

CROWDS The first three weeks in August are as crowded as the rest of the summer. Crowds diminish beginning the third week in August as kids start the new school year and are the lowest of the summer in the final week. Guests with flexible schedules are best served waiting until September when crowds are significantly lower.

REFURBISHMENTS Rare.

SPECIAL EVENTS THAT MAY AFFECT CROWDS OR YOUR STAY:

- None.

BEST TIME TO VISIT The last week in August is the least crowded since early May.

September

COST September sees a mixture of Value, Fall, and Regular price seasons. All prices are below average.

WEATHER September is just barely cooler than the summer months with an average high of 89 and an average low of 74 degrees. Humidity remains extremely high, and there is a good chance thunderstorms or rain will disrupt most afternoons and some evenings. Historically, it rains 40% of days in September. Peak hurricane season continues.

CROWDS Crowds are at their lowest levels of the year during the first three weeks in September. The only time you may find less people in the parks is certain days toward the end of January and the first two weeks in February, making it an excellent time to visit as far as crowds are concerned. September 1–3 will be the busiest days due to the Labor Day holiday, but even those three days will have significantly smaller crowds than any of the days over the summer.

REFURBISHMENTS The frequency of attraction refurbishments increases with the lower crowds. Expect a few rides to be down.

SPECIAL EVENTS THAT MAY AFFECT CROWDS OR YOUR STAY:

- *Mickey's Not So Scary Halloween Party* includes several dates throughout September beginning the first of the month. It requires a separate ticket to attend. The Party runs from 7pm until midnight, with ticket holders typically allowed to enter as early as 4pm. The Party's main features are a unique parade, fireworks show, and trick-or-treating throughout the park. Most rides are operating. This event closes the Magic Kingdom at 7pm for visitors without a ticket to the Halloween Party. The Magic Kingdom is actually less busy on days when there is a Halloween Party because it closes early. If you have park hopper tickets, you may want to start at Magic Kingdom and then hop to another park to end the day. Without a park hopper, consider a reservation at one of the resorts connected by the monorail or watercraft and, then proceed to the beach or lookout area at the resort to watch the fireworks. Tuesday Parties are the least crowded.

- *Night of Joy* is a contemporary Christian concert inside Magic Kingdom from 7:30pm–1am, held on Friday, September 5, and on Saturday, September 6, in 2014. Like the Halloween Party, Night of Joy closes Magic Kingdom at 7pm for everyone who has not purchased an additional ticket to the event. Night of Joy tickets are good for entry beginning at 4pm, which increases crowds in the park after 5pm. Crowds are low before then. Avoid traveling to Magic Kingdom on the monorail or ferry after 4pm because buses and buses of kids will be in line.

- *The Epcot Food and Wine Festival* officially begins on September 19, with most World Showcase food and wine booths opening on the 18th. It runs every day through November 10. There are also bands performing throughout the Festival outside at the American Gardens Theater for free. It's a fun event with interesting food, educational classes, and several expensive dinners. During the Festival, Epcot is extremely busy on weekends, and weekdays in World Showcase are also busier.

BEST TIME TO VISIT Any date from September 3–18 will have low crowds and some of the lowest prices of the year, especially when considering the likelihood of significant discounts. Beginning September 19, crowds pick up a bit, particularly on the weekends at Epcot with the Food and Wine Festival beginning. Any date from the 19th to the beginning of October is still more than do-able with well below-average crowds, other than the weekends at Epcot.

October

COST Most of October is a mix of Fall season and Regular season 2, with pricing slightly below average. Columbus Day weekend is the exception, with average pricing.

WEATHER Weather cools slightly with an average high of 84 and an average low of 68 degrees. Precipitation is much lower than the summer months, with a 26% chance of showers on any given day. Peak hurricane season ends early in the month.

CROWDS Crowds are heavier in October than in past years with domestic school schedules moving towards week-long fall breaks. South American attendance is also higher in the first two weeks, culminating in the largest crowds of the month over Columbus Day weekend. Still, they won't be anywhere near as bad as summer or other holiday weekends. If you are flexible with your dates, hold off until after October 19.

REFURBISHMENTS Expect a couple minor attractions to be closed briefly throughout the month.

SPECIAL EVENTS THAT MAY AFFECT CROWDS OR YOUR STAY:

- *The Twilight Zone Tower of Terror 10-Miler* returns after hours on the 4th. After the run is a villains-themed party at the Studios. The event closes the Studios at 6pm, which in turn causes crowds to be lower during the day.
- *The Gartner Symposium* returns to the Swan, Dolphin, Beach Club, and Yacht Club from October 5–October 9. All of the Epcot-area

resorts will be sold out, and most of the restaurants in the area will be booked solid for those dates. The convention does not affect theme park attendance, except for Epcot, which is busier in the evenings.

- *Mickey's Not So Scary Halloween Party* includes many dates throughout October. See "September" for details.

- *Epcot's International Food and Wine Festival* continues daily through November 10. See "September" for details.

BEST TIME TO VISIT Sunday October 26–Sunday November 2 is the best week to visit in October, with average crowds, cooler weather, and plenty of opportunities to enjoy Mickey's Not So Scary Halloween Party and the Food and Wine Festival.

November

COST With the exception of Thanksgiving week, all of November is Fall season, with pricing slightly higher than Value season 2 and lower than Regular season. Thanksgiving week sees pricing about equal to a weekend during Regular season, which is less than Peak season and other major holidays.

WEATHER It's noticeably cooler than September and October, with an average high of 76 and an average low of 59 degrees. November introduces more variability in high and low temperatures than the summer. Humidity is also substantially lower, with a 23% chance of precipitation. For those who like warm, but not uncomfortably hot temperatures, November is the perfect month to visit.

CROWDS Crowds are surprisingly light for the majority of November, with two major exceptions. The first is November 4–11, due to a phenomenon known as "Jersey Week" combining with Veteran's Day weekend and the Wine and Dine Half Marathon. All New Jersey schools are off the Thursday and Friday of the first full week of November, and many families from the state travel to Disney World during that week and/or weekend. This raises crowd levels significantly, particularly at Epcot and Magic Kingdom from November 7–10. Second, Thanksgiving week is very crowded.

REFURBISHMENTS Typically a few minor attractions.

SPECIAL EVENTS THAT MAY AFFECT CROWDS OR YOUR STAY:

- *Mickey's Very Merry Christmas Party* begins November 7 and happens several other evenings throughout the month. It requires a separate ticket to attend. Like Mickey's Not So Scary Halloween Party, this Party includes a unique parade, fireworks show, and several special stage shows. Cocoa and cookies take the place of trick-or-treating candy. The Party runs from 7pm–12am, with Party ticket holders allowed to enter as early as 4pm. Because of the 7pm closures for regular guests, other nights with late closures, fireworks, and the evening parade are wildly crowded at the Magic Kingdom.

- *The Wine and Dine Marathon* is scheduled after hours on Saturday, November 8. It begins at 10pm at the ESPN Wide World of Sports and finishes at Epcot for the after-party, which runs (no pun intended) through 3am. Spectators may purchase separate tickets to just the Party.

- *Epcot's International Food and Wine Festival* continues daily through November 10. See "September" for details.

- *Holidays Around the World* in Epcot begins on Friday, November 28. Disney brings in storytellers to tell holiday stories and explain unique traditions in many of the World Showcase countries. Santa Claus meets in the U.S. Pavilion. In addition, the Candlelight Processional is an amazing stage show featuring the voices of famous celebrities, a large choir, and a 50-piece orchestra. The show, which tells the story of Christmas, is put on three times throughout the night (5pm, 6:45pm, and 8pm) and lasts about 40 minutes. Illuminations, the nightly fireworks and laser show, also includes several holiday-only effects that you won't want to miss. Holidays Around the World will increase crowds to the World Showcase in the evening, especially on the weekends.

- At Hollywood Studios, beginning November 7, the *Osborne Family Spectacle of Dancing Lights* features over 5 million lights carefully set up throughout the Streets of America. The lights are up every evening (unless a private event closes Hollywood Studios early) and don't affect day-time crowds. A lighting ceremony occurs nightly around 6pm. The best time to view the Lights is from about 15 minutes before the Studios closes through 60 minutes after the Studios officially "closes" because the lights continue to dance.

BEST TIME TO VISIT November 12–22 is the best time to visit with the lowest crowds of the month and low resort pricing. You'll have plenty of opportunities to see the Osborne Lights, Magic Kingdom Castle Lighting, and have an opportunity to attend Mickey's Very Merry Christmas Party. Consider a visit over the first week in November if you'd prefer to attend the Food and Wine Festival.

December

COST Fall Season continues with prices slightly below average through December 11, 2014. Peak season, with well-above-average pricing, begins the 12th and continues through the 18th, followed by the most expensive pricing of the year through January 1.

WEATHER Expect erratic temperatures throughout December. It is not uncommon for one day to be in the low 60s and the next day to be in the high 70s. Nonetheless, the average high is 72 and the average low is 53 degrees, making most afternoons comfortable and most evenings a little chilly. Precipitation remains low with a 22% chance.

CROWDS Crowds are slightly below average to average through December 18. Beginning December 19, some of the heaviest crowds of the year arrive, with the highest crowds of the year from December 25–31.

REFURBISHMENTS Expect a few minor attraction closures for brief stints.

SPECIAL EVENTS THAT MAY AFFECT CROWDS OR YOUR STAY:

- The ABC Christmas Day Parade taping is scheduled for December 5 and 6. Most of Main Street will be closed off December 6. Expect additional delays in Frontierland and Liberty Square as the floats are moved to Main Street, on top of incredibly heavy crowds due to the fact it's a Saturday with long hours and night-time entertainment in the midst of Mickey's Party season. December 6 is best avoided, while the 5th is less impacted as the bulk of the taping occurs before park opening.

- Pop Warner brings its youth football Super Bowl to Disney World over the first full week of December. Pop Warner does not have a substantial impact on theme park attendance, but it does have a serious impact at the resorts where kids and their families stay. Pop Warner families typically receive hefty discounts at the All-Stars, Coronado Springs, and Caribbean Beach. If planning a trip over the first full week of December, consider booking another resort to avoid thousands of largely unchaperoned kids.

- Mickey's Christmas Party continues through the first three weeks in December. See "November" for details.

- Holidays Around the World in Epcot runs through December 30. See "November" for details.

- Osborne Spectacle of Dancing Lights continues throughout December. See "November" for details.

NEW YEAR'S EVE CELEBRATIONS Magic Kingdom hosts identical fireworks December 30 and 31. The 30th is slightly less crowded, but both days should fill to capacity in the afternoon. Epcot hosts a special IllumiNations on the 31st with several minutes of outstanding fireworks at the end. Dance parties throughout World Showcase continue into the late night. Hollywood Studios shoots fireworks off from behind Mickey's Sorcerer's Hat to live music. The Studios' show is the easiest to see, and Animal Kingdom is the least crowded park to visit during the day.

BEST TIME TO VISIT Try to end the trip by December 12 to take advantage of below-average crowds, below-average resort pricing, and everything the Christmas season has to offer.

When to Go if it's Your Only Visit

A family looking at a once-in-a-lifetime trip should aim to visit at a less crowded time when refurbishments and weather are less likely to negatively impact the trip. Based on both this and the delights of the Disney Christmas program, Dave has ranked all the weeks of the year for first-timers who may never return, in this chart:

2014 Weeks to Visit Rankings

Arrival Date	Week Rank	Comments	Crowd Ranking	Crowds	Values Prices	Moderates Prices	Deluxes Prices	Other
Bold=Recommended Week								
January 4, 2014	50		3	Low	Lower	Lowest	Lower	Ride Closures Common
January 11, 2014	51	Marathon	4	Low-plus	Lower	Lowest	Lower	Ride Closures Common
January 18, 2014	49	MLK Day 1/20	3	Low	Lower	Lowest	Lower	Ride Closures Common
January 25, 2014	48		1	Lowest	Lowest	Lowest	Lowest	Ride Closures Common
February 1, 2014	47		1	Lowest	Lowest	Lowest	Lowest	Some Ride Closures
February 8, 2014	52		4	Low-plus	Moderate-minus	Moderate-minus	Moderate	Some Ride Closures
February 15, 2014	42	President's Day 2/17	10	Higher	Higher	Higher	Higher	
February 22, 2014	**11**		3	Low	Moderate	Moderate	Moderate-plus	
March 1, 2014	**13**		4	Low-plus	Moderate-plus	Moderate	Moderate-plus	
March 8, 2014	41		10	Higher	Higher	High	High	
March 15, 2014	39		9	High	Higher	High	High	
March 22, 2014	38		9	High	Higher	High	High	
March 29, 2014	17		5	Moderate-minus	Higher	High	High	
April 5, 2014	**12**		3	Low	Higher	High	High	
April 12, 2014	44	Easter 4/20	11	Highest	Highest	Highest	Highest	
April 19, 2014	30	Easter 4/20	8	High-minus	Higher	Higher	Higher	
April 26, 2014	**6**		2	Lower	Moderate-plus	Moderate	Moderate-plus	
May 3, 2014	**5**		2	Lower	Moderate	Moderate	Moderate	
May 10, 2014	**10**		3	Low	Moderate	Moderate	Moderate	
May 17, 2014	16		5	Moderate-minus	Moderate	Moderate	Moderate	
May 24, 2014	31	Memorial Day 5/26	9	High	Moderate-plus	Moderate-minus	Moderate	
May 31, 2014	19		7	Moderate-plus	High	Moderate-minus	Moderate-minus	
June 7, 2014	29		8	High-minus	High	Moderate-minus	Moderate-minus	
June 14, 2014	35		9	High	High	Moderate-minus	Moderate-minus	
June 21, 2014	36		9	High	High	Moderate-minus	Moderate-minus	
June 28, 2014	40	Fourth of July 7/4	10	Higher	High	Moderate-minus	Moderate-minus	
July 5, 2014	43	Fourth of July 7/4	11	Highest	High	Moderate-minus	Moderate-minus	
July 12, 2014	34		9	High	High	Moderate-minus	Lowest	
July 19, 2014	33		9	High	High	Moderate-minus	Lowest	
July 26, 2014	32		9	High	High	Moderate-minus	Lowest	
August 2, 2014	28		8	High-minus	Low	Lower	Lowest	
August 9, 2014	18		7	Moderate-plus	Lower	Lower	Lowest	
August 16, 2014	27		6	Moderate	Lower	Lower	Lowest	Peak Hurricane Season
August 23, 2014	23		3	Low	Lower	Lower	Lowest	Peak Hurricane Season
August 30, 2014	21	Labor Day 9/1	2	Lower	Lower	Lower	Lowest	Peak Hurricane Season
September 6, 2014	20		1	Lowest	Lower	Lower	Lowest	Peak Hurricane Season
September 13, 2014	24		3	Low	Low	Low	Lowest	Peak Hurricane Season
September 20, 2014	22		2	Lower	Low	Low	Lower	Peak Hurricane Season
September 27, 2014	26		3	Low	Low	Low	Moderate	Peak Hurricane Season
October 4, 2014	25		3	Low	Low	Low	Moderate	Peak Hurricane Season
October 11, 2014	15	Columbus Day 10/13	5	Moderate-minus	Moderate-minus	Low	Moderate	
October 18, 2014	**7**		3	Low	Low	Low	Low	
October 25, 2014	**8**		3	Low	Low	Low	Low	
November 1, 2014	14	Jersey Week	5	Moderate-minus	Low	Low	Low	
November 8, 2014	**4**		2	Lower	Low	Low	Low	
November 15, 2014	**9**		3	Low	Low	Low	Low	
November 22, 2014	37	Thanksgiving 11/27	9	High	High	Moderate	Moderate	Some Xmas Program
November 29, 2014	**1**		3	Low	Low	Low	Low	Xmas Program
December 6, 2014	**3**	Pop Warner Week	4	Low-plus	Moderate-minus	Moderate-minus	Moderate	Xmas Program
December 13, 2014	**2**		3	Low	Higher	Higher	Higher	Xmas Program
December 20, 2014	46		11	Highest	Highest	Highest	Highest	Xmas Program
December 27, 2014	45		11	Highest	Highest	Highest	Highest	Xmas Program
Arrival Date	Week Rank	Comments	Crowd Ranking	Crowds	Values Prices	Moderates Prices	Deluxes Prices	Other

Choosing dates is easiest for those with flexible schedules. For vacationers with school-age children unwilling to take them out of school, or other date constraints, picking a date among the less desirable times of year may be a bit daunting. The good news is that you're in the best possible position to make an informed decision. From there, we'll help you save money and time in the following chapters, regardless of when you ultimately choose to visit.

Where to Stay

In this chapter we suggest that you stay in a Disney-owned resort hotel, either a value, moderate, or deluxe resort, based on your budget. Specifically, we recommend:

- **VALUE** Art of Animation, Pop Century
- **MODERATE** Port Orleans French Quarter, Port Orleans Riverside
- **DELUXE** Grand Floridian, Wilderness Lodge, Contemporary. (The Polynesian will join this list after construction is completed in early 2015.)

The chapter begins by addressing the advantages and disadvantages of staying on-site in a Disney-owned hotel. We then discuss the key differences between Disney's value, moderate, and deluxe classes, and take a look at what specifically differentiates resorts within each class. Next we provide detailed reviews by resort class. The chapter finishes with alternatives to staying in a Disney resort.

Stay at a Walt Disney World Owned Resort

More than 20 Disney-owned resorts dot the 40+ square miles that comprise Walt Disney World.

Another dozen hotels owned by third parties are also on Disney World property. Most third-party hotels are located in the far northeast corner of Disney World near Downtown Disney. Third-party hotels that are closer to the parks include the Swan and Dolphin, both about a ten-minute walk to Epcot and about 15 minutes away from Hollywood Studios. Another is Shades of Green, an armed forces recreation center with lodging for military personnel and their families, conveniently located right across the street from the Polynesian. Finally, Four Seasons is scheduled to open in 2014 between Fort Wilderness and Port Orleans

Riverside. It will offer some of the best on-site amenities with pricing expected to be similar to Disney's flagship resort, the Grand Floridian Resort & Spa. There's more on these non-Disney owned hotels on Disney World property, and also on off-site options, near the end of this chapter.

The Disney-owned resorts are more expensive than hotels operated by third parties, but they are also typically:

- Much more fun
- Much more convenient
- Much more "Disney"

The Disney-owned hotels offer a laundry list of unique perks that third-party operators could never dream of providing. The most advantageous perks include:

- Free airport transport to and from your hotel via Disney's Magical Express.
- Free and frequent transport from your hotel to the parks, water-parks, and Downtown Disney.
- Free parking at both your hotel and the parks.
- The right to book dining ten days further out than non-Disney guests, which can be critical for high-demand meals like dinner at Be Our Guest Restaurant.
- The right to book FastPass+ reservations for key attractions beginning 60 days in advance of arrival. Non-Disney guests can book only up to 30 days before use—which may mean some attractions aren't available for pre-booking, and others may be available only at less convenient times.
- Access to the various Disney Dining Plans, which are a conve-nient budgeting tool if your family eats the way they are designed to feed you, and may save you a bit if your kids are younger than ten and you plan on several character meals.
- Keeping Disney magic real and definite: while it's easy to read a list of definable resort perks, it's more difficult to describe to a first-time visitor how it feels to be caught up in the completely immersive atmosphere of the Walt Disney World bubble. There are very few vacation destinations in the world that truly allow visitors to escape the harsh realities of life and instead be immersed in the fun and fantasy of a make-believe world. An inclusive on-property stay offers just that—from the time Magical Express picks you up at the airport to the moment they drop you off again, there's nothing to worry about at Disney World. Just keep your credit card handy.

THE PERK WE RARELY RECOMMEND

Extra Magic Hours (EMH) are one the best known perks offered to guests staying at Disney-owned resorts, as well as at the Swan, Dolphin, Shades of Green, Downtown Disney Hilton, and likely the Four Seasons once it opens in later 2014.

There are two varieties of Extra Magic Hours: morning and evening. Morning Extra Magic Hour is limited to one hour immediately before a park's regular open. Evening Extra Magic Hours are two hours long and begin immediately after a park's regular close. Most popular rides operate during both Morning and Evening Extra Magic, though the selection is wider during the evening. The participating attractions are listed in Chapter 6. At least one park offers Extra Magic Hours virtually every day, with the most common schedule being:

Sunday: Magic Kingdom evening

Monday: Animal Kingdom morning, Hollywood Studios evening

Tuesday: Epcot morning

Wednesday: Animal Kingdom morning

Thursday: Magic Kingdom morning

Friday: Epcot evening

Saturday: Hollywood Studios morning

Seasonal or special events may alter the schedule slightly, so always check the park calendars. Most notably:

- During Star Wars Weekends from the middle of May to the middle of June, Hollywood Studios offers morning EMH on Wednesday, and the Animal Kingdom morning EMH moves from then to Saturday.

- During the Food and Wine Festival from mid-September to early November, Epcot offers evening EMH on Wednesdays, and Animal Kingdom moves its Wednesday morning EMH to Fridays.

- During the Mickey's Party Season from early September to mid-December, Magic Kingdom and Hollywood Studios commonly swap evening EMH nights

So why is the park with such a great benefit so rarely recommended? Over 25,000 rooms on property have the opportunity to "take advantage of EMH" and every guest checking in will receive a Times Guide with the Extra Magic Hours schedule for the week clearly listed. "Up to two exclusive hours inside the park" sounds so overwhelmingly positive that the majority of the 75,000+ resort guests staying on property choose the park with the "extra magic". In turn, the park(s) with Extra Magic Hours are usually the busiest from 10am–7pm because they attract so many extra people. Simply choosing a different park avoids these resort guests.

In addition, Morning EMHs begin at 7am or 8am, and it's awfully hard to get the family up, bathed, clothed, fed, and on the way in time to actually take advantage of the extra time. Arriving late to the park with EMH completely negates any benefit. Evening EMHs are often late at night, making it more difficult to arrive at the park the next day before open when waits are often much shorter. Because Hollywood Studios and Epcot offer so few rides during EMH, wait times at them are usually just as long during evening EMH as they are during the day, negating much of the benefit.

There are a few ways to make Extra Magic Hours work:

- If you actually arrive in time to take advantage of the full morning EMH and can park hop away from it in the afternoon, then you can have a tremendous amount of success during the extra hour, particularly at Magic Kingdom and Animal Kingdom. The morning EMH park will be busier than other days from 10am–7pm, and staying in the park during that time will lessen the benefit of the extra hour.

- Evening EMHs are less busy in the final hour, particularly at Magic Kingdom where numerous attractions are operating. Those able to park hop to the evening EMH park at night and stay through close often enjoy themselves if they begin with the anytime attractions.

It's easier to simply avoid the park with EMH and instead visit the less busy parks. You'll also be better rested and better able to enjoy the parks in the morning during a regular day.

How to Pick Your Disney Resort Hotel

The most important factor is budget. Standard value resort rooms range in price from $96/weeknight at the All-Stars during value season all the way up to $221/night at Art of Animation over Christmas. Standard rooms at the deluxes start at $319 at Animal Kingdom Lodge in the value season and go up to $856/night for a standard view at the Grand Floridian over the holidays. Larger rooms, better locations, and better views cost even more.

There are five different types of Disney resorts:

- **VALUE RESORTS** Lowest prices, smallest rooms, fewest amenities, no table service restaurants. (Value resort "Family Suite" rooms, available at Art of Animation and All-Star Music, come in at about twice the size of a standard room, but cost more than twice as much.)

- **MODERATE RESORTS** Middle-of-the-road prices, room sizes, and amenities. Table service restaurants at all but Port Orleans French Quarter.

- **DELUXE RESORTS** Highest prices, largest rooms, most amenities, plentiful dining.

- **DISNEY VACATION CLUB RESORTS** There are multiple deluxe-level room types: "Studios" are similar to deluxe rooms; "Villas" are larger and have full kitchens, and, at the two-bedroom and larger sizes, sleep eight people plus.

- **THE CAMPSITES AT DISNEY'S FORT WILDERNESS RESORT** Campgrounds for tent and RV campers (the Cabins at Fort Wilderness are grouped in the moderate class).

The vast majority of first time visitors stay in one of the first three resort types. The table below shows more detailed distinctions among them. Take heed of the footnotes that follow...none of this is as easy as we'd all wish!

RESORT FEATURES BY PRICE CLASS

Value Resorts*	Moderate Resorts*	Deluxe Resorts*
All Value Resorts Have:	**Some Moderate Resorts Have:**	**Some Deluxe Resorts Have:**
Basic, very small rooms	Beds for 5***	Spa services
Price** of $110-$132/night	Full-sized beds	Childcare clubs
Beds for 4***	Marina	Beds for 4***
Full-sized beds		
Split baths	**Most Moderate Resorts Have:**	**Most Deluxe Resorts Have:**
Single sinks	Two sinks	Varied transportation, not just buses
260 square foot rooms	Queen beds	Beach access
Room doors on exterior corridors	Indoor bar	Marina
Basic exteriors	Table-service restaurants	Hot tub
Basic landscaping	Elevators	Workout gym
Basic pools	Beds for 4***	Beds for 5***
Larger than life sculptures		Balconies
Hourly luggage assistance	**All Moderate Resorts Have:**	Counter-service food
Bus service to parks	Nicer, large-enough rooms	Table-service restaurants
Elevators	Price** of $203/night	Split baths
Pizza delivery	Split baths	
Some clothes storage	314 square foot rooms	**All Deluxe Resorts Have:**
Counter-service food	Room doors on exterior corridors	Lovely rooms
	Coffeemakers	Price** of $361-$568/night
	Lovely exteriors	Queen beds
	Lovely landscaping	Two sinks
	Nice pools with slides	344-476 square feet rooms
	Bell luggage service	Room doors on interior corridors
	Bus service to parks	Indoor bar
	Pizza delivery	Elevators
	Enough clothes storage	Coffeemakers
	Hot tub	Lovely exteriors
	Counter-service food	Lovely landscaping
		Proximity to at least one theme park
		Concierge and suite options
		Really nice pools with slides
		Bell luggage service
		Valet parking
		Room service
		Plenty of clothes storage

*Excludes Family Suites, Cabins at Fort Wilderness, and Disney Vacation Club resorts
**Fall season 2014 weeknight rate for a standard view room
***One additional child younger than three at check-in can also occupy the room

Once you've set your budget, there's no one size fits all answer, but the material in this section, and detailed reviews later in this chapter, should help paint a clearer picture of which resort is the best fit for your group. The reviews focus on the standard room options at each of Disney's resorts, and also the popular family suites at Art of Animation and All-Star Music. For a more comprehensive look at the various Disney Vacation Club Villas and updates on the comings and goings of the resorts throughout the year, visit Dave's YOURFIRSTVISIT.NET.

Dave suggests picking hotels based first on overall kid appeal, mainly visual, and then on transportation convenience in a trip where the Magic Kingdom sees the most visits. Convenience to Epcot is prioritized second.

The chart below is derived from this methodology, with Dave's top picks at the top and on the right. Note that the Polynesian is undergoing extensive renovations and additions. The Polynesian's lobby, quick service dining, check-in area, main pool, and parts of the beach will be renovated, closed, or walled off in phases throughout 2014 into early 2015. This will likely diminish the Polynesian's overall tranquility and ambiance—by quite a bit. Consider another resort if your trip falls before March 2015, when the majority of the projects will be completed.

Bold=Value Resort

Italic=Moderate Resort

<u>Underline</u>=Deluxe Resort/DVC

RESORTS SORTED BY CONVENIENCE AND KID APPEAL

CONVENIENCE	<u>Grand Floridian</u>	<u>Contemporary</u>	<u>Polynesian</u>
Very Convenient			(after March 2015)
Convenient	<u>BoardWalk Inn and Villas</u> <u>Beach Club and Villas</u> <u>Yacht Club</u>		<u>Wilderness Lodge and Villas</u> <u>Animal Kingdom Lodge and Villas</u> **Art of Animation** **Pop Century**
Somewhat Convenient	*Port Orleans Riverside* *Port Orleans French Quarter* <u>Old Key West</u> <u>Saratoga Springs</u> *Fort Wilderness*	*Caribbean Beach* *Coronado Springs*	**All-Star Sports** **All-Star Movies** **All-Star Music**
KID APPEAL	Slight Kid Appeal	Some Kid Appeal	**Great Kid Appeal**

Josh ranks resorts on a wider set of criteria, but largely arrives at the same results.

VALUE RESORTS

Art of Animation and Pop Century are the top two choices.

The distinctive features of the value resorts are their tiny 260-square-foot standard rooms, their terrific—but garish to the eyes of many adults—kid appeal, and their short list of resort amenities compared to what you'll find at the moderates and deluxes. For instance, a lot of first-time visitors are surprised that standard value rooms don't have coffeemakers. You also won't find bikes and other leisure activity rentals or table service restaurants at the values.

Standard value resort rooms sleep four in two full beds. You may also add a child three or younger in a crib. These rooms fit the needs of many first-time family visitors looking for low prices, as they won't be spending much time in them other than sleeping.

Family Suites at the All-Star Music (520 square feet) and Art of Animation (565 square feet) resorts are much larger, sleep six, and include coffee-makers in every room, but cost more than double the price of standard rooms.

Dave favors Art of Animation with its oversized icons of some of Disney's most popular contemporary properties like *Cars* and *Finding Nemo* that are sure to excite kids. Rooms are bright and cheery, from the deep red clam-shell-themed chairs to the oversize Ariel motif on the shower curtain. Josh loves Animation's detailed theming, but all its standard rooms are located in the Little Mermaid section, which is a five to seven minute walk from the main building. This is less of a concern if you're already planning to stay in one of its more convenient family suites. Pop rooms are blander and more generic looking with little in-room decoration. Some families and couples may prefer the subdued theming at Pop, while others favor the over-the-top décor at Animation. Otherwise, Pop standard rooms usually run $10-$15 less per night than standard rooms at Art of Animation. Both resorts are newer than the All-Stars, provide dedicated bus service, offer elevated fare at the quick services, and feature more robust Disney-inspired theming.

The other value resorts—All-Star Sports, All-Star Music, and All-Star Movies—cost about $10 per night less than Pop, but they're also significantly farther away from Magic Kingdom and Epcot. The three All-Stars often share buses and none of their themes (except Movies) are overtly "Disney", though each features smaller character scenes around the resort. Finally, their food courts offer lower quality, less inspired fare.

MODERATE RESORTS

Port Orleans French Quarter and Port Orleans Riverside are the best choices.

Standard moderate rooms are found in all moderates except the Cabins at Fort Wilderness. They cost about $80/night more than standard value rooms and $350/night less than a standard room at the Polynesian. Your extra $80/night buys you about 50 more square feet than value rooms, in addition to queen beds (except Caribbean Beach which will have full beds until its 2014 renovation including queen beds is complete), double sinks (except at Coronado Springs), a coffee-maker, a table service restaurant (except at French Quarter), an indoor lounge (except at Caribbean Beach), a pool slide, and hot tubs. The moderates also provide the most cost-effective way to sleep five (in the Alligator Bayou section of Riverside, and, we believe, in Caribbean Beach after its 2014 rehab) and the most cost-effective way to get a full kitchen (in The Cabins at Disney's Fort Wilderness Resort). Compared to the deluxes, the moderates have limited dining options, no character meals, are less convenient to at least one theme park, and have far fewer services and amenities. Fortunately, living areas are more comparable in size to those in the deluxes than you might expect, especially when considering deluxe resorts with smaller room sizes like those at Animal Kingdom and Wilderness Lodges.

Of the moderates, all but Port Orleans French Quarter are large and spread out, with dozens of guest buildings spread out over hundreds of acres. All have multiple bus stops (including shared buses at POFQ). All have more amenities than the values, but fewer than the deluxes. Coronado Springs offers the most amenities, including a salon, gym, nightclub, a strong room service menu, and the largest hot tub on property. French Quarter offers the fewest, including the smallest feature pool, no quiet pools, and no sit-down restaurant. Luckily, all those amenities and more are a short walk or boat ride away at Port Orleans Riverside.

Moderate resorts favor tranquility and a more sublime atmosphere when compared to the values, but don't offer the lushness and detail of the deluxes. This may translate to less overt kid appeal. There are no 50-foot-tall Mickey Mouse icons at the moderates, and other than some subtle references, nothing about them screams Disney World. Of the moderates, the vast majority of kids prefer Caribbean Beach Resort, with its beautiful white sand beaches, hammocks, and colorful guest houses. It also features a pirate-themed pool and play area that kids adore.

Our preference for Port Orleans French Quarter comes largely from its being so much easier to get around than any other moderate, and the relative ease in getting from it to the Magic Kingdom. Among the less convenient moderates, Port Orleans Riverside beats out Caribbean Beach because of its better transportation and queen rather than Caribbean Beach's current full beds—being replaced by queens in 2014. It beats out Coronado Springs because of its more family-friendly atmosphere and dining.

(The Cabins at Fort Wilderness are so different than any other moderate that we refer you to the detailed review later in this chapter. However, we do not recommend them for first-time visitors.)

DELUXE RESORTS

The Grand Floridian, Wilderness Lodge, and Contemporary are the best choices. (The Polynesian will join this list after construction is completed in early 2015.)

Compared to other Walt Disney World options, the deluxe resorts are distinguished by having the:

- Most amenities, with the Contemporary and Grand Floridian at the top of this list.
- Nicest views, especially at the Contemporary, Polynesian, Grand Floridian, and Animal Kingdom Lodge.
- Best in-resort and nearby dining options, especially at the four Magic Kingdom-area resorts—the Contemporary, Polynesian, Grand Floridian, and Wilderness Lodge. The Epcot resorts—the BoardWalk Inn, Yacht Club, and Beach Club—have access to many nearby restaurants, but most of them are undistinguished for either kids or parents. The restaurants in the Animal Kingdom Lodge are marvelous, but there's no character dining, and no easy access to more dining at other resorts.
- Best pools, especially at the Beach Club, Yacht Club, Wilderness Lodge, and Animal Kingdom Lodge.
- Best transportation, especially at the Contemporary, Polynesian, and Grand Floridian that share the resort monorail. The Polynesian is most convenient overall. It has resort monorail and boat access to Magic Kingdom, and it's also possible to walk from the Polynesian to the Transportation and Ticket Center (TTC) to catch the Epcot monorail, which eliminates the lengthy monorail ride to the TTC before then having to switch monorails. The Contemporary is just a ten minute walk away from the Magic Kingdom, making it most convenient for a Magic-Kingdom-centric vacation. The Beach Club, located just a five minute walk or boat ride away from Epcot's International Gateway entrance, is the most convenient for an Epcot-centric vacation, particularly during the Food and Wine Festival in the fall.
- Largest standard rooms, with those in the monorail resorts the largest, and those at the Wilderness and Animal Kingdom Lodges the smallest.
- Highest prices for standard rooms, with the monorail resorts the highest, and Wilderness and Animal Kingdom Lodges the lowest.

- Mixed kid appeal, with the Wilderness Lodge and Animal Kingdom Lodge the highest, the Polynesian next (although its kid appeal will be greatly diminished when its main pool is closed for rehab from late July 2014 through March 2015), and the Yacht Club and BoardWalk Inn the lowest.

As perhaps is clear by now, there are much bigger differences across the deluxes than in the other price classes. The detailed reviews later in this chapter cover these differences.

Until Polynesian renovations are complete, we recommend the Wilderness Lodge. Its location across Bay Lake puts it a fun boat ride or just a short bus ride to Magic Kingdom. It offers one of the most family-friendly restaurants in Whispering Canyon Café. Artist Point is a delightful Northwest-inspired signature restaurant away from the hustle and bustle of the monorail resorts. And Territory Lounge, with terrific Northwest beer on draft and a menu that features appetizers that come out of the kitchen it shares with Artist Point, is among the best on property. The pool is fantastically themed and there's even a geyser that erupts throughout the day near the outdoor bar. One deterrent—rooms are smaller than at most other deluxes, but prices are in turn lower.

Among the rest, Beach Club is the best choice for an Epcot-focused visit—which most first visits aren't. It's closer to Epcot and less uppity than neighboring Yacht Club. It also shares with the Yacht Club the best pool complex on property and is more convenient to the limited Epcot-area quick service dining.

The Value Resorts

DISNEY'S ART OF ANIMATION RESORT

Disney's Art of Animation Resort ("AofA") is themed on four wildly popular Disney animated films—*Cars*, *The Lion King*, *Finding Nemo*, and *The Little Mermaid*. Like Disney's other value resorts, this theming is partly achieved with larger-than-life sculptures, but much more than the other values, the theming is also suffused into the landscape and into the rooms themselves. This makes it the most "Disney" of any Disney World hotel, wonderfully so to kids, and unrelentingly and garishly so to some adults.

You'll find at AofA four lodging areas, each with two or three buildings framed around one of the movies, and two distinct room types. Family Suites sleeping six are found in the Cars, Lion King, and Finding Nemo areas, and standard rooms similar to those at the other value resorts (except for their much deeper Disney theming) are in the more distant Little Mermaid area. Found in Animation Hall near the entrance to the resort are dining, shops, and guest services. The main "Big Blue" pool, just outside Animation Hall, is the best pool among the values. You'll find two smaller pools as well—a tiny one in the Cars area, and a larger one in the Little Mermaid section. (You need to bring towels from your room to any of these pools; housekeeping can get you more towels if you need them.)

All transport to theme parks, water parks, and Downtown Disney is via bus. AofA is one of only two resorts at Walt Disney World with one bus stop and no shared buses, making total transit time shorter— nearby Pop Century is the other. Because at full capacity AofA holds fewer people than Pop does, AofA is the clear convenience winner among the values. AofA (and Pop Century) are just next to and south of the Epcot Area resort Caribbean Beach, but Disney way-finding seems to be morphing to identifying them as ESPN Wide World of Sports Area resorts. Regardless, these are the two most centrally-located of Disney's value resorts, though neither is particularly close to anything.

AofA's rich and detailed theming gives it the highest kid appeal, by far, among the values, and perhaps of any Disney World resort—at least for kids into one the movies it showcases. As with all the values, adult appeal is mixed, with some finding it fun, and others garish.

At AofA, there are two very different room types in four very different themed areas.

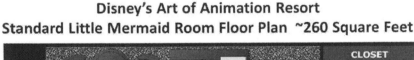

Disney's Art of Animation Resort
Standard Little Mermaid Room Floor Plan ~260 Square Feet

One room type is standard rooms sleeping four on two full beds (almost identical except in decoration to what you'll find at the other value resorts). These are all found in the Little Mermaid area, which is also the farthest area from the main pool, Animation Hall, and bus stops. At about 260 square feet, these standard rooms may be the smallest four-person rooms you will ever see in the U.S. outside of historic center-city hotels. Besides the two full beds, you'll find in the sleeping area a table and two chairs, a TV/dresser combo, and a mini-fridge. There are no coffee-makers in these standard rooms. In the divided bath, you'll find a clothes hanging area, hair dryer, and single sink separated from the rest of the room by a fabric curtain. Next to this you'll find the toilet and tub in their own room. Unlike the other value resorts, which have little room theming, the *Little Mermaid* gang is quite present in these rooms. No rooms at Art of Animation have balconies. All Little Mermaid rooms are accessed from exterior corridors.

Disney's Art of Animation Resort
Family Suite Floor Plan ~565 Square Feet

The rest of the rooms at AofA are Family Suites, found in three themed areas—Cars, Finding Nemo, and the Lion King. (No standard rooms are in these three areas, and no family suites are in the Little Mermaid area.) AofA Family Suites sleep six in more than twice the area of standard rooms, and contain a living room with a couch that folds out into a full bed, a dining area with a full bed that folds down, a master bedroom with a queen, two full baths (one connected to the master bedroom) and a kitchenette with a mini-fridge, microwave, and coffee-maker. Each of these rooms is deeply themed to its respective movie. Family Suites are accessed via interior corridors—more comfortable than exterior ones, but potentially more noisy.

Dining is in Animation Hall at the food court, Landscape of Flavors, the most ambitious of Disney's food courts in terms of adventuresome menus and fresh preparation. (Josh finds it unreliable and easily over-pressed by guests—if you do too, the food court at Pop Century is just over the bridge between the two resorts.) There's no indoor bar, but you'll find an outdoor bar by the main pool. There is no table service restaurant at any value, nor any character meals.

Amenities available at the resort include nightly movies, jogging trails, playgrounds, and an arcade. Art of Animation and Pop Century are the only value resorts on a lake, but the only water recreation available is bird-watching.

At AofA there are no "preferred" rooms or upcharges for views.

Standard four-person rooms are $132/night on weekdays and $155/night on Fridays and Saturdays during the 2014 Fall season. 2014 peak prices for these rooms are $221 and prices bottom out at $118/night. These prices are about $9-12 per night more expensive than Pop Century, and around $20 more per night than the All-Stars.

Six-person family suites are $317/night on weekdays and $358/night on Fridays and Saturdays during the 2014 Fall season. 2014 peak prices for these rooms are $511 and prices bottom out at $298/night. These prices are about $70 per night more expensive than the only other value resort Family Suites at All-Star Music.

DISNEY'S POP CENTURY RESORT

Disney's Pop Century Resort ("Pop") is themed around the toys, cultural icons, and Disney characters popular in the second half of the twentieth century. Think larger-than-life icons of Roger Rabbit, yo-yos, and a Mickey phone with Mickey, too. Pop has five themed lodging areas, each with one to three buildings framed around one decade—the 50s, 60s, 70s, 80s, and one lonely building representing the 90s. All this is more fun than it sounds, and the characters—Roger Rabbit, Mickey, Mowgli and Balou, Lady and Tramp—add Disney sparkle. Found in Classic Hall near the entrance to the resort are dining, shops, and guest services. The main Hippy Dippy Pool is just outside Classic Hall. You'll find two additional, smaller—but still plenty big—pools, the Bowling Pin pool in the 50s area, and the Computer Pool in the 80s and 90s area. Among these three pools, Pop has the largest area of pool and sunbathing space of any value. (You need to bring towels from your room to any of these pools; housekeeping can get you more towels if you need them.)

All transport to theme parks, water parks, and Downtown Disney is via bus. Pop is one of only two resorts at Walt Disney World with one bus stop and no shared buses, making total transit time shorter (nearby AofA is the other). Because at full capacity AofA holds fewer people than Pop does, AofA is the clear convenience winner among the values, but Pop is a close second. Pop is just next to and south of the Epcot Area resort Caribbean Beach, but Disney way-finding seems to be morphing to identifying it as an ESPN Wide World of Sports Area resort. Regardless, Pop and AofA are the two most centrally-located of Disney's value resorts, though neither is particularly close to anything.

Not so deeply themed as Art of Animation, especially in the rooms, but more Disney than any of the All-Star resorts except, possibly, All-Star Movies, Pop has high kid appeal, and is a little less busy to parental eyes than AofA.

Standard rooms at Pop sleep four on two full beds (almost identical to what you'll find in the standard rooms at the other value resorts). At about 260 square feet, these standard rooms may be the smallest four-person rooms you will ever stay in. Besides the two full beds, you'll find in the sleeping area a table and two chairs, a TV/dresser combo, and a mini-fridge. There are no coffee-makers in these standard rooms. In the divided bath, you'll find a clothes hanging area, hair dryer, and single sink separated from the rest of the room by a fabric curtain. Next to this you'll find the toilet and tub in their own room. The rooms themselves have next to no theming. No rooms at Pop have balconies, and all are accessed from exterior corridors.

Dining is in Classic Hall at the food court Everything Pop. In terms of size and menu, Everything Pop is well above average among the values. There's no indoor bar, but you'll find an outdoor bar by the main pool. There is no table service restaurant at any value, nor any character meals.

Amenities available at the resort include nightly movies, jogging trails, playgrounds, and an arcade. Art of Animation and Pop Century are the only value resorts on a lake, but the only water recreation available is bird-watching.

At Pop you can pay extras for "preferred" rooms closer to Animation Hall and for pool views. Standard view, non-preferred four-person rooms are $121/night on weekdays and $146/night on Fridays and Saturdays during the 2014 Fall season. 2014 peak prices for these rooms are $209 and prices bottom out at $106/night. These prices are about $9-12 per night less expensive than AofA, and around $10 more per night than the All-Stars.

DISNEY'S ALL-STAR MOVIES RESORT

Disney's All-Star Movies Resort ("Movies") is themed around five movies—*Toy Story, The Mighty Ducks, Fantasia, The Love Bug,* and *101 Dalmatians,* with two accommodation buildings in each theme. These films are represented by much-larger-than-life icons of characters and objects from them. Found in Cinema Hall near the entrance to the resort are dining, shops, and guest services. The main Fantasia Pool is just outside Cinema Hall. You'll find a smaller—but still plenty big—hockey-themed pool in the Mighty Ducks area. (You need to bring towels from your room to any of these pools; housekeeping can get you more towels if you need them.)

All transport to theme parks, water parks, and Downtown Disney is via bus. Movies shares most buses most of the year (except to the Magic Kingdom) with sister resorts All-Star Music and All-Star Sports. Buses stop at Sports first and Movies last—which at times has meant the buses were filled by the time they got to Movies. At press time, it was unclear how Disney's new, 50% larger articulated buses might affect this issue. Until the impact of the new buses becomes clear, Movies has to be considered the least convenient of the values. The All-Star resorts are Animal Kingdom Area resorts, and are the least conveniently located of the values.

Movies is much more Disney-themed than the other All-Stars, but does not have so rich a set of kid-appealing movies in its themes as AofA, nor are many of its movies as widely kid appealing as the Disney characters and the toys at Pop. The rooms themselves have only the lightest theming related to their area. Adults may find the theming garish, or may warm to the represented movies.

Standard rooms at Movies sleep four on two full beds (almost identical to what you'll find in the standard rooms at the other value resorts, although the All-Stars and AofA are a little less crowded at the entry door, and a little more crowded by the bath wall, than are standard rooms at Pop). At about 260 square feet, these standard rooms are very, very small. Besides the two full beds, you'll find in the sleeping area a table and two chairs, a TV/dresser combo, and a mini-fridge. There are no coffee-makers in these standard rooms. In the divided bath, you'll find a clothes hanging area, hair dryer, and single sink separated from the rest of the room by a fabric curtain. Next to this you'll find the toilet and tub in their own room. No rooms at Movies have balconies, and all are accessed from exterior corridors.

Dining is in Cinema Hall at the World Premiere food court. In terms of size and menu, Movies has the best food court among the All-Stars, making it average among the values. The bar is set in the exterior wall between the food court and the pool, and serves guests from both areas. There is no table service restaurant at any value, nor any character meals.

Amenities available at the resort include nightly movies, jogging trails, playgrounds, and an arcade.

At Movies, you can pay extra for "preferred" rooms closer to Cinema Hall. Non-preferred rooms are $110/night on weekdays and $133/night on Fridays and Saturdays during the 2014 Fall season. 2014 peak prices for these rooms are $198 and prices bottom out at $96/night. These prices are the same as similar rooms at the other All-Stars, about $20-22 per night less expensive than AofA, and around $10 less per night than Pop.

DISNEY'S ALL-STAR SPORTS RESORT

Disney's All-Star Sports Resort ("Sports") is themed around five sports—baseball, basketball, tennis, football, and surfing, with two accommodation buildings in each theme. These sports are represented by much-larger-than-life icons of sports objects, and by theming of the spaces between the two buildings of each theme to the playing field of the respective sport. Found in Stadium Hall near the entrance to the resort are dining, shops, and guest services. The main Surf's Up pool is just outside Stadium Hall. You'll find a smaller—but still plenty big—baseball field-themed pool in the baseball area. (You need to bring towels from your room to any of these pools; housekeeping can get you more towels if you need them.)

All transport to theme parks, water parks, and Downtown Disney is via bus. Sports shares most buses most of the year (except to the Magic Kingdom) with sister resorts All-Star Music and All-Star Movies. Buses stop at Sports first and Movies last—which means that Sports guests are most likely to get a seat, making Sports the most convenient of the All-Stars, and of average convenience among the values. The All-Star resorts are Animal Kingdom Area resorts, and are the least conveniently located of the values.

Sports appeals to kids interested in its specific themes, but is otherwise thin on general kid appeal. The rooms themselves have only the lightest theming related to their area. Adults may find the theming garish, or may warm to the represented sports. All the All-Stars can be overrun with kids competing in events at ESPN Wide World of Sports, and this seems most common at Sports.

Standard rooms at Sports sleep four on two full beds in rooms pretty much identical to what you'll find at the other All-Stars. At about 260 square feet, these standard rooms are teeny but adequate for sleeping. Besides the two full beds, you'll find in the sleeping area a table and two chairs, a TV/dresser combo, and a mini-fridge. There are no coffee-makers in these rooms. In the divided bath, you'll find a clothes hanging area, hair dryer, and single sink separated from the rest of the room by a fabric curtain. Next to this you'll find the toilet and tub in their own room. No rooms at Sports have balconies, and all are accessed from exterior corridors.

Dining is in Stadium Hall at the End Zone food court. Recently renovated, this space is still too small for the guests it tries to serve, and is below average among the values. The bar is set in the exterior wall between the food court and the pool, and serves guests from both areas. There is no table service restaurant at any value, nor any character meals.

Amenities available at the resort include nightly movies, jogging trails, playgrounds, and an arcade.

At Sports you can pay extra for "preferred" rooms closer to Stadium Hall. Non-preferred rooms are $110/night on weekdays and $133/night on Fridays and Saturdays during the 2014 Fall season. 2014 peak prices for these rooms are $198 and prices bottom out at $96/night. These prices are the same as similar rooms at the other All-Stars, about $20-22 per night less expensive than AofA, and around $10 less per night than Pop.

DISNEY'S ALL-STAR MUSIC RESORT

Disney's All-Star Music Resort ("Music") is themed around five musical genres—calypso, jazz, Broadway, rock, and country, with two accommodation buildings in each theme. These genres are represented by much-larger-than-life icons of musical instruments and other objects related to the theme, e.g., cowboy boots in the country music area, and by a bit of theming here and there of the spaces between the two buildings to the musical genre. Found in Melody Hall near the entrance to the resort are dining, shops, and guest services. The main Guitar pool is just outside Melody Hall. You'll find a smaller—but still plenty big—piano-themed pool deeper in the resort. (You need to bring towels from your room to any of these pools; housekeeping can get you more towels if you need them.)

All transport to theme parks, water parks, and Downtown Disney is via bus. Music shares most buses most of the year (except to the Magic Kingdom) with sister resorts All-Star Movies and All-Star Sports. Buses stop at Sports first and Movies last—which means that Music guest are less likely than Sports guests to get a seat, but more likely than Movies guests. This makes Music of average convenience among the All-Stars, and of below-average convenience among the values. The All-Star resorts are Animal Kingdom Area resorts, and are the least conveniently located of the values.

Music appeals to kids interested in its specific themes, but is otherwise quite thin on general kid appeal. The rooms themselves have only the lightest theming related to their area. Adults will find it the loveliest of the values, and its overall layout the easiest to understand and navigate.

Music has two very different room types: standard four-person rooms found in all its themed areas, and six-person family suites in the Calypso and Jazz areas.

Standard rooms at Music sleep four on two full beds in rooms pretty much identical to what you'll find at the other All-Stars. At about 260 square feet, these standard rooms are really small but adequate for sleeping. Besides the two full beds, you'll find in the sleeping area a table and two chairs, a TV/dresser combo, and a mini-fridge. There are no coffee-makers in these standard rooms. In the divided bath, you'll find a clothes hanging area, hair dryer, and single sink separated from the rest of the room by a fabric curtain. Next to this you'll find the toilet and tub in their own room. No rooms at Music have balconies, and all are accessed from exterior corridors.

Family Suites at Music sleep six in twice the area of standard rooms, and contain a living room with three furniture items that fold out into beds—a couch that folds out into a full, and a chair and an ottoman that each fold out into twins. It also has a master bedroom with a queen and two full baths, each accessible to anyone in the room, plus a kitchenette with a mini-fridge, microwave, and coffee-maker. These rooms are not nearly as much fun as the suites at AofA, and the fold-out beds are not nearly as comfortable for older/heavier guests. But some families will appreciate the more flexible number of sleeping spots, and others the fact that these suites are typically $70/night less expensive than those at AofA.

Dining is in Melody Hall at the Intermission food court. This space is too small for the guests it tries to serve, and is below average among the values. The bar is set in the exterior wall between the food court and the pool, and serves guests from both areas. There is no table service restaurant at any value, nor any character meals.

Amenities available at the resort include nightly movies, jogging trails, playgrounds, and an arcade.

At Music you can pay extra for "preferred" standard rooms closer to Melody Hall. Non-preferred standard rooms are $110/night on week-days and $133/night on Fridays and Saturdays during the 2014 Fall season. 2014 peak prices for these rooms are $198 and prices bottom out at $96/night. These prices are the same as similar rooms at the other All-Stars, about $20-22 per night less expensive than AofA, and around $10 less per night than Pop.

Family Suites at Music are all the same cost, whether in Jazz or Calypso. Family Suites are $253/night on weekdays and $292/night on Fridays and Saturdays during the 2014 Fall season. 2014 peak prices for these rooms are $448 and prices bottom out at $239/night. These suites are about $70 less per night than at AofA.

The Moderate Resorts

DISNEY'S PORT ORLEANS FRENCH QUARTER RESORT

Disney's Port Orleans French Quarter Resort ("POFQ") is one of two moderates with "Port Orleans" in the name—the other is Port Orleans Riverside Resort. Some mistakenly call these one resort. The only point of commonality most guests will ever notice is that guests at either are welcome to share the other's pools. The confusion comes from Disney shutting down, more than a decade ago, the table service restaurant and boat and bike rentals at what was then known as Port Orleans Resort, and is now POFQ, and then renaming both resorts as Port Orleans— indicating to guests that these amenities weren't really missing, but just more distant, at Port Orleans Riverside, part of the same resort now...

Disney does not much bother with this distinction any more—other than making it clear to guests that they are welcome to partake in everything offered at both. It turns out that despite the missing ame-nities at Port Orleans French Quarter, it is the most highly valued of the Disney moderates—which is why alone among the moderates it is almost never included in Disney's discounts and other special offers.

POFQ has as its theme New Orleans and Mardi Gras, combining lacy wrought iron, lovely gardens, and cobblestoned streets. You'll also find Mardi Gras figures and decorations scattered about, especially in the food court and near the main pool. POFQ has half as many rooms as the other traditional moderates, and has—with no lake or river in the middle—a much more compact footprint for those rooms. As a result, it is, by far, the easiest moderate to get around. It has no real separate areas for its seven accommodations buildings, although you'll see North Quarter and South Quarter signage meant to help you find your building. Near the entrance at the center you'll find dining, shops, and guest services in the Port Orleans Mint building. The only pool, the Mardi-Gras themed Doubloon Lagoon, is just steps away, and the sole bus stop is right out front. One pool may seem like not enough, but the main pool area at POFQ has 65% of the area that Port Orleans Riverside's main pool has, but only half as many rooms, and the pool volume at POFQ is almost 40% larger. Most times of the year POFQ shares buses (except to the Magic Kingdom) with Riverside, but the single bus stop on the Magic Kingdom route makes it overall the most convenient of the moderates.

All transport to theme parks and water parks is via buses. Downtown Disney is accessible by both boat and bus. POFQ, like Riverside, is labeled as a Downtown Disney Area Resort in Disney's way-finding material, but is more centrally located than that implies. The Magic Kingdom, Epcot, and Disney's Hollywood Studios are all close.

There's no special kid appeal at POFQ, and in fact the Mardi Gras theming—including, for example, an enormous depiction of a dragon/snake at the pool—wigs some kids out. But POFQ is the loveliest and most romantic of the moderates, and that, when combined with the ease of getting around and to the parks, makes it a great favorite of adults among the moderates.

Disney's Port Orleans French Quarter Resort Floor Plan ~314 Square Feet

Rooms at POFQ are typical of those at the traditional moderates. They sleep four on two queens in about 314 square feet, and all come with a table and two chairs, a dresser/mini-fridge, coffee-maker, hair-dryer, and a divided, family-friendly bath. In the bath, the two sinks and closet/dressing area are shielded from the sleeping part of the room by a curtain, and the tub and toilet have their own room. All buildings have elevators. No rooms have balconies. All rooms are accessed from exterior corridors.

The only dining at POFQ is at the food court Sassagoula Floatworks Food Company, which is well above average among the moderates, and has a nice sprinkling of themed offerings—for example, beignets, Po Boys, jambalaya, and BBQ ribs served with collard greens. (You can. of course. walk to the table service Boatwright's at Riverside.) The indoor bar, the Scat Cats Lounge, is not as rollicking as the River Roost Lounge at Riverside, but one should always have the option to not rollick. There are no character meals.

Amenities are thinner than at the other moderates, although most that are missing are nearby at Riverside. On site, you'll find (besides the pool) an arcade, playground, and nightly movies.

At POFQ there are no "preferred" rooms—itself an indication of how easy it is to get around for a moderate—but you can still pay extra for king beds, for garden views, for pool views, and for water views. Standard view rooms are $203/night on weekdays and $226/night on Fridays and Saturdays during the 2014 Fall season. 2014 peak prices for these rooms are $284 and prices bottom out $182/night.

DISNEY'S PORT ORLEANS RIVERSIDE RESORT

Disney's Port Orleans Riverside Resort ("POR") is one of two moderates with "Port Orleans" in the name—the other is Port Orleans French Quarter. Some mistakenly call these one resort. The only point of commonality most guests will ever notice is that guests at either are welcome to share the other's pools and other amenities.

POR has as its theme the 19th century American South, particularly the bayou and riverine areas of Louisiana. Rooms in the massive resort are in two areas, Magnolia Bend, with four large buildings meant to be reminiscent of plantation mansions, and Alligator Bayou, with many smaller buildings meant to evoke a more rural feel. Found in the Sassagoula Steamship Company area near the entrance to the resort are dining, shops, and guest services. The main pool, located on a central island, has a bit of saw-mill theming, and is average among moderate pools. Testifying to the sprawl of the resort and the distance of many rooms from Ol' Man Island, you'll find five additional smaller pools around the resort. The resort proper has four bus stops, but most times of the year shares buses (except to the Magic Kingdom) with nearby Port Orleans French Quarter, making it less convenient than either Coronado Springs or Port Orleans French Quarter. The overall accommodations footprint of POR is larger than that of Coronado Springs, but, because it has no central lake, the main services at POR are more central than those at Coronado Springs.

All transport to theme parks and water parks is via bus. Downtown Disney is accessible by both boat and bus. POR is labeled as a Downtown Disney Area Resort in Disney's way-finding material, but is more centrally located than that implies. Before the Animal Kingdom and Blizzard Beach opened, the two Port Orleans Resorts were in fact the most centrally located moderates, and the Magic Kingdom, Epcot, and Disney's Hollywood Studios are still all close—at least after the buses finally get out of the resort itself. The resort itself is massive, and some rooms are a hike from the main services, and others from the main pool...some from both.

There's no special kid appeal at POR compared to that at Caribbean Beach, and no special adult appeal compared to that at Coronado Springs and POFQ. But even so, POR is likely the best-loved, most frequently recommended, and most loyally defended of all the moderate resorts.

There are three very different room types at POR. All are about the same size as those at the other traditional moderates, about 314 square feet, and all come with a table and two chairs, a dresser/TV/mini-fridge combo, coffee-maker, hair-dryer, and a divided, family-friendly bath. In the bath, the two sinks and closet/dressing area are shielded from the sleeping part of the room by a curtain, and the tub and toilet have their own room. The two story buildings in Alligator Bayou have no elevators, but the taller Magnolia Bend buildings do. No rooms have balconies. All rooms are accessed from exterior corridors.

Rooms in the Alligator Bayou section of POR are the only traditional moderate rooms that sleep five—two each in two queens, and the fifth in a small murphy bed (about 66 inches long by 31 inches wide, and meant for a kid ten or younger) that folds down beneath the TV. (Caribbean Beach's 2014 rehab is expected to add fifth sleeping spots there, too.)

Rooms in half the Magnolia Bend section have "Royal" theming, and are more expensive. These rooms sleep 4 in two queens, and have much prince and (especially) princess detail, including a lovely headboard light show based on the *Princess and the Frog* triggered by an easy-to-miss button on the side.

Rooms in the other half of Magnolia Bend also sleep 4 in two queens, but do not have the special royal theming—nor its extra cost. They are also largely more convenient than the Royal Rooms, and, if you don't need the fifth sleeping spot, more livable than the Alligator Bend rooms.

Dining is at Sassagoula Steamship Company, with a food court that's average among the moderates and a table service restaurant, Boatwright's Dining Hall, that's also average. The food court is too small for the crowds it faces, and has little special on its standard menu to reflect the theming other than grits at breakfast and a Cajun chicken sandwich. The indoor bar, the River Roost Lounge, has a widely loved family-friendly show from "Ye Haa" Bob Jackson most Wednesday through Saturday evenings. There's also a bar at the main pool. There are no character meals.

Amenities available at the resort include nightly movies, campfires, bike rental, fishing, jogging trails, playgrounds, and an arcade (watercraft rental closed in March 2014). The main pool is far too small for the resort, and can't fit everyone who would like to be there.

At POR you can pay more for preferred locations that are a closer walk to the Sassagoula Steamship Company, for the Royal rooms, for king beds, for garden views, and for water views. Standard view, non-preferred rooms are $203/night on weekdays and $226/night on Fridays and Saturdays during the 2014 Fall season. 2014 peak prices for these rooms are $284 and prices bottom out at $182/night.

DISNEY'S CARIBBEAN BEACH RESORT

Disney's Caribbean Beach Resort ("CB") is themed around Caribbean islands, their beaches, and the pirates who once voyaged among them. Rooms in the massive resort are found in six "villages" ringing a lake, all named after Caribbean destinations: Trinidad North, Trinidad South, Martinique, Barbados, Aruba and Jamaica. Each colorful village has (or at Martinique, shares) palm-tree lined beaches, and each has its own pool and bus stop. The central Old Port Royale area includes the main pool at the resort, the pirate-themed Fuentes del Morro Pool—the best pool of the Disney World moderate resorts—as well as dining, shops, yet another bus stop, and some guest services. (Other guest services are located in the out-of-the-way Customs House.)

Seven pools and seven bus stops may sound like an abundance of riches. They are not.

Rather, there are this many pools and bus stops because of design flaws that make CB large and hard to get around—especially for guests staying at Trinidad South, and to a lesser extent, at Barbados. This is the resort's major negative. All transport to theme parks, water parks, and Downtown Disney is via buses. Because of the number of required bus stops, CB is not particularly convenient to anywhere, but is closest to Disney's Hollywood Studios and Epcot.

A second major negative is that CB is the only remaining "traditional" moderate with full beds—although queen beds will be increasingly available as part of a general rehab that began in 2014.

All of the rooms at CB have Disney theming—a light touch of *Finding Nemo* in most, and deep pirate theming in the distant (and overly expensive) Trinidad South area. The combination of Disney-themed rooms, sparkling beaches, bright colors, swaying palms, and the pirate-themed main pool give CB high kid appeal among the moderates. Adults like most of this, too, but can be frustrated by the full-sized beds, walking distances, and all the bus stops.

Standard rooms at CB hold four people on two full beds (queens in re-done rooms) in about 314 square feet. This makes them—other than bed size—similar to what you'll find at the other traditional moderates. These rooms are plenty large for four. They come with a table and two chairs, a dresser/TV/mini-fridge combo, coffee-maker, hair-dryer, a smaller storage chest, and a divided, family-friendly bath. In the bath, the sinks and closet/dressing area are shielded from the rest of the room by a curtain, and the tub and toilet have their own room. The two-story buildings that hold these rooms have no elevators, and no rooms have balconies. All rooms are accessed from exterior corridors.

CB's 2014 rehab will bring not only queen beds, but also, it's expected, to some rooms fifth sleeping spots—likely as a murphy bed similar to what's available in the Alligator Bayou section of POR.

Dining is at Old Port Royale, with a food court that's a little below average among the moderates and too small for peak crowds, and a table service restaurant, Shutters, that's been revitalized with more Caribbean and seafood flair since new chef Mike Reitzler signed on. There's no dedicated indoor bar—the only bar is outdoors near the main pool. There are no character meals.

Other amenities available at the resort include nightly movies, campfires, bike rental, fishing, a Pirate Adventure cruise, great jogging trails, playgrounds, and an arcade (watercraft rental closed in March 2014). The main pirate-themed pool is not small, but is so popular that it can't fit everyone who would like to be there.

At CB, you can pay more for preferred locations that are closer to Old Port Royale, for the Pirate rooms that are quite a hike, for king beds, and for water views. Standard view, non-preferred rooms are $203/night on weekdays and $226/night on Fridays and Saturdays during the 2014 Fall season. 2014 peak prices for these rooms are $284 and prices bottom out at $182/night.

Preferred rooms and a rental car would make up for the inconveniences of CB, but may add $80 per night or more, depending on the hotel price season and seasonal rental car rates.

DISNEY'S CORONADO SPRINGS RESORT

Disney's Coronado Springs Resort's ("CS") theme is based on the American Southwest, Spanish-colonial Mexico, and the architectural remnants of Mesoamerican civilizations. Rooms in the massive resort are found in three areas surrounding a lake: the Casitas, elegant colonnaded three- and four-story buildings; the Ranchos, a sharply contrasting, desert-inspired area; and the Cabanas, a beach-house themed area with beaches, too—fewer than at Caribbean Beach, but more than at any other moderate. The El Centro area, between the Casitas and Cabanas, includes dining, shopping, and guest services, and leads to the Coronado Springs Convention Center. Away from El Centro, and near the actual center of the resort—and most convenient to the Cabanas and Ranchos—is the Mesoamerican-themed main pool, the Lost City of Cibola, in the Dig Site area, the second-best pool among the moderates. Each of the three room areas has its own smaller pool (the Casitas pool has the only lap pool at Disney World), as well as a bus stop. A fourth bus stop is at El Centro.

All transport to theme parks, water parks, and Downtown Disney is via buses (or your rental car). CS is labeled as an Animal Kingdom Area Resort in Disney's way-finding material, but is in fact the most centrally-located of all the moderate resorts. This, combined with its "only" four bus stops, makes it the second most convenient of the moderates—among them, only Port Orleans French Quarter is more convenient for park travel. The resort itself is massive, and some buildings in the Ranchos in particular are quite distant from El Centro.

Coronado Springs is the only moderate with convention facilities. This has led to much fussing, largely unfair. The same number of rooms occupied by conventioneers rather than families means fewer people in total at the resort (because conventioneers average fewer people per room) and fewer people at the bus stops and pools (as the fewer conventioneers are in meetings, not going to the parks or the pools). Most of the time, except breakfast, there's also fewer people in CS's public dining spaces, as most meetings have meals served as part of the meeting program. However, when a thousand people leave a meeting at once, and all want to go someplace, things clot up quickly.

On the other hand, because of the demands of the business travelers at the convention center, Coronado Springs has a much higher level of services and amenities than at the other moderates. There are the usual nightly movies, campfires, bike rental, fishing, playgrounds, and arcade. In addition, uniquely at CS among the moderates, you'll find watercraft rental, a health club, spa services, real room service, a main pool menu with real food, the largest hot tub at Disney World, multiple bars, and a business center. The effect of these extra services is to make Coronado Springs quite attractive to adults. Kids like the beach-themed Cabanas, the Dig Site area and main pool, and, if they aren't familiar with the geography, the exotic Southwest theming.

Standard rooms at CS hold four people on two queen beds in about 314 square feet. They are similarly sized to those at the other traditional moderates, but have no Disney theming—and are in fact the most stark rooms among the moderates. In a concession to convention travelers, they come with a desk rather than the table and two chairs you'll find in the other traditional moderates. Most other room amenities are similar—a dresser/TV/mini-fridge combo, coffee-maker, and hair dryer. The bath is divided and family friendly, but also designed so a conventioneer can use both parts at once. As a result, it has one sink rather than two, and sliding wooden doors separating it from the sleeping area, rather than the fabric curtains of the other traditional moderates. All buildings have elevators, and no rooms have balconies. All rooms are accessed from exterior corridors.

Dining is at El Centro, and, unless you are on the dining plan, is more expensive than at the other moderates. The food court, Pepper Market, used to be the best food court among the Disney World hotels, but while still good has gotten less interesting recently. The table service restaurant, Maya Grill, has a menu suited to the Southwest theming of the resort, but is overpriced. The indoor bar, Rix Lounge, is the closest thing to a club you'll find in a Disney-owned hotel; there's an additional outdoor lakeside bar, and yet another bar by the pool. There are no character meals.

The extra amenities at CS come, most times of the year, at a cost of $3-6/night more than the other traditional moderates. You can pay more for preferred locations that are a closer walk to El Centro, for king beds, and for water views. Standard view, non-preferred rooms are $203/night on weekdays and $226/night on Fridays and Saturdays during the 2014 Fall season. 2014 peak prices for these rooms are $290, and prices bottom out at $187/night.

THE CABINS AT DISNEY'S FORT WILDERNESS RESORT

Disney has had some trouble over the years communicating what's in the Cabins at Disney's Fort Wilderness Resort. The cabins—each its own little building—are distinctive spaces, sleeping six in two rooms, and with full kitchens. There used to be a "home away from home" category which the Cabins were in, but everything else in this group was a "deluxe" class room, and the Cabins didn't match up well with them.

So to eliminate the confusion about amenities, in 2009 Disney re-classed these Cabins as "moderates". This is a fair description of room-level amenities and spaciousness, but there's really few other ways that the Cabins are like the other moderates (inconvenience is one, and thin kid appeal another). As a result, the phrase "traditional moderate" started being used for all the moderates except the Cabins.

The Cabins are one of two lodging options at Disney's Fort Wilderness Campground and Resort—the other being campsites. Fort Wilderness is one of America's great campgrounds, and the Cabins share in all the wonderful recreational activities available in the rest of this resort. The Cabins are each small, standalone buildings, looking on the outside like a rustic cabin, and on the inside like a nice small wood-paneled mobile home. If driving—and you should have a car to stay in these—you park right in front. Each cabin also has an outdoor barbecue grill and a big deck with picnic table.

As you walk in, you'll find first the full kitchen, then a small dining table and small living room. A near-full-sized bed folds down from a wall in the living room, so this space sleeps two—typically the parents. Further back is a full bath. It's not divided, and is a bit short on hot water, so it doesn't well suit the six people that these cabins can sleep. Beyond this is the back bedroom, with a tight-fitting full bed on one side and a pair of bunk beds on the other.

The Cabins are not the least expensive way to get a Disney room for six—a family suite at All-Star Music or Art of Animation is that. But they are the least expensive way to get moderate-level fittings and fixtures for six, and are by far the least expensive way to get a full kitchen.

The challenge, though, is some crowding, especially around the bath, thin kid appeal—unless your kids love campgrounds—and great inconvenience. If you don't have a car, it takes two transport acts to get off Fort Wilderness and to a park—the first bus gets you to another bus stop or boat dock, from which you go to your final destination. We couldn't imagine staying here if you don't have a car.

Fort Wilderness has some wonderfully family-friendly table service dining—the storied Hoop-Dee-Doo Revue and Mickey's Backyard

The Cabins at Disney's Fort Wilderness Resort
Floor Plan ~504 Square Feet

Barbecue. There's also Trails End restaurant. Plus you have that kitchen. But there's not much in the way of counter service, and to get to these table service venues from the Cabins, you need to take a bus.

The resort has two pools. One is dull but within walking distance of the Cabins; the other, the main pool, was themed in 2009 but remains the weakest among the moderates. This pool is farther (a bus trip for most), and is in the same Meadows area as where you'll find many of Fort Wilderness's other amenities. At the Settlement end of Fort Wilderness, you'll find (via bus...you can't drive to these) the beach, marina, boat docks (with boat service to the Magic Kingdom, and to the nearby Wilderness Lodge and Contemporary resorts), and the dining noted above.

If you need the lowest-priced kitchen you can find, need to sleep six, and have a car, the Cabins are great options. Otherwise, not so much.

The Cabins have no extra price options for views and such. They are $367/night on weekdays and $393/night on Fridays and Saturdays during the 2014 Fall season. 2014 peak prices for these rooms are $562/night, and prices bottom out at $330/night.

The Deluxe Resorts

DISNEY'S POLYNESIAN RESORT

Disney's Polynesian Resort ("Poly"), a monorail resort, is themed around the Pacific islands of Polynesia. Theming at the Polynesian is pervasive and detailed, but more subtle than that of the jaw-dropping Wilderness Lodge and Animal Kingdom Lodge. Lush landscaping, lovely beaches, flaming torches, and exotically styled and named "longhouses" (where you find the rooms) create a delightful impression. In the Great Ceremonial House ("GCH") near the entrance to the resort are dining, shops, guest services, and, on the second floor, access to the resort monorail with service to the Magic Kingdom, the other monorail resorts, and the Transportation and Ticket Center (TTC). The often-crowded main Nanea Volcano Pool is just outside the GCH, and nearby is a second pool, good-sized but short on sunbathing space.

With travel to the Magic Kingdom available via both monorail and boat, and many rooms at the Polynesian within easy walking distance of the TTC and its Epcot monorail, the Polynesian is the most convenient Disney World resort. Transportation to the other parks and Downtown Disney is via buses, typically shared with one or two other Magic Kingdom area resorts.

Construction has been ongoing at the Polynesian since 2013, affecting its eastern beaches and longhouses, and is widely expected to greatly expand in mid-2014, leading to closures of the main pool, more of the beach, and parts of GCH. If this happens, first-timers will still find a pool, but one not so fun or large as Nanea; a free ticket to Blizzard Beach; and most, but not all of, what makes the Poly visually special, larded with some construction activity, off-theme visuals, and mild noise.

All standard rooms at the Poly were refurbished in 2013, and sleep five on two queens and a sofa that flips into a twin. Rooms are about 415 square feet, among the largest at Disney World. (Larger rooms at the Polynesian are being converted into DVC rooms.) Besides the two queens and couch, you'll find an easy chair and ottoman, a desk with a small rolling table underneath, desk chair, mini-fridge, TV/dresser combo, two closets, and a coffeemaker. The spacious bath includes two sinks and a hair dryer, but is not divided, making it a little less family friendly than you'll find in more recently built hotels (the Polynesian was built in the early 70s). Second-floor standard rooms don't have balconies; other floors have patios or balconies. All rooms are accessed from interior corridors. Like the other deluxe resorts, you can also reserve concierge-supported rooms (Disney calls these "club" rooms) and suites.

The Poly has three table service restaurants and one quick service option. Dining is in GCH, except for the Luau which has its own building at the northwest edge of the resort. 'Ohana is a great family restaurant that features well-loved character breakfasts with Mickey, Lilo, and Stitch. Kona Café has a lousy setting, but terrific and under-appreciated food. The Luau fills any need you may have for a Polynesian-themed dinner show. The quick service location is Captain Jacks, too small for the resort but convenient to the pool. More great dining is just a monorail ride away at the Grand Floridian and Contemporary. There's a bar outside of 'Ohana, and another at the pool.

Amenities available at the resort include beaches, nightly movies, campfires, jogging trails, playgrounds, boat rental, bike rental, fishing, a volleyball court, and an arcade. Poly guests can use the spa and health club Senses on the Poly side of the Grand Floridian. Oddly, the Poly is alone among the deluxes in having no hot tub. The beaches are a popular spot for watching the fireworks for the Magic Kingdom across the Seven Seas lagoon—parts of these are already closed for construction, and more may be. The Poly is one of only three Disney deluxe resorts (the Wilderness and Animal Kingdom Lodges are the others) that are not convention hotels.

At the Poly you can pay extras for views. Standard view five-person rooms are $510/night on weekdays and $574/night on Fridays and Saturdays during the 2014 Fall season. 2014 peak prices for these rooms are $760 and prices bottom out at $482/night.

DISNEY'S GRAND FLORIDIAN RESORT & SPA

Disney's Grand Floridian Resort & Spa ("GF"), a monorail resort inspired by the Hotel Del Coronado in San Diego, is a lovely mix of gorgeous landscaping, white Victorian shapes and details, and red roofs. It visually enchants adults but does nothing in particular for kids. At opening, it supplanted Disney's Contemporary Resort as Disney World's flagship-- and most expensive—hotel, leading some Contemporary Cast Members to refer to GF as the "red roof inn". (Remind yourself of this if GF ever seems too stuffy or self-satisfied.) There are three basic areas at GF: the main building, the outer buildings, and the Disney Vacation Club Villas. The main building has most dining, all shops, guest services, some suites, and several types of "club" rooms (Disney-speak for concierge rooms). The five outer buildings have more club rooms, more suites, all standard rooms, and some smaller but high-ceilinged Dormer Rooms. The Villas are at the southern edge of the resort grounds. From the second floor of the main building, GF guests can access the resort monorail with service to the Magic Kingdom, the other monorail resorts, and the Transportation and Ticket Center (TTC). The uninteresting but large main pool is in a beautifully landscaped area between the main building and the outer buildings, and the smaller but more fun Beach Pool is between the main building and the Villas.

Transportation to the Magic Kingdom is by the resort monorail or a boat shared with the Polynesian. Transportation to Epcot is via the Epcot monorail at TTC, accessible by the resort monorail. Transportation to the other parks and Downtown Disney is via buses, typically shared with one or two other Magic Kingdom area resorts. Transportation convenience is above average among the deluxes for a Magic Kingdom focused trip, but not as good as sister monorail resorts the Contemporary and Polynesian.

Adults generally love the exterior and grounds of GF, while reactions to interior decorating choices are mixed, with some finding them stuffy. Kids often don't get the theme—a hotel themed as a hotel?—or it fails to delight them.

Guest rooms at the Grand Floridian are being refurbished in 2014. All standard rooms at GF sleep five on two queens and a sofa that flips into a twin bed. Standard rooms are about 440 square feet—larger than the typical rooms at any other Disney-owned hotel. Besides the two queens and couch, you'll find an easy chair, a desk with a small rolling table underneath, a desk chair, mini-fridge, TV, dresser, closet (with robes!), and a coffee-maker. The spacious divided bath includes two sinks and a hair dryer, and a toilet and tub in a separate room. Rooms in the nearby Villas are also available for rent to the general public. Of the four room types at the Villas, studios are most comparable to standard GF rooms. They sleep five in a smaller overall space, but one with a better bath, on a queen, fold-out couch, and flip-down 72" long murphy bed. All rooms are accessed from interior corridors, and all rooms have balconies or patios.

The Grand Floridian has the best adult dining of any Disney resort, some attractive kid dining, and easy access to other great options at the other monorail resorts. GF has five table service restaurants and one quick service option. Three are on the second floor of the main building. Victoria and Albert's is by far the best and most expensive restaurant at Disney World. Kids under ten are not allowed, and jackets are required. Citricos is a seafood-focused establishment with inspired modern fare. "Resort casual" is the appropriate dress. On the first floor is 1900 Park Fare, with character meals at breakfast and dinner—Mary Poppins and others in the morning, and Cinderella and her family in the evening. Also on the first floor is the unpretentious and unambitious Grand Floridian Café—with no dress code, no characters, and no fancy dining, it's usually the easiest to book, but also the least interesting for kids or adults. The fifth table service restaurant, Narcoossee's, fronts the Seven Seas Lagoon near the boat dock, specializes in seafood, and has a resort casual dress code. The quick service option is in the main building but only accessible from outside, and is one of the best quick service options among the deluxes. There's a bar on the second floor of the main building, and another at each pool.

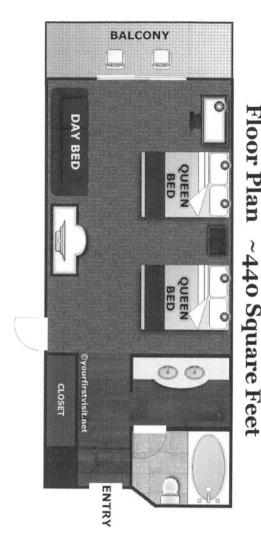

Disney's Grand Floridian Resort & Spa Floor Plan ~440 Square Feet

The Grand Floridian has an extensive set of amenities, including beaches, nightly movies, campfires, jogging trails, playgrounds, a pirate cruise, boat rental, fishing, a great spa and fitness center, hot tubs, a volleyball court, and an arcade.

At the Grand Floridian you can pay extra for views. Standard view (Outer Building Garden View) five-person rooms are $568/night on weekdays and $636/night on Fridays and Saturdays during the 2014 Fall season. 2014 peak prices for these rooms are $856 and prices bottom out at $549/night.

DISNEY'S WILDERNESS LODGE

Disney's Wilderness Lodge ("WL"), near the Magic Kingdom, is inspired by the great U.S. National Park Lodges, and celebrates them and the mountain West. Its astonishing theming begins with its jaw-dropping lobby and continues with extensive detail everywhere in the resort. Nearby is the Disney Vacation Club Villas at the Wilderness Lodge, also available to all for rent. Guest services, a shop, and most dining are accessed from the lobby. Most rooms are in two wings off the lobby that enclose a mountain-stream-themed courtyard that ends in the delightful main pool. A smaller pool is between the WL and the Villas.

The Wilderness Lodge is on Bay Lake near the Magic Kingdom, which is a ten-minute boat ride away. Boats also connect the Wilderness Lodge with the nearby Contemporary Resort and Fort Wilderness, giving easy access to the great dining options at those resorts. The other theme parks, water parks, and Downtown Disney are accessed via shared buses that can take a while. The Wilderness Lodge is well located for a Magic Kingdom-focused trip.

The exterior architecture, lobby, detailing, and pools make the Wilderness Lodge an astonishingly kid-appealing resort. Adults enjoy it as well, although they might find its rooms smaller than expected.

Disney's Wilderness Lodge   ~340 Square Feet
Floor Plan from yourfirstvisit.net

Standard guest rooms at WL, with about 340 square feet, are tied with those at Disney's Animal Kingdom Lodge as the smallest deluxe rooms on property (they are also the least expensive such rooms). No five-person rooms are available—standard rooms sleep four on two queens. You'll also find a table and two chairs, mini-fridge, TV, dresser, closet, and a coffee-maker. The divided bath includes two sinks and a hair dryer, and a toilet and tub in a separate room. Of the three room types at the Villas, studios are most comparable to standard WL rooms. They sleep five in a slightly larger space, on a queen, a fold-out couch, and a fold-down smaller bed. Disney markets the fifth sleeping spot as a "twin", but we expect it to be closer to 30 inches by 72 inches. These five-person studio rooms will be great choices for five-person families looking for Wilderness Lodge kid appeal who can fit in their beds. Rooms have balconies or patios, and are accessed from interior corridors. Like the other deluxe resorts, you can also reserve concierge-supported rooms (Disney call these "club" rooms) and suites, and WL also has larger "deluxe rooms" that sleep six.

There are two table service restaurants at WL. Artist Point has a resort casual dress code, and offers a Pacific Northwest inspired menu. Whispering Canyon provides raucous fun and family-friendly dining. There are no character meals here, but these and other kid and adult-appealing meals are available at the Contemporary and Fort Wilderness—each just a boat ride away. WL has one of the better counter service options among the deluxes, and the best bar of the Magic Kingdom resorts. There's another bar at the pool.

Amenities include a beach, nightly movies, campfires, jogging trails, playgrounds, boat rental, fishing, a spa/fitness center, hot tubs, volleyball, and arcades. More water sports and a pirate cruise are at the nearby Contemporary. WL is one of three deluxe resorts (the Polynesian and Animal Kingdom Lodge are the others) that are not convention hotels.

At the Wilderness Lodge you can pay extra for views. Standard view rooms are $336/night on weekdays and $407/night on Fridays and Saturdays during the 2014 Fall season. 2014 peak prices for these rooms are $561 and prices bottom out at $325/night.

DISNEY'S CONTEMPORARY RESORT

Disney's Contemporary Resort ("Contemporary"), a monorail resort, is essentially un-themed but still iconic, and, on first impression, visually striking. The massive concrete A-frame with monorails passing through the middle is stunning at first view. However, the spare masses and geometric landscaping quickly fades from notice, and there's not much interesting detail earning a second glance. There are three basic areas at the Contemporary—the Tower, which is what most people mean when they think of it; the South Garden Wing, low-rise rooms without balconies; and Bay Lake Tower, the Disney Vacation Club offering. Found in the Tower are dining, shops, guest services, and, from a dedicated escalator on the fourth floor, access to the resort monorail with service to the Magic Kingdom, the other monorail resorts, and the Transportation and Ticket Center (TTC). The dull but large main pool is outside the Tower, and there's a second dull and somewhat smaller pool between the main pool and Bay Lake. The Contemporary is the only Disney resort from which you can walk to and from the Magic Kingdom. With travel to the Magic Kingdom available via both monorail and walking, the Contemporary is, by far, the most convenient Disney World resort for trips focused solely on that park.

Transportation to Epcot is via the Epcot monorail at TTC, accessible by the resort monorail. Transportation to the other parks and Downtown Disney is via buses, typically shared with one or two other Magic Kingdom area resorts. There's also boat service among the three Bay Lake resorts—the Contemporary, Wilderness Lodge, and Fort Wilderness.

The Contemporary has nothing of the visual kid appeal of the Polynesian or the Wilderness or Animal Kingdom Lodges, but it does make a strong first impression, and some kids continue to be fascinated by the monorail running through the middle.

Standard rooms at the Contemporary were refurbished in 2013, and sleep five on two queens and a sofa that flips into a twin bed. Most rooms are about 400 square feet, among the largest at Disney World. Besides the two queens and couch, you'll find a very large L-shaped desk that is too large to fit gracefully where it is placed, with a small rolling table underneath, a desk chair, mini-fridge, TV, two closets, and a coffee-maker. Clothes storage drawers are in the corner of the desk area, making them a little less usable than those in rooms with more central storage. The spacious bath includes two sinks and a hair dryer, but is not divided, making it a little less family friendly than you'll find in more recently built hotels (the Contemporary was built in the early 70s). Views from the Tower rooms of the Magic Kingdom or Bay Lake are marvelous, and, because it is Disney World's only high-rise hotel, guests in Tower rooms will also find it the most compact Disney hotel to navigate. All Tower rooms have balconies. Garden Wing rooms have similar size and furnishings to Tower rooms, but are much more spread out, and without the views—or balconies—of the Tower rooms. They are also much less expensive. Of the four room types in the Disney Vacation Club at Bay

Lake Tower, studios are most comparable to Tower rooms, but sleep only four in a cramped space with a queen and fold-out couch. All rooms are accessed from interior corridors. Like the other deluxe resorts, you can also reserve concierge-supported Tower rooms (Disney call these "club" rooms) and suites in both the Tower and the Garden Wing.

The Contemporary has three table service restaurants and one quick service option. All dining is in the Tower. The first floor Wave of American Flavors focuses on locally grown and organic offerings. Chef Mickey's on the fourth floor offers a wildly popular buffet attended by Mickey, Minnie, Donald, Goofy, and Pluto. The top-floor California Grill was revamped in 2013, and offers fine modern American and sushi dining with a great view of the Magic Kingdom, especially if you are there during the fireworks. The quick service location is the fourth-floor Contempo Café. More great dining is just a monorail ride away at the Grand Floridian and Polynesian, and a boat ride away at the Wilderness Lodge and Fort Wilderness. There's a weak-looking and mis-placed bar on the fourth floor, a fine setting for a bar at the California Grill, and a pool bar.

The fourth floor of the Contemporary is the center of much of its action, and elevators there can be quite crowded. Guests headed from there to the first floor should consider the escalators.

The Contemporary has as broad a set of amenities as you will find at a Disney resort. They include beaches, nightly movies, campfires, jogging trails, playgrounds, boat rental, bike rental, parasailing, waterskiing, wakeboarding, tubing, tennis, fishing, a spa and fitness center, hot tubs, a Pirate cruise, a volleyball court, and an arcade.

At the Contemporary you can pay extra for views. Standard (Bay Lake) view five-person tower rooms are $560/night on weekdays and $636/night on Fridays and Saturdays during the 2014 Fall season. 2014 peak prices for these rooms are $743 and prices bottom out at $533/night.

DISNEY'S BEACH CLUB RESORT

Disney's Beach Club Resort ("BC"), an Epcot resort, is themed to recollect images of New England Victorian seaside cottages and hotels. The exterior architecture is particularly charming, and of high appeal to adults. Kids don't much get its theming until they see the Stormalong Bay pool and its associated beaches and playgrounds. After that, that's all they see... The Beach Club occupies half of an enormous, long-corridored building, with sister resort The Yacht Club taking up the other half. Nearby you'll find the Disney Vacation Club Villas at the Beach Club Villas. In the center of the enormous building are kitchens and other back-of-the house areas, then on either side the table service restaurants of the two resorts, then the guest service areas (one for each) and shops. Near Crescent Lake you'll find Stormalong Bay pool, shared with the Yacht Club—actually three separate pools, each with its own focus: a sand-bottomed shallow pool delightful for little ones; a pool perfect for drifting or tubing; and a pool for swimming. Fun water slides accessed from a shipwreck (!) on a beach splash down at one end of this pool. Some call Stormalong Bay a "mini water park". That's a stretch yet does capture the difference between it and every other Disney World pool. There's two smaller pools at BC—the better one back by the Villas—and another at the very far end of the Yacht Club.

The Beach Club is near the back entrance to Epcot, the International Gateway. For Epcot, walk or take a boat. For most BC rooms, the boats are a long walk away, so walking is often the better choice. Hollywood Studios is best accessed by boat, and the other theme parks, water parks, and Downtown Disney via shared buses that can take a while. The Beach Club is wonderfully located for trips centered on Epcot, and a favorite of many returning family visitors. It's not so well located for a Magic Kingdom focused trip.

Adults generally love the architecture and convenience to Epcot of BC, while kids often don't get the theme—a hotel themed as a cottage?—but just don't care after they see the pool.

Guest rooms at the BC are expected to be refurbished in 2014. Most standard rooms at BC sleep five on two queens and a daybed (some rooms omit the daybed). Standard rooms are about 380 square feet—in the middle of the deluxe range, but well-appointed and proportioned. Five-person rooms have beside the beds a desk with a small rolling table underneath, a desk chair, mini-fridge, TV, dresser, closet, and a coffee-maker. The divided bath includes two sinks and a hair dryer, and a toilet and tub in a separate room. Four-person rooms have the same size, omit the daybed, but add an easy chair. Rooms in the nearby Villas are also available for rent to the general public. Of the three room types at the Villas, studios are most comparable to standard BC rooms. They sleep four in a smaller overall space, on a queen and fold-out couch. All rooms are accessed from interior corridors. Most BC standard rooms have small balconies or patios that seat two, but many BC rooms have tiny balconies with barely room to stand. This choice adds interest and grace to the façade, but impedes livability. Like the other deluxe resorts, you can also reserve concierge-supported rooms (Disney call these "club" rooms) and suites.

BC has two table service restaurants. The Cape May Café (the New Jersey name of which confuses the New England theming) offers a character breakfast with Goofy, and other characters like Minnie,

Chip and Dale, but not Mickey. In the evening, Cape May converts to a no-character "clambake" buffet. Seafood can be good from a buffet—but it can't be great. By the pool is the glorious Beaches and Cream ice cream and burger-focused establishment, with not remotely enough seats. There's no real counter service here, just a few options in the back of the gift shop. You can walk to sister resort the Yacht Club or the nearby Epcot resort the BoardWalk Inn, but you won't find any counter service at either, nor any kid-appealing table service restaurants. Dining in Epcot is also an option, but may be impractical for families without hopper tickets. There's an indoor bar and another at the pool.

Among them, the three Epcot resorts—the Beach and Yacht Clubs, and BoardWalk Inn—provide within walking distance access to almost any amenity, including beaches, nightly movies, campfires, jogging trails, playgrounds, a pirate cruise, boat rental, fishing, a spa/fitness center, tennis, hot tubs, volleyball, a business center, and arcades.

At the Beach Club you can pay extra for views. Standard view rooms are $436/night on weekdays and $481/night on Fridays and Saturdays during the 2014 Fall season. 2014 peak prices for these rooms are $671 and prices bottom out at $400/night.

DISNEY'S ANIMAL KINGDOM LODGE

Disney's Animal Kingdom Lodge ("AKL"), near the Animal Kingdom theme park, shares with the Wilderness Lodge astonishingly detailed theming and a jaw-dropping lobby, based in its case on African park lodges. It is also near-surrounded with parklands (Disney calls them "savannas") displaying animals. These animals are visible from savanna-view rooms and also from multiple public viewing areas. On several upper floors of the main building (Jambo House) you'll also find Disney Vacation Club spaces, the Jambo House Villas, and, a long walk or short bus ride away, even more DVC Villas at Kidani Village, all available for rent. Guest services and a shop are accessed from the main AKL Jambo lobby. Dining is at a lower level. (Kidani has another lobby, shop, and restaurant.) Most Jambo rooms are in two long-corridored semi-circular wings off the lobby that enclose animal savannas. The main pool is as good as any Disney pool except Stormalong Bay at the Yacht and Beach Clubs. A slightly smaller but still wonderful pool serves Kidani.

The Animal Kingdom Lodge is at the far southeast corner of Walt Disney World. Uniquely among the deluxes, all transport to the theme parks, water parks, and Downtown Disney is via buses shared with Kidani. Included in this is the Animal Kingdom park—you can't walk there. AKL thus is not particularly well located.

The animals, exterior architecture, lobby, detailing, and pools make AKL an astonishingly kid-appealing resort. Adults enjoy it as well, although they might find its rooms smaller than expected.

Standard guest rooms at AKL, with about 340 square feet, are tied with those at Disney's Wilderness Lodge as the smallest deluxe rooms on property (standard view rooms also are—for a Disney deluxe—inexpensive). Most first-time visitors ought not to pay for views, as they won't be in their rooms enough, but they should pay for savanna views at AKL. No five-person rooms are available—standard rooms sleep four on two queens. You'll also find a table and two chairs, mini-fridge, TV, dresser, closet, and a coffee-maker. The divided bath includes two sinks and a hair dryer, and a toilet and tub in a separate room. Of the four room types at the Disney Vacation Club Jambo and Kidani Villas, studios are most comparable to standard AKL rooms. They sleep four in a slightly larger space, on a queen and a fold-out couch. Jambo studios are the better choice than Kidani studios, as the Jambo building is much better themed, and dining is much more convenient. Rooms have balconies or patios, and are accessed from interior corridors. Like the other deluxe resorts, you can also reserve concierge-supported rooms (Disney call these "club" rooms) and suites.

There are two table service restaurants at in the main Jambo building, and another at Kidani. In Jambo, Jiko nears the top of many "best Disney dining" lists, has a resort casual dress code, and offers an eclectic African-inspired menu. Next-door Boma is more family friendly, with a wide-ranging buffet. At Kidani, the underappreciated gem Sanaa has an African/Indian inspired menu. AKL also has one of the better counter service options among the deluxes, and one of Disney World's best bars. There's another bar at each pool. Unlike the other deluxes, there's no easy access to more great dining at another hotel.

Amenities include nightly movies, campfires, jogging trails, playgrounds, a spa/fitness center, hot tubs, and arcades. AKL is alone among the Disney deluxe resorts in not being on water, having no beach, and offering no easy access to water sports. AKL is one of three deluxe resorts (the Polynesian and Wilderness Lodge are the others) that are not convention hotels.

At the Animal Kingdoms Lodge you should pay extra for savanna views. Savanna view rooms are $457/night on weekdays and $513/night on Fridays and Saturdays during the 2014 Fall season. 2014 peak prices for these rooms are $670 and prices bottom out at $409/night. These prices are typically around $100/night more than standard view rooms.

DISNEY'S YACHT CLUB RESORT

Disney's Yacht Club Resort ("YC"), an Epcot resort, is themed to resemble a formal New England yacht club. The dull gray exterior does little to accomplish this, but there are some nautical decorative elements in the public areas and rooms. Neither kids nor adults much get its theming. Kids, though, are delighted by Stormalong Bay pool and its associated beaches and playgrounds. The Yacht Club occupies half of an enormous long-corridored building, with sister resort The Beach Club—warmer, more charming, and more inviting—taking up the other half. In the center of the enormous building are kitchens and other back-of-the house areas, then on either side the table service restaurants of the two resorts, then the guest service areas (one for each) and shops. Near Crescent Lake you'll find Stormalong Bay pool, shared with the Beach Club—actually three separate pools, each with its own focus: a sand-bottomed shallow pool delightful for little ones; a pool perfect for drifting or tubing; and a pool for swimming. Fun water slides accessed from a shipwreck (!) on a beach splash down at one end of this pool. Some call Stormalong Bay a "mini water park". That's a stretch yet does capture the difference between it and every other Disney World pool. There's one smaller pool at the far west end of YC, and two smaller ones near the east end of BC.

The Yacht Club is near the back entrance to Epcot, the International Gateway. You can walk or take a boat to Epcot. Hollywood Studios is accessed by a long walk or by boat, and the other theme parks, water parks, and Downtown Disney via shared buses that can take a while. The Yacht Club is well located for trips centered on Epcot, but not so well located for a Magic Kingdom focused trip.

All of Disney's marketing material stresses the "formality" of the Yacht Club and the "fun" of the Beach Club. Both points are overstated, but result in families self-selecting into the prettier Beach Club, and conventioneers (both hotels are convention hotels) into the duller Yacht Club. This is fine—the Beach Club is the better family choice on any relevant measure except balconies: all YC rooms have large balconies, while BC rooms have either small or almost uselessly tiny ones.

Guest rooms at the YC are identical to those in BC except for decorations and balconies. Most standard rooms at YC sleep five on two queens and a daybed (some rooms omit the daybed and sleep four). Standard rooms are about 380 square feet—in the middle of the deluxe range, but well-appointed and proportioned. Five-person rooms have, beside the beds, a desk with a small rolling table underneath, a desk chair, mini-fridge, TV, dresser, closet, and a coffee-maker. The divided bath includes two sinks and a hair dryer, and a toilet and tub in a separate room. Four-person rooms have the same size, omit the daybed, but add an easy chair. All rooms are accessed from interior corridors. Like the other deluxe resorts, you can also reserve concierge-supported rooms (Disney call these "club" rooms) and suites.

YC has two table service restaurants. The Yachtsman Steak House is a top-notch venue with steaks as good as any Disney restaurant. It has a resort casual dress code. The other table service restaurant, Captain's Grille, is tied with the Grand Floridian Café for being the most uninteresting resort restaurant on property. There's no counter service at all. You can walk to the nearby Beach Club and find a character breakfast at Cape May Café, great burger and ice cream dining at Beaches and Cream, and very weak counter service. The nearby BoardWalk Inn has neither meaningful counter service nor any kid-appealing table service restaurants. Dining in Epcot is also an option, but may be impractical for families without hopper tickets. There's a bar inside and another at the pool.

Among them, the three Epcot resorts—the Beach and Yacht Clubs, and BoardWalk Inn—provide within walking distance access to almost any amenity, including beaches, nightly movies, campfires, jogging trails, playgrounds, a pirate cruise, boat rental, fishing, a spa/fitness center, tennis, hot tubs, volleyball, a business center, and arcades.

At the Yacht Club you can pay extra for views. Standard view rooms are $436/night on weekdays and $481/night on Fridays and Saturdays during the 2014 Fall season. 2014 peak prices for these rooms are $671 and prices bottom out at $400/night.

DISNEY'S BOARDWALK INN

Disney's BoardWalk Inn ("BWI"), an Epcot resort, has a split visual personality. One part of it, facing Crescent Lake, is themed to recall Atlantic coast boardwalk vacation settings. The rest—including the areas with the most rooms—is themed to recall a quieter and more peaceful Colonial-revival style resort with garden courtyards. The BoardWalk Inn is Disney's smallest deluxe resort, but some corridors are as long as those at sister Epcot resorts the Yacht and Beach Clubs. Cutting across the courtyards saves much walking. Connected through the lobby of the BoardWalk Inn is the enormous Disney Vacation Club property Disney's BoardWalk Villas, also available to all for rent. Guest services and a small shop are in the lobby, and more shopping is downstairs on the BoardWalk. Dining is a little weird—there's next to none "in" the BoardWalk Inn, but several restaurants are accessible just outside on the Boardwalk. In the Villas area you'll find the fun amusement-park themed main pool and a second smaller pool. A third pool, also small, is in an internal courtyard of the Inn.

The BoardWalk Inn is near the back entrance to Epcot, the International Gateway, and is as near Epcot as is the Beach Club, and nearer to Disney's Hollywood Studios. You can walk to either park from it, though most take the boat to the Studios. The other theme parks, water parks, and Downtown Disney are reached via shared buses that can take a while. The BoardWalk Inn is well located for trips centered on Epcot and the Studios, but not so well located for a Magic Kingdom-focused trip.

From its interior courtyards, the BoardWalk Inn is the loveliest and most compact of the Epcot resorts, and is highly popular with honeymooners. Kids don't get its theme, and the main pool, while fine, isn't at the standard of the pool at the Beach Club, making the Beach Club a better choice for most families. But adults love it, and the resulting demand means BWI is typically a little more expensive than the Beach Club.

Standard guest rooms at BWI, with about 370 square feet, are similar to those in the Yacht Club and Beach Club, mid-sized among the deluxes but well-proportioned and appointed, sleeping four on two queens or five with an added couch. Rooms also have a desk with a small rolling table underneath, a desk chair, mini-fridge, TV, dresser, closet, and a coffee-maker. The divided bath includes two sinks and a hair dryer, and a toilet and tub in a separate room. Four-person rooms have the same size, omit the couch, but add an easy chair. Of the four room types at the Villas, studios are most comparable to standard BWI rooms. They sleep four in a similar space on a queen and fold-out couch, but can be quite a hike. Rooms have balconies or patios, and are accessed from interior corridors. Like the other deluxe resorts, you can also reserve concierge-supported rooms (Disney call these "club" rooms) and suites, and BW also has larger "deluxe rooms" that sleep six, and Garden Cottages best suited to couples.

The BoardWalk Inn itself has next to no dining, but several restaurants of zero kid appeal are right outside on the BoardWalk itself. These include the sports-bar style ESPN Club; Kouzzinas, with Mediterranean cuisine; high-end, expensive seafood at the Flying Fish Café; and the brew pub Big River Grille. There are no character meals, nor any real counter service. More table service dining is at the Yacht and Beach Clubs, and dining in Epcot is also an option, but may be impractical for families without hopper tickets. There's a great bar inside and another at the pool.

Among them, the three Epcot resorts—the Beach and Yacht Clubs, and BoardWalk Inn—provide within walking distance access to almost any amenity, including beaches, nightly movies, campfires, jogging trails, playgrounds, a pirate cruise, boat rental, fishing, a spa/fitness center, tennis, hot tubs, volleyball, a business center, and arcades.

At the BoardWalk Inn you can pay extra for views. Standard view rooms are $446/night on weekdays and $482/night on Fridays and Saturdays during the 2014 Fall season. 2014 peak prices for these rooms are $682 and prices bottom out at $411/night.

Other Disney World Lodging Options

Besides the Disney-owned value, moderate and deluxe resorts, there are other options as well—none of which we particularly recommend:

- The Disney-owned multi-room spaces at the Disney Vacation club resorts.
- The Disney-owned Campsites at Fort Wilderness.
- The on-property, non-Disney-owned hotels: the Swan, Dolphin, Shades of Green, Four Seasons (opening late summer 2014), and the hotels of the Downtown Disney Resort Area.
- Everything else—the offsite hotels and vacation homes.

The positives and negatives of these choices vary, so we'll comment briefly on each.

THE MULTI-ROOM VILLAS AT THE
DISNEY VACATION CLUB RESORTS

The Disney Vacation Club ("DVC") Resorts at Walt Disney World are time-shares with rooms that can also be booked via cash reservations, just like any other Disney World resort hotel room.

Except for the studios, which we've already discussed in the "Deluxe Resorts" section, above, what's distinct about these resorts is the extra space and large kitchens—neither of which will be used much during a first visit.

These villas can also be reserved (usually at a huge cost saving) by privately renting "points" from Disney Vacation Club members.

For most first-time family visitors, the Disney Vacation Club Resorts are worth considering only under a few circumstances:

- Large families, especially those aimed at a deluxe property, who are not willing to bet on actually getting connecting rooms. (You can request connecting rooms at WDW, but getting them is not guaranteed.) Villas, which can sleep 8, 9, and 12 people, are available.
- Smaller families looking to spread out into a One or Two-Bedroom Villa, despite the higher price.

- Families aimed at a deluxe hotel, but who can only pull it off through the cost savings of renting DVC points.
- Families who have targeted a resort with which a DVC property is paired, find it is sold out, but can get into the DVC resort.
- People who already are DVC owners.

THE CAMPSITES AT FORT WILDERNESS

The Campsites at Disney's Fort Wilderness Resort, while wonderful for returning visitors who like to camp or own an RV, are not recommended for typical first-time family visitors to Walt Disney World. The wilderness and backwoodsy theming of this resort, while charming, is so subtle that it will fly over the heads of most kids. Mickey and other Disney themes are almost entirely absent.

Also, the Campsites at Disney's Fort Wilderness Resort are remarkably inconvenient compared to the other Walt Disney World resorts. While often thought of as out of the way, the resort is actually located just across Bay Lake and Seven Seas Lagoon from the Magic Kingdom. Its inconvenience comes not from its location, but rather from the internal bus system that the sprawling Fort Wilderness Resort uses.

To get to any theme park, two transportation actions are required: an internal bus to the appropriate transfer point, and then an external bus or boat to the park itself. This can easily add half an hour or more to daily transportation times—adding up to seven or eight extra hours wasted on internal bus trips over the course of an eight-night visit.

Moreover, simply moving around the seven-hundred acre resort—getting to the pool, the shops, the playgrounds—can be a chore. Even if you have a car, you are discouraged from using it in the campground itself, both officially and by the lack of parking spaces in places you might want to go.

OTHER ON-PROPERTY HOTELS

There are two groups of resorts operated by third parties on Disney property.

First, there's a group of three that are comparable to the Disney deluxe resorts in room size, quality, amenities, and location. These are Shades of Green, the Swan, and the Dolphin. (Four Seasons will join this group when it opens later in 2014).

- **Shades of Green** is an inexpensive deluxe-level resort near the Polynesian for U.S. service members, career military retirees, other eligible guests, and their families and sponsored friends. For more on Shades of Green, see SHADESOFGREEN.ORG and Steve Bell's MILITARYDISNEYTIPS.COM.

- **The Swan and Dolphin** are deluxe hotels near the Epcot resorts—a little closer to Hollywood Studios than Epcot, compared to the other Epcot resorts. The Swan and Dolphin are known for unusual exteriors, hardly any Disney theming, conventions, great and varied restaurants, wider and more varied discounts than at the Disney properties, and for a wonderful shared pool complex. With about 2,200 rooms in all, both resorts are competitively priced, but suffer from a daily $17 resort fee, in addition to $15 per day for parking.

Second, there's a group of half a dozen or so hotels in the Downtown Disney Resort Area. While their prices may initially seem attractive, high resort and parking fees typically push the price up by $30 or more per night. The Downtown Disney Resort Area isn't convenient to anything but shopping, and these hotels have their own, often disappointing, park transportation. Opinions of these hotels vary and change, but none but the Hilton has a track record of strong reviews.

At press time, none of these non-Disney hotels participate in the Disney Dining Plan, in Disney's Magical Express, in MagicBands, or are able to book FastPass+ 60 days ahead of arrival.

- Guests at Shades of Green, the Swan and the Dolphin, and the Hilton get to participate in the Extra Magic Hours program. No other non-Disney owned hotels besides these four offer the Extra Magic Hours program.
- Guests at the Swan and Dolphin use the Disney transportation system for travel to the theme parks.

OFF-PROPERTY HOTELS AND VACATION HOMES

An off-site stay may remain attractive due to significantly lower prices, especially when considering the cost for a family of five to stay on property. While it's theoretically possible for a family of five to stay at the Riverside in an Alligator Bayou room, we're still talking about five people sharing a single bathroom and 314 square feet of total space. Disney's idea of a moderately priced family suite at Art of Animation starts at $298 per night and skyrockets up to $511/night over the holidays.

However, staying off-site presents another set of costs and challenges. First, any scheduled shuttle transportation from most off-site resorts can be as weak as one bus in the morning and one bus at night. These times are often rigid and inconvenient, whether the bus arrives after park opening or departs long before the night-time entertainment or the park closes. Miss the bus and it's an expensive cab ride. Off-site guests often rent cars, but that reduces convenience and increases costs. Parking at the theme parks is $17 per day (due only *once* per day, if you keep your receipt), in addition to potential parking costs back at the hotel. Second, resort fees that typically cost $15-$20 per night are another concern. For some families, the price discount may be too much to overlook this trip, and there's nothing wrong with that. But be sure to consider all the costs associated with a stay that may not be included in the initial price.

There are literally thousands of off-site hotels, motels, campgrounds, vacation homes, condos, etc., in and around Orlando. Target your search to the Highway 192/West Irlo Bronson Highway and/or the Downtown Disney Resort Areas to narrow your search to convenient locations. The value of honing in on these two areas is simple: from almost any place in Walt Disney World, you can find directional signage to 192, and directional signage to Downtown Disney.

Walt Disney World is much more complicated than many first-time visitors imagine, and your first few days of finding your way around will be made simpler by this signage.

- The street address of hotels on 192 will include either "Highway 192" and/or the words "Irlo Bronson Highway".
- The street address of hotels in the Downtown Disney Resort Area will include "Hotel Plaza Boulevard".

It's possible to find multiple-bedroom vacation homes available for short-term rentals in the Orlando area for a fraction of the price you'd pay to stay in some of the deluxe large family options at Walt Disney World, even counting your rental car costs. Airbnb is also becoming more accepted in Orlando.

First-time visitors benefit most from staying on property at a Disney owned and operated resort. While more expensive than their off-site counterparts, it's hard to put a price on the convenience and peace of mind that an on-site stay in a Disney resort offers.

How to Spend Your Time

6

This chapter:

- Provides example, pre-made itineraries for guests arriving on a Saturday and planning to spend nine days in Orlando.
- Presents introductions to touring each of the major theme parks, with reviews and insight into every single theme park attraction.
- Follows with Cheat Sheets that cover everything you need to bring with you to the theme parks. These include what to expect at park open, detailed touring plans including when you can expect to arrive and depart each attraction, FastPass+ priority so you know which experiences will save you the most time, and advice on how to see the night-time spectaculars with the least hassle. Color copies of the newest versions of these Cheat Sheets are available at WWW.EASYWDW.COM/EASY-GUIDE.

We open with a discussion of one of Disney's newest and most expensive innovations, FastPass+, and how it has transformed the theme park experience in positive and negative ways. Maximizing FastPass+ is an important strategic advantage and we'll cover the best methods to save you hours in line every day.

Next, we focus on itinerary planning, including:

- Deciding how many days to visit each park.
- Picking the best park to visit each day based on crowds and entertainment offerings.
- Creating a daily touring plan that blends easy morning touring, strategically chosen FastPass+ experiences, and the best dining choices.

Example itineraries are provided to give you an idea about how best to plan your vacation in its entirety. Modifications can easily be made depending on where you want to go and what you want to do.

This is the lengthiest chapter because the theme parks are what a Walt Disney World vacation is all about. Plan to digest it over several sessions.

FastPass+ at Walt Disney World

Disney world attractions have one or two entrances:

- At those with just one entrance, called the standby entrance in Disney-speak, guests arrive, get in line (the standby line), and enter the attraction in order of arrival.

- Attractions with two entrances have both a standby entrance and a FastPass+ entrance...and this changes everything.

Disney's FastPass+ system, fully initiated in early 2014 but still, at press time, being tested and revised, is a digital system that replaces Disney's old FASTPASS paper system (now often called "legacy" FASTPASS).

At attractions with both types of entrances, guests with a FastPass+ can experience an attraction with priority boarding. Attractions like Tower of Terror and Toy Story Mania admit as many as seven FastPass+ riders for every one standby rider. Thus, those with FastPass+ wait much less than those in standby lines, and push up standby waits because they receive priority boarding, even if they arrive long after a standby rider.

Disney bills FastPass+ as an "easy way to reserve some of your must-do fun before you leave home". Indeed, all guests with tickets may book three FastPass+ experiences either 60 days in advance (guests staying in Disney-owned hotels) or up to 30 days in advance (all other guests). This is one of the most positive features of the program—guests may schedule headlining attractions like Toy Story Mania, Test Track, Soarin', Space Mountain, and the Princess Fairytale Hall Meet and Greets from the comfort of their home long before they arrive in Orlando, or even the day of a visit to the theme park from their smartphone or in-park kiosk. But there are two major negatives:

1. Guests must select a specific one-hour window on a specific day. Based on the ride reviews that follow, you may decide that the group wants to meet Ariel at Ariel's Grotto in Magic Kingdom. But you'll need to pick a specific date and time—August 27 from 2:15pm–3:15pm, for example. (The rest of this chapter helps with all these choices—which days, which rides, which FastPass+, and which times.)

2. Some attractions distribute an extremely limited number of FastPass+ opportunities, making booking 30 to 60 days in advance necessary.

Later in this chapter, we'll discuss the importance of choosing which theme park to visit based on crowds and entertainment. This goes hand in hand with Chapter 7, which discusses restaurant reservations, some of which must be booked a whopping six months in advance. Combined with the FastPass+ priority discussion next, picking attractions and theme parks is easy, but being forced to select specific hour-long windows for each ride can feel like too much micro-managing and reduce spontaneity.

There is no such thing as legacy FASTPASS inside the theme parks anymore, which—for those who have visited before-- means no more paper FASTPASS tickets. Legacy FASTPASS tickets were generally distributed at each attraction that offered it, necessitating backtracking and long walks to collect FASTPASSes over the course of the day. The good news is that FastPass+ eliminates the need to visit each attraction for which you'd like a FastPass+. Gone are the days of sending Dad to Splash Mountain with everyone's park tickets while the rest of the group rides Buzz Lightyear's Space Ranger Spin 20 minutes away. FastPass+ also brings new attractions onto the system, including parades, nighttime entertainment like Fantasmic! and IllumiNations, in addition to character meet and greets like Rapunzel and Mickey Mouse.

The introductions to each theme park below, along with the Cheat Sheets, include a list of the attractions that offer FastPass+ and also their priority, which is generally based on how much waiting time using one will save in the late morning and afternoon when waits peak. Wait times remain short early in the morning and most guests will find easy touring in most "standby lines" through at least 10am. Once guests use their initial three FastPass+, they may select a fourth FastPass+ based on availability. Once they use that one, they can book a fifth FastPass+, and so on. At press time, all FastPass+ experiences after the third need to be made on the day of visit at an in-park kiosk where the attraction is located. For example, if you've booked your three FastPass+ experiences at Epcot and would like to make a fourth at Hollywood Studios, someone in the group would need to physically travel to Hollywood Studios to book that experience. Disney may add the ability to book the fourth, fifth, etc. FastPass+ experiences via your phone in the future.

Because FastPass+ experiences can be booked in advance, the new program adds certainty to your schedules and also makes arriving late at a theme park much easier than with the legacy FASTPASS system. Prior to FastPass+, Toy Story Mania legacy FASTPASSes would typically be gone before 11am, with return times well into the evening by 9:45am most days. This meant guests needed to arrive early to secure FASTPASSes with an unknown return time, or find themselves in a 75+ minute standby line at some point later in the day. Now you can leave home knowing you have Toy Story Mania booked in the afternoon, and no longer need to arrive at the park early to assure you can enjoy it.

Unfortunately, Disney has instituted a tiering system at Epcot and Hollywood Studios, which means guests at those parks can initially reserve only one high priority attraction in advance. At Epcot, guests choose between Soarin' and Test Track, among three other lesser choices. At Hollywood Studios, the major decision is between Toy Story Mania and Rock 'n' Roller Coaster, where guests can only initially choose one. Riding both Soarin' and Test Track in one day is easy if you head to one right at park open and then use FastPass+ for the other later in the day. But riding both over the course of one day with a late arrival will be more difficult since both attractions ordinarily see 60 to 100 minute waits over the course of the day. It's possible that these attractions will be available to book as a fourth FastPass+ selection at a kiosk in the afternoon, but it's unlikely on busier days and return times will be severely limited.

There's more in Chapter 9 on how to book FastPass+. For now, let's stay focused on the parks!

Designing Your Own Walt Disney World Itinerary

The art of itinerary design has three parts: dividing your time among the parks, picking the best days to see each park, and shaping what you do each day to minimize time spent waiting in line.

ALLOCATING YOUR TIME AMONG THE PARKS

Chapter 3 covered in-depth how to divide your time depending on party size, makeup, and length of vacation. As a refresher, most guests will spend the most time at Magic Kingdom, with Epcot being a close second except for those traveling with the youngest children. Most guests spend about a day each at Hollywood Studios and Animal Kingdom, though guests spending just a few days at Disney World may not have time for all four parks.

PICKING THE BEST DAYS TO VISIT THE PARKS

There are several factors that contribute to the decision on which theme park to visit each day, including expected crowds and nighttime entertainment. Daily advice is available at EASYWDW.COM/CATEGORY/CALENDAR beginning about six and a half months ahead of a given date. For each day of your visit, you'll find overall crowd levels, recommended parks, night-time entertainment, and a daily explanation of what to expect.

In general, the longer a theme park is open and the more nightly entertainment it offers, the busier it will be. This is particularly true at Magic Kingdom, which can see wildly different operating hours and entertainment offerings, particularly during Mickey's Party Season from September 1 through the third week in December. It's not uncommon for Magic Kingdom to be open from 9am–7pm and offer no evening fireworks or parades three or four days per week, while the other days it's open as late as 1am with fireworks and two night-time parades. The days with longer hours are significantly more crowded because people equate longer hours with more bang for their buck. This isn't necessarily true. While a longer day does offer more time in the park, it also brings with it longer lines, increased congestion in common areas, and a more stressful overall experience. With two days at Magic Kingdom, most guests will want to visit on one less crowded day to hammer out the priority attractions and also visit on a day that they can enjoy the nighttime entertainment.

- Animal Kingdom is typically least busy early in the week, particularly on Tuesdays. It's busiest on Wednesday and Fridays, particularly on days with morning Extra Magic Hours.

- Hollywood Studios is least crowded early in the week on days it doesn't offer Extra Magic Hours, particularly Sundays and Tuesdays (Sundays are quite crowded during the annual mid-May to mid-June Star Wars Weekends.) Wednesdays and Saturdays are typically busiest otherwise.

- Epcot is generally least busy on Mondays, Thursdays, and weekends (except during the Food and Wine Festival in the fall, when weekends are quite busy).

- Magic Kingdom is typically busiest on Sundays, Mondays, Thursdays, and Saturdays.

One of the reasons why Magic Kingdom tends to be busiest on weekends and Mondays, and the other theme parks are less crowded on those days, is the number of people that arrive over the weekend and head to the Most Magical Place on Earth first thing. We recommend putting off Magic Kingdom for a Tuesday or Wednesday not only because it's less crowded and more enjoyable, but also because seeing it first might spoil the very different experiences found at the other theme parks. While much of Magic Kingdom is an exercise in excitement and sensory overload, Epcot in particular takes more time and thought to discover the richness that it offers. This isn't to say the other theme parks are "bad", but it can be difficult to get young kids excited about an educational boat ride focused on horticulture after experiencing the 50-foot plunge on Splash Mountain the day before.

But there are exceptions to these general guidelines, which is where the daily crowd calendars and recommended parks come into play. Be sure to check out your dates as soon as possible. Crowd calendars are typically available at EASYWDW.COM/CATEGORY/CALENDAR about 200 days in advance, just after Disney releases its operating schedules.

Once you've sorted out which parks you will see on which days, begin entering the details in the planning sheet, on the opposite page. (There's room in it for dining as well, which is coming in Chapter 7.)

DESIGNING YOUR PARK APPROACH FOR EACH DAY

After you've divided your days among the parks, and picked days to visit each park, your final step is designing your approach for each day.

There are two easy ways to go about this:

1. Model your visit around the daily agendas you'll find linked to from the itineraries on YOURFIRSTVISIT.NET/ITINERARIES. We give two examples of these itineraries after the worksheet.

2. Use the park overviews and ride reviews that come just after the example itineraries, to tailor the easyWDW Cheat Sheets to a trip that's perfectly adapted to your group and the length of your trip!

Example Itineraries for Walt Disney World

If you have chosen to do an eight-night, nine-day trip with a Saturday arrival, and your kids are at least 8 years old and 48 inches tall, then you'll find an itinerary for dates within the next six or so months (they are released as Disney releases its operating calendar) at YOURFIRST-VISIT.NET/ITINERARIES. Scan down the dates at that link and click to the itinerary suggested for that date—taking special note of words like "but see this for required changes...".

When you do so, you'll find an itinerary like one of the two examples that follow, and with it links to daily touring plans based on that itinerary and a tailored To-Do List with suggested FastPass+. While the examples below will give you an idea about what we're looking at, they do change based on different weekly schedules. The list at YOURFIRSTVISIT. NET/ITINERARIES will be updated with itineraries for each specific week.

Disney World Itinerary Planning Worksheet

	_____ day	_____ day	_____ day
Meals:			
Breakfast			
Lunch			
Dinner			
Parks, Etc:			
Early Morning			
Late Morning			
Early Afternoon			
Late Afternoon			
Evening			
Late Evening			
Notes:			
Parade			
Fireworks			
Park-Open Target			
FastPass+ Target			

	_____ day	_____ day	_____ day
Meals:			
Breakfast			
Lunch			
Dinner			
Parks, Etc:			
Early Morning			
Late Morning			
Early Afternoon			
Late Afternoon			
Evening			
Late Evening			
Notes:			
Parade			
Fireworks			
Park-Open Target			
FastPass+ Target			

Underline =
Counter/Quick Service

Bold =
Table Service

Italic =
Cash, not Dining Plan

Red =
Character Meal

"FastPass+ Target" is the Tier One Fastpass+ to aim for, at time of writing, only Epcot and Hollywood Studios have tiered FastPass+

EXAMPLE ITINERARY: TYPICAL HIGHER-CROWD WEEKS

Disney World FastPass+ High Crowd Itinerary
from yourfirstvisit.net

	Saturday	Sunday	Monday	Tuesday
Meals:				
Breakfast		*Hotel Room**	*Hotel Room**	*Hotel Room**
Lunch	*Travel*	Backlot Express	Sunshine Seasons	Hotel or Hollywood Studios Counter
Dinner	7p Akershus or San Angel Inn	Hotel Counter	Hotel or Epcot Counter	7p 50's Prime Time Cafe
Parks, Etc:				
Early Morning	*Travel*	At Hollywood Studios by 8.15a	At Epcot by 8.15a	Off
Late Morning	*Travel*	Hollywood Studios	Epcot	Off
Early Afternoon	Check In/Epcot ASAP	Hollywood Studios	Epcot	Hollywood Studios by 2p or so
Late Afternoon	Epcot	Hollywood Studios	Epcot	Hollywood Studios
Evening	Epcot	Off	(Optional) Epcot	Hollywood Studios
Late Evening				
Notes:				
Parade				
Fireworks	Illuminations			Fantasmic
Park-Open Target	N/A	Rock 'N Roller Coaster	Test Track	N/A
FastPass+ Target	Illuminations	Toy Story Midway Mania	Soarin	Fantasmic

	Wednesday	Thursday	Friday	Saturday	Sunday
Meals:					
Breakfast	*Hotel Room**	*Hotel Room**	*Hotel Room**	*Hotel Room**	*Hotel Room**
Lunch	TBD Cinderella's Royal Table**	Flame Tree Barbecue	Chef Mickey's 11a	Magic Kingdom or Hotel Counter	*Travel*
Dinner	6.15p Hoop-Dee-Doo Revue**	Yak and Yeti	Magic Kingdom or Hotel Counter	7p Crystal Palace	*Travel*
Parks, Etc:					
Early Morning	Magic Kingdom by 8.15a	Off	Magic Kingdom by 8.15a	Magic Kingdom by 8.15a	Animal Kingdom by 8.15a
Late Morning	Magic Kingdom	Off	Magic Kingdom	Magic Kingdom	Animal Kingdom
Early Afternoon	Animal Kingdom by noon	Animal Kingdom	Magic Kingdom	Off	*Travel*
Late Afternoon	Animal Kingdom	Animal Kingdom	Off	Off	*Travel*
Evening	Animal Kingdom	Off	Magic Kingdom by 6p	Magic Kingdom by 6p	*Travel*
Late Evening	Hoop-Dee-Doo Revue		Magic Kingdom	Magic Kingdom	
Notes:					
Parade	Afternoon Parade	Afternoon Parade		Evening Parade	Afternoon Parade
Fireworks		N/A		Wishes	N/A
Park-Open Target	Peter Pan	Kali River Rapids	Space Mountain	Big Thunder Mountain	Expedition Everest
FastPass+ Target	Seven Dwarfs Mine Train	Enchanted Tales with Belle	Enchanted Tales with Belle	Splash Mountain	Kilimanjaro Safaris

Legend:
- Underline = Counter/Quick Service
- **Bold** = Table Service
- *Italic* = Cash, not Dining Plan
- Reds = Character Meal

*Cereal, fruit, juice etc. in room   **Two Table Service credits

Version 12/13; thanks to Josh of easyWDW.com for help and permission to use his findings...but errors are mine alone.

EXAMPLE ITINERARY: TYPICAL LOWER-CROWD WEEKS

Disney World FastPass+ Lower-Crowd Itinerary v2 from yourfirstvisit.net

This does not work for all dates!! See yourfirstvisit.net/itineraries

Meals:	Saturday	Sunday	Monday	Tuesday
Breakfast	*Travel*	*Hotel Room**	*Hotel Room**	*Hotel Room**
Lunch	*Travel*	Backlot Express	Sunshine Seasons	Flame Tree Barbecue
Dinner	**7p Akershus or San Angel Inn**	**6p 50s Prime Time Café**	Hotel or Epcot Counter	**Yak and Yeti**
Parks, Etc:				
Early Morning	Travel	Off	At Epcot by 8.15a	Off
Late Morning	Travel	Off	Epcot	Off
Early Afternoon	Check In/At Epcot ASAP	At Hollywood Studios by noon	Epcot	At Animal Kingdom by noon
Late Afternoon	Epcot	Hollywood Studios	Epcot	Animal Kingdom
Evening	Epcot	Hollywood Studios	(Optional) Epcot	
Late Evening				
Notes:				
Park-Open Target	n/a	n/a	Test Track	n/a
Fireworks	Illuminations	Illuminations	n/a	
FastPass+ Target	Illuminations	Toy Story Midway Mania	Soarin	Expedition Everest

Meals:	Wednesday	Thursday	Friday	Saturday	Sunday
Breakfast	*Hotel Room**	*Hotel Room**	*Hotel Room**	*Hotel Room**	*Hotel Room**
Lunch	**Chef Mickey's 11a**	Hotel Counter	TBD **Cinderella's Royal Table****	*Magic Kingdom or Hotel Counter*	*Travel*
Dinner	*Magic Kingdom or Hotel Counter*	Hollywood Studios Counter	**6.15p Hoop-Dee-Doo Revue****	**6p Crystal Palace**	*Travel*
Parks, Etc:					
Early Morning	Off	Off	At Magic Kingdom by 8.15a	At Magic Kingdom by 8.15a	At Animal Kingdom by 8.15a
Late Morning	Off	Off	Magic Kingdom	Magic Kingdom	Animal Kingdom
Early Afternoon	At Magic Kingdom by noon	At Hollywood Studios by noon	Magic Kingdom	Off	Off
Late Afternoon	Magic Kingdom	Hollywood Studios	Magic Kingdom	Off	Off
Evening	Magic Kingdom	Hollywood Studios	Hoop Dee Doo Revue	Magic Kingdom	Travel
Late Evening				Magic Kingdom	Travel
Notes:					
Parade	Afternoon Parade	Fantasmic		Evening Parade	Afternoon Parade
Fireworks	n/a	n/a		Wishes	
Park-Open Target			Peter Pan	Big Thunder Mountain	Kilimanjaro or Everest
FastPass+ Target	Space Mountain	Rock 'n' Roller Coaster	Seven Dwarfs Mine Train	Splash Mountain	Festival of the Lion King

Bold = Table Service
Underline = Counter/Quick Service
Italic = Cash, not Dining Plan
Red = Character Meal

*Cereal, fruit, juice etc. in room   **Two Table Service credits

"FastPass Target" is the Tier One Fastpass+ to aim for; at time of writing, only Epcot and Hollywood Studios have tiered FastPass+

Version 5/14; thanks to Josh of easyWDW.com for help and permission to build on his findings...but conclusions are mostly mine, and errors are mine alone

Disney's Animal Kingdom

Disney's newest major theme park is also its easiest to tour. Each of the headliner attractions (except the over-rated Kali River Rapids) enjoys healthy capacity and relatively short peak waits. On the downside, the park's circular layout may require backtracking to visit all the rides and shows. The Animal Kindom Cheat Sheet at the end of this chapter minimizes walking and waits as much as possible.

With FastPass+, a late arrival at Animal Kingdom can be just as effective as an early arrival. Animal Kingdom tends to empty by 4pm, leaving waits at the major attractions short from then until close. This may be tempered somewhat by the fact that Animal Kingdom often closes by 5 or 6pm. Still, Expedition Everest, Kali River Rapids, and the DinoLand attractions all see reduced waits in these periods, to the point where ride vehicles often leave partially empty because there aren't enough people around to fill a vehicle.

FASTPASS+ AT ANIMAL KINGDOM

Nine attractions at Animal Kingdom offer FastPass+, from among which you can pre-book three. On hot days, FastPass+ is best used at Kali River Rapids in the afternoon when waits are longest and temperatures highest. For guests that need to meet Mickey, The Adventurers Outpost Meet and Greet has a limited capacity and is another priority. The best uses on cooler days without Mickey are at Kilimanjaro Safaris and Expedition Everest.

FastPass+ Priority

1. Kali River Rapids (when highs are 80+ degrees)
2. Adventurers Outpost Mickey and Minnie Meet
3. Kilimanjaro Safaris
4. Expedition Everest
5. Kali River Rapids (when highs are less than 80 degrees)
6. Primeval Whirl
7. DINOSAUR
8. Finding Nemo the Musical
9. It's Tough to Be a Bug

ARRIVING AT ANIMAL KINGDOM

Arriving 45 minutes before open puts you in the best position to enjoy the shortest waits possible first thing in the morning as well as have an opportunity to re-ride Expedition Everest, DINOSAUR, Kali River Rapids, or other attractions a second time in the standby line before considerable waits begin to develop. Believe it or not, a 9am arrival is actually "late" and thousands of guests will already be in line at Kilimanjaro Safaris and Expedition Everest before you even scan your ticket.

Almost all guests arrive by Disney bus or their own transportation. Guests parking early can easily walk to the main entrance. Guests arriving later and parking farther out have the option of walking or taking a tram. Those arriving via Disney bus will be dropped off just a minute or two walk away from the main entrance.

Bag check precedes the ticket windows. Ticket windows generally have nonexistent lines because it's rare that a group begins their vacation at Animal Kingdom. Guest Services is located on the far left both inside and outside the main entrance. Stroller and wheelchair rental are located on the right just inside the main entrance.

Rainforest Café sits on the left with an entrance/exit both inside and outside the park. Theme park admission is thus not required to dine at the restaurant, which is only convenient as you enter or exit the park.

THE OASIS

Unlike the entry into any other Disney theme park, The Oasis is completely devoid of shops, restaurants, and loud stimuli. Instead, the area works to transition visitors into the lush, tropical, animal-filled surroundings that set the tone for the rest of the park. Expansive animal habitats display iguanas, anteaters, macaws, ducks, and a variety of other animals amidst rushing waterfalls, dense vegetation, and a burgeoning canopy. Guests arriving prior to park opening will want to breeze through the Oasis with plans to return either in the afternoon or on the way out. Time spent here at open will only result in thousands of people passing you and filling the queues for the major attractions, in turn pushing up wait times. With an afternoon arrival, plan to slowly meander around the winding pathways, taking in the various exhibits for 15 to 30 minutes.

DISCOVERY ISLAND

After The Oasis, guests cross a bridge to Discovery Island, the central hub for the entire park. Discovery Island circles the 14-story hand-carved Tree of Life, the park's central icon and an easy marker for guests trying to make their way back to the main drag from one of the peripheral lands. DinoLand and Asia are off to the right, in addition to the Adventurer's Outpost Mickey and Minnie meet and greet, It's Tough to Be a Bug 4D show, and Flame Tree Barbecue, the park's best quick service. Off to the left is Pizzafari, another quick service option—much less interesting than Flame Tree, but air-conditioned. Past Pizzafari is Africa, one of the three major lands. (Camp Minnie-Mickey closed in 2013.)

Discovery Island is where you'll find the bulk of the shopping opportunities, with Island Mercantile and Disney Outfitters supplying the widest selection. Virtually anything you would find in any of the smaller stores can be found here. Plan to return in the afternoon for some air-conditioned perusing when few people are shopping and the waits at the attractions are longer. Like the major stores at the other theme parks, Island Mercantile and Disney Outfitters remain open for at least 30 minutes after close, allowing for last-minute impulse buys.

Adventurers Outpost

RANKING Don't miss for those that want to meet Mickey and Minnie together; skippable otherwise. **EMH** No. **FP+** Yes. High priority for guests wanting to meet the characters. **TYPE** Meet-and-greet. **REQUIREMENTS** None.

WHAT TO EXPECT Guests line up outside the winding queue before entering a small air-conditioned room prior to the meet and greet. Mickey and Minnie greet together in their safari outfits with a fun adventurer's background. **SCARY FACTOR** None.

WHEN TO GO Before 9:45am, one hour before close, or with FastPass+.
EXPECT TO WAIT Peak afternoon waits are typically 25 to 40 minutes.
LENGTH About two minutes of signing, mingling, and picture taking.

It's Tough to Be a Bug

RANKING Minor attraction. **EMH** Morning. **FP+** Yes. Low priority. **TYPE** 4D Show. **REQUIREMENTS** None.

WHAT TO EXPECT The theater is dark, loud, and there are a number of effects that "add" to the experience. Otherwise, It's Tough to Be a Bug is a fun 3D theater show (in-theater special effects make it "4D") based on *It's a Bugs Life* that most guests enjoy. **SCARY FACTOR (WITH MINOR SPOILERS)** Low for most people 12 and older, but it may frighten kids younger than that. Animatronic spiders, termites, beetles, hornets, and more make appearances; several effects add to the anxiety including smoke, a "sting" from the back of the seat, insects dropping from the ceiling, and the sensation that bugs are running under your feet. If you're scared of bugs, this show may not be for you. At the same time, all of the bugs are "cartoony" like in the movie and not particularly realistic.

WHEN TO GO Afternoon when crowds have peaked elsewhere. **EXPECT TO WAIT** Only as long as it takes for the next show to start. **LENGTH** 8 minutes. **WHERE TO SIT** Target the back few rows and let guests fill about half the row before entering. With apprehensive kids, instead sit at the end of a row for an easy exit.

AFRICA

Home to Kilimanjaro Safaris, Festival of the Lion King, Pangani Forest Exploration Trail, and the Wildlife Express Train to Rafiki's Planet Watch, Africa is Animal Kingdom's largest, and arguably most immersive, land. Guests enter through Harambe, a rural African marketplace surrounded by buildings inspired by the ones Disney Imagineers saw throughout their travels across the continent. You'll see everything from a fortress reminiscent of Zanzibar to thatched huts built by the Zulu in South Africa

Tusker House Restaurant with its fun character breakfasts and lunches, Harambe Popcorn, Dawa Bar, and Tamu Tamu Refreshments are the first buildings guests see as they cross the bridge over to Africa. Farther back, Mombasa Marketplace is the large store on the right, offering authentic African crafts, Animal Kingdom merchandise, and African wines. Kusafiri Bakery is on the left with Harambe Market a bit farther up on the right. Both serve drinks, treats, snacks, and the like. The entrance to Kilimanjaro Safaris is straight back with the entrance to Pangani Forest Exploration Trail around to the right near the Wildlife Express Train station. If you're interested in food and drink, stick to the front half of Africa. For the attractions, continue to the back.

Festival of the Lion King

RANKING Major attraction. **EMH** No. **FP+** Yes. Low priority. **TYPE** Musical theater show. **REQUIREMENTS** None.

WHAT TO EXPECT Lion King reopens in the summer of 2014. The show reprises songs and characters from the movie and features acrobatics, Animatronics, singing, dancing, fire, theater, and the most elaborate costumes and sets you'll find at Disney World. With more than 50 performers, there is almost too much to take in. **SCARY FACTOR** Zero.

WHEN TO GO First and last shows are least crowded. **EXPECT TO WAIT** Arrive 10 to 20 minutes early. **LENGTH** 30 minutes. **WHERE TO SIT** The section you choose isn't as important as the row you select. Higher than the eighth row provides a better view of the various floats and sets.

Kilimanjaro Safaris

RANKING Don't miss. **EMH** Morning. **FP+** Yes. High priority.**TYPE** Safari ride. **REQUIREMENTS** None.

WHAT TO EXPECT Riders board a 32-passenger open-air safari truck and take a mildly bumpy, fully narrated trip through the 100-acre Harambe Wildlife Reserve. It's basically a simulated, shortened safari through lifelike savannas populated with rare animals, including black and white rhinoceroses, cheetahs, flamingos, lions, giraffes, warthogs, zebras, wildebeests, ostriches, crocodiles, antelopes, and more. The animals aren't always "out" and your viewing may be limited by the time of day and simple luck of the draw. **SCARY FACTOR** None. **CAN WE HANDLE IT?** Mild jostling. If you have back or neck problems, request a front row where it's less bumpy.

WHEN TO GO Immediately after park open, in the final hour of operation, or with FastPass+. Safaris closes before dusk. Check for the "last safari" time—you need to be in line before this time to ride. **EXPECT TO WAIT** 35 to 70 minutes in the afternoon. **LENGTH** 20 minutes. **WHERE TO SIT** Those sitting on the ends of the rows have the most unobstructed views. Otherwise, the driver's side seems to offer the best view overall.

Pangani Forest Exploration Trail

RANKING Minor attraction. **EMH** Morning. **FP+** No. **TYPE** Self-guided walking tour, zoo exhibit. **REQUIREMENTS** None.

WHAT TO EXPECT Visitors walk along the path and enter various enclosures and exhibits that show off the animals in their native habitats. Expect to see hippopotamuses, meerkats, naked mole rats, gorillas, okapi (the only known relative of the giraffe), and an extensive number of rare African bird species. **SCARY FACTOR** Zero.

WHEN TO GO Last hour of operation, which may be earlier than park close. Kilimanjaro Safaris spits out thousands of guests an hour right at the doors to Pangani, causing crowding from 9:30am to 4pm along the narrow paths. The gorillas are also out more consistently in the late afternoon. Closes shortly before dusk. **EXPECT TO WAIT** No waits. **LENGTH** Pangani Trail is a little less than a half mile long. Most visitors spend about 30 minutes moving through the trail and the various exhibits.

Rafiki's Planet Watch

RANKING Fun but skippable. **EMH** No. **FP+** No. **TYPE** Zoological exhibits and interactive experiences. **REQUIREMENTS** None.

WHAT TO EXPECT Rafiki's Planet Watch is a collection of nicely air-conditioned diversions from long waits in the hot sun. You'll find a variety of exhibits that you'll need to take some time with if you want to get anything out of them. There are no rides, thrills, or excitement at Planet Watch—just educational exhibits. Here's what's available:

- *Affection Section*, a petting zoo. The animals here are mostly species that are endangered or otherwise at risk.
- *Sounds of the Rainforest*, a five-minute auditory exhibit narrated by Grandmother Willow from *Pocahontas*.
- *Conservation Station*, the main building at Rafiki's Planet Watch housing the majority of the live and hands-on exhibits. Veterinarians and wildlife experts will answer questions and give insight into how the Animal Kingdom operates. You can view live-camera feeds of backstage areas where the animals are kept, as well as a variety of other exhibits featuring a wealth of information on conservation efforts around the globe. Exhibits and activities can change on a daily basis because the area is actually used for live preparation and animal surgeries, so you never know what you'll see.
- *Character Meet and Greets*: Rafiki and friends are often on hand to meet guests to short lines.

SCARY FACTOR Minimal. There is a snake or two and the mornings may feature intensive veterinary procedures on the wildlife, but both are easily avoided.

WHEN TO GO Between 11am and 3pm when crowds and temperatures peak. There are no waits and the main building offers plentiful air conditioning. Closes shortly before dusk. **EXPECT TO WAIT** Riders must board the Wildlife Express in the back right corner of Africa. Expect to wait up to ten minutes to board the train and another seven minutes to ride over. **LENGTH** As little or as long as you want. Most guests spend about 30 minutes.

Wildlife Express Train

RANKING Fun but skippable. **EMH** No. **FP+** No. **TYPE** Slow-moving transportation. **REQUIREMENTS** None.

WHAT TO EXPECT Guests wait at the station for the slow-moving train that arrives every eight-or-so minutes. All guests seated on the train sit facing the sights on the side of the train as it slowly travels through backstage areas where riders have an opportunity to see where the elephants sleep, among other things. This is the only way to travel to and from Rafiki's Planet Watch. **SCARY FACTOR** Zero.

WHEN TO GO Between 11am and 3pm when crowds and temperatures peak elsewhere is best. Begins operation 30 minutes after regular park open and closes shortly before dusk. **EXPECT TO WAIT** Between two and ten minutes. **LENGTH** The trip lasts about seven minutes.

ASIA

Home to perhaps Disney's best roller coaster, in addition to a white water rafting ride, jungle trek, and the underrated Flights of Wonder, Asia has a lot to offer underneath its dense vegetation and gorgeously detailed theming. Asia is accessible via Discovery Island, a path from Africa, or DinoLand. Guests arriving from Africa or Discovery Island will first happen upon Flights of Wonder, which is located in a nondescript theater on the left. Continuing on, Yak & Yeti Restaurant and quick service are located on the left. Both serve very good Pan-Asian fare, though the quick service arm only offers outdoor seating that is uncomfortable in the summer heat and rain. Just past Yak & Yeti on the left is the walkway to Kali River Rapids and Maharajah Jungle Trek. Free lockers are available near Kali River Rapids to keep belongings dry while enjoying the ride. Continue ahead and Expedition Everest is unmistakable in the distance. The ride entrance is again on the left. Passing Everest will take you to The Theater in the Wild, home of *Finding Nemo–The Musical*, and then on to the rest of DinoLand.

Shopping is thin through Asia, though you don't want to miss the clever Yak & Yeti-themed merchandise to the right of the quick service, or all the Expedition Everest-themed merchandise at the attraction's exit.

Expedition Everest

RANKING Don't miss. **EMH** Morning. **FP+** Yes. High priority. **TYPE** Roller coaster. **REQUIREMENTS** 44" or taller.

WHAT TO EXPECT Interesting artifacts in the queue create the back story of a mysterious beast that resides in the sacred mountains. Riders board (two per row) a train that traverses high speed twists, turns, and drops before a final confrontation with the Yeti. **SCARY FACTOR** Medium-High. Guests plummet down an 80-foot drop at speeds up to 50 miles per hour in the dark, but it could be worse. **CAN WE HANDLE IT?** If you enjoyed Rock 'n' Roller Coaster, or any other "big coaster," you shouldn't have a problem with Expedition Everest. It is more intense than Space Mountain, but not so intense that the younger crowd won't be jumping up and down begging to ride. Some motion sickness risk, but no loops or inversions. Little jostling or jerkiness.

WHEN TO GO At park open, in the final hour of operation, or with FastPass+. **EXPECT TO WAIT** 35 to 60 minutes in the afternoon. **LENGTH** 3 minutes. **WHERE TO SIT** The first row provides the best view, but the last provides the wildest ride. There really isn't a bad seat on the train. **SINGLE RIDER LINE**: Yes, to the right of standby entrance.

Flights of Wonder

RANKING Minor attraction. **EMH** No. **FP+** No. **TYPE** Stage show. **REQUIRE-MENTS** None.

WHAT TO EXPECT Guests enter a covered outdoor theater and find seats on bleacher-style benches without backs. A skilled trainer introduces viewers to over 20 species of birds, including a Great Horned Owl, Harris Hawk, and bald eagle. Tour Group Leader Guana Joe (or Jane) and his intense fear of birds provides comic relief throughout the show that includes several incredible tricks. We think it's under-rated. **SCARY FACTOR** Low for anyone without ornithophobia.

WHEN TO GO One of the last two shows will minimize crowds without wasting precious morning touring time. Otherwise, whenever it's convenient. **EXPECT TO WAIT** Arrive ten minutes early. **LENGTH** 30 minutes. **WHERE TO SIT** At least half way back in the center section is best, though there isn't a bad seat in the house.

Kali River Rapids

RANKING Major attraction. **EMH** Morning. **FP+** Yes. High priority when temperatures are 80+. **TYPE** Flume ride. **REQUIREMENTS** 38" or taller.

WHAT TO EXPECT Expect to get drenched on Kali, which follows a story about the destruction caused by illegal forestry. Riders board large rafts that seat 12 people in a circle around the outside perimeter of the raft. Your raft will be pulled up a 90 foot hill and then be released to freely but briefly float down the rapids, passing through geysers, waterfalls, and beautiful tropical jungles before plummeting down a 30-foot waterfall. The drop isn't fast or particularly thrilling, but it is still fun. Our opinion is that it's not worth the wait or the possible discomfort of wet socks and clothes. Complimentary lockers are located across from the entrance. Put everything you don't want getting wet inside before riding. **SCARY FACTOR** The ride starts off with a 90 foot uphill ascent, but there are no steep drops.

WHEN TO GO When it's hot, visit before 10am or in the last hour of operation. **EXPECT TO WAIT** 35 to 70 minutes in the afternoon when it's hot; 15 to 20 minutes when temperatures are under 70. **LENGTH** 5 minutes total, 2 of which are spent on the initial lift. **WHERE TO SIT** Anywhere.

Maharajah Jungle Trek

RANKING Minor attraction. **EMH** No. **FP+** No. **TYPE** Self-guided walking tour, zoo exhibit. **REQUIREMENTS** None.

WHAT TO EXPECT Maharajah Jungle Trek does not suffer from several of the problems that plague the Pangani Trail—the trail is wider, there is more room to view the animals, and the walkways aren't as crowded.

This makes Maharajah more pleasant in the afternoon. Otherwise, like Pangani, Maharajah is a trail that takes visitors through several zoo-like exhibits and enclosures. You'll see Bengal tigers, the world's largest Komodo dragon, Malayan tapirs, Blackbuck and Elds deer, and hundreds of exotic birds. Bats are located in a separate house that's easy to skip if you prefer. **SCARY FACTOR** None.

WHEN TO GO Much of the Trek is shaded and cooler than other areas in the Animal Kingdom, which makes it a good choice during the afternoon heat when attraction lines elsewhere are longest. Closes shortly before dusk. **EXPECT TO WAIT** No waits. **LENGTH** Maharajah is a little longer than a third of a mile and most visitors spend about 20 minutes walking through it.

DINOLAND USA

By far the least appreciated land in any domestic Disney theme park, DinoLand follows the story of the Dino Institute and their Time Rover Tours. The fictitious backstory is that, in 1947, researchers found dinosaur fossils in Diggs County and "Dino fever" took hold of the area, bringing in thousands of tourists. A local entrepreneurial couple, Chester and Hester, took advantage of the influx by building Chester and Hester's Dino-Rama, a collection of cheap carnival games, gaudy colors, and off-the-shelf rides.

Indeed, much of DinoLand is themed to a cheap carnival built on top of a parking lot—on purpose. Whether it works is another debate, but the Imagineers that designed the park would tell you it took more time and energy to make the parking lot look old and decrepit than it did to install much of the vegetation around the park.

Guests walking from Asia will first see The Theater in the Wild on their left. This houses one of Disney's most elaborate stage shows, *Finding Nemo–The Musical*. In the center of DinoLand sits Primeval Whirl and TriceraTop Spin. TriceraTop Spin is a spinner similar to Dumbo and Aladdin's Magical Carpets, while Primeval Whirl is an off-the-shelf wild-mouse-style coaster. Farther back to the left of Restaurantosaurus is DINOSAUR, the land's major attraction and a fun dark ride that transports lucky riders back to the end of the late Cretaceous period. Restaurantosaurus itself is a burger-and-nugget quick service option with fun theming.

Chester & Hester's Dinosaur Treasures shop is located near TriceraTop Spin's exit. There's nothing here that isn't available elsewhere. Another small store is located at DINOSAUR's exit. Here, you'll find some fun dinosaur-themed merchandise.

DINOSAUR

RANKING Don't miss. **EMH** Morning. **FP+** Yes. Medium priority. **TYPE** Dark ride. **REQUIREMENTS** 40" or taller.

WHAT TO EXPECT DINOSAUR is located in the Dino Institute, an elaborately themed queue area with authentic dinosaur fossils. After you move through the queue, you will be taken to watch a short video where the storyline is explained. Once the pre-show concludes, you will move to the next area where you board a 12-person (three rows with four people in each row) Time Rover vehicle. Once strapped in, you will embark on your wild ride through time and space. **SCARY FACTOR** High. DINOSAUR is one dark, loud, bumpy ride. Although there are no drops more than a few feet and the vehicles don't move particularly fast, this may still prove to be the scariest ride at Animal Kingdom. **CAN WE HANDLE IT?** Besides being scary and bumpy, DINOSAUR is rough on those with even moderate motion sickness.

WHEN TO GO Before 10:30am or two hours before park close. **EXPECT TO WAIT** 25 to 40 minutes in the afternoon. **LENGTH** 4 minutes. **WHERE TO SIT** Put apprehensive kids in the middle seats. The front row affords the best view.

Finding Nemo the Musical

RANKING Major attraction. **EMH** No. **FP+** Yes. Low priority. **TYPE** Musical theater show. **REQUIREMENTS** None.

WHAT TO EXPECT Featuring the *Finding Nemo* characters, the show is housed in an air-conditioned theater with fairly comfortable bench seats with backs. Tony Award-winner Robert Lopez and his wife Kristen Anderson-Lopez (now of "Let It Go" fame) penned 16 original songs for the show, and Michael Curry, who helped design the wildly successful *Lion King* Broadway show, served as lead designer. The actors and puppeteers wear costumes and are just as much a part of the show as the puppets themselves. Don't be put off by this being "just a puppet show" because it's much, much more than that. **SCARY FACTOR** Low. Nemo gets into some trouble with a shark puppet, but that's about it.

WHEN TO GO First and last shows are least crowded. **EXPECT TO WAIT** You'll want to be lined up about 20 minutes before it begins. **LENGTH** 40 minutes. **WHERE TO SIT** Plan to sit at least half way up in the middle seating section. Sitting any closer may result in a cropped view of the stage that requires a lot of head turning to see the action.

Primeval Whirl

RANKING Fun but skippable. **EMH** Morning. **FP+** Yes. Medium priority. **TYPE** Wild mouse coaster. **REQUIREMENTS** 48" or taller.

WHAT TO EXPECT Riders board four-person spinning ride vehicles reminiscent of Mad Tea Party. The vehicles travel up a steep incline before being unleashed on the track that features no serious drops or g-forces. It is a herky-jerky ride with the occasional neck-snapping stop. **SCARY FACTOR** Medium. While technically less intense than other coasters, the spinning can be disconcerting and it "feels" like you're higher up than you are. **CAN WE HANDLE IT?** The ride can be incredibly hard on necks and backs. Anyone with pain should skip the ride.

WHEN TO GO Before 10:30am or two hours before park close. **EXPECT TO WAIT** 15 to 30 minutes in the afternoon. **LENGTH** 3 minutes. **WHERE TO SIT** The common advice is to evenly distribute weight on each side of the vehicle for less spinning. Or conversely, stick two heavier people on one side and two lighter people on the other for more spinning. Does it have an effect? Probably not, but it might make you feel better.

The Boneyard

RANKING Fun for kids, skippable for everyone else. **EMH** No. **FP+** No. **TYPE** Playground. **REQUIREMENTS** None.

WHAT TO EXPECT The Boneyard is an elaborately themed playground aimed at young kids and has several stories of sand pits, swings, and things to climb on. **SCARY FACTOR** None.

WHEN TO GO Visit with youngsters when the bigger kids are riding Primeval Whirl and DINOSAUR. Otherwise, visit in the late morning or afternoon when waits elsewhere peak. The Boneyard does get hot, so save it for the end of the day during the summer. **EXPECT TO WAIT** Very rarely any wait. **LENGTH** As long as it takes to pry Junior away.

TriceraTop Spin

RANKING Fun diversion, especially with kids. **EMH** Morning. **FP+** No. **TYPE** Spinning ride. **REQUIREMENTS** None.

WHAT TO EXPECT Riders enter four-person dinosaur-themed vehicles with two rows of two people. Each row has a joystick that can slightly alter the way the vehicle moves: either up and down or back and forth. The ride vehicles slowly move around the base of the ride in a circle. **SCARY FACTOR** Minimal. Although the ride does move up, down, and side to side, it's geared towards young children and it shouldn't frighten anyone.

WHEN TO GO Before 11am or about two hours before park close. **EXPECT TO WAIT** Peak waits of 10 to 15 minutes are common. It's a walk-on, early and late. **LENGTH** 90 seconds. **WHERE TO SIT** Your choice, though young kids will be asked to sit on the inside so they won't accidentally fall out. Riders in the front can reach behind and use the joystick in the back row if there's nobody back there.

Epcot

Epcot is Walt Disney World's second most popular theme park and a quintessential part of any theme park vacation. Most guests with older kids will want to prioritize a second day here over a second day at Animal Kingdom or Hollywood Studios due to Epcot's vast size and the time it takes to experience many of its attractions. Epcot is unlike any other theme park, and many of its attractions take time and a little effort to enjoy.

Epcot consists of two very different pieces– Future World and World Showcase. Future World is where you'll find the headlining rides like Soarin' and Test Track, in addition to the bulk of the secondary attractions. It's the area located just inside the main entrance and consumes the north half of the park. World Showcase is home to most of the dining and shopping experiences, in addition to the emphasis on the cultures of the world that the park is so famous for providing.

Future World almost always operates from 9am (rarely, it opens at 8am) through regular park close, although the Imagination Pavilion, Energy Pavilion, both Innoventions buildings, and all the attractions inside them typically close at 7pm. World Showcase usually operates from 11am through park close, though Akershus Royal Banquet Hall in Norway serves breakfast beginning at 8am and the bakery in France usually begins operating at regular park open.

FASTPASS+ AT EPCOT

FastPass+ at Epcot is divided into two tiers. In Tier 1 are Soarin', Test Track, IllumiNations, and Living with the Land. Guests may initially select only one Tier 1 experience. Soarin' is the top priority because it's more convenient to ride it in the afternoon with FastPass+.

FastPass+ Priority

1. Mission: SPACE Orange
2. Spaceship Earth
3. Character Spot
4. Maelstrom
5. Mission: SPACE Green
6. Turtle Talk with Crush
7. The Seas with Nemo and Friends
8. Journey into Imagination with Figment
9. Captain EO

Note that Mission: SPACE does not require you to select Orange or Green when booking the experience, but guests planning on using it for the Orange side will want to prioritize it higher than those planning the Green side.

ARRIVING AT EPCOT

Guests aiming to take advantage of shorter morning waits should arrive at the main entrance at least 45 minutes before open, or at the International Gateway at least 30 minutes before open.

Most guests arrive at the main entrance via Disney bus or their own automobile. Guests staying at the Beach Club, Yacht Club, BoardWalk Inn, Swan, and Dolphin have the option of walking from their resort or taking the boat to the International Gateway entrance in the World Showcase between the Canada and France Pavilions. Guests transferring from Magic Kingdom or the Magic Kingdom parking lot (Transportation and Ticket Center) arrive at the main entrance via the monorail.

Guest Services outside the main entrance is on the far right, while Guest Services inside is on the far left past Spaceship Earth. Wheelchair and ECV rental are on the left just inside the entrance. At the International Gateway, Guest Services is located next to the ticket booths on the left outside bag check. Wheelchairs and EVCs are available for rental inside on the left.

FUTURE WORLD EAST

Future World East is where you'll find three of Epcot's four top priority attractions: Test Track, Sum of All Thrills, and Mission: SPACE. Most guests visiting only for one day will want to start on this side, and guests spending two or more days will also want to plan a morning starting with Test Track or a late arrival with Test Track as a FastPass+ selection.

Bypass Spaceship Earth, the park's icon, first thing in the morning. The iconic structure that looks like a giant golf ball enjoys lower peak waits than the headliners and sees short waits in the late afternoon and evening. Many uninformed guests ride Spaceship Earth first thing, putting them at a great disadvantage as they won't arrive at Test Track until at least 9:30am, when waits will already be hitting 30+ minutes.

Dining choices are slim—Electric Umbrella is really it, and it serves a limited menu featuring Disney's standard burgers, chicken nuggets, and meatball sandwiches. Various stands serve snacks, including pretzels, churros, and beer.

Mouse Gear is the largest store in Epcot, offering the widest assortment of theme park merchandise outside of World of Disney at Downtown Disney.

Ellen's Energy Adventure

RANKING Minor attraction. **EMH** No. **FP+** No. **TYPE** Dark ride. **REQUIRE-MENTS** None.

WHAT TO EXPECT A 45-minute experience begins when riders are seated in what looks like a conventional theater where they will be shown the first of several films featuring Ellen DeGeneres and Bill Nye. After that, your section of the theater will break away from the other ride vehicles and you will slowly be taken through a variety of Animatronic scenes and films. **SCARY FACTOR** Low. Some young children may find Animatronic dinosaurs startling.

WHEN TO GO In the afternoon, or with a shorter child while the rest of the group rides the thrill rides. Usually closes at 7pm. **EXPECT TO WAIT** Less than ten minutes. **LENGTH** 45 minutes, with no way to exit in the middle. **WHERE TO SIT** Around the fourth row, which makes it easier to see the films.

Innoventions East (excluding Sum of All Thrills)

RANKING Afternoon diversion. **EMH** No. **FP+** No. **TYPE** Exhibits and interactive experiences. **REQUIREMENTS** None.

WHAT TO EXPECT Mostly a collection of interactive experiences; each exhibit will take 15–30 minutes to complete. **SCARY FACTOR** Low. *Storm Struck* is a 4D film that simulates a storm in a small theater, but nothing else is frightening.

WHEN TO GO In the afternoon. Usually closes at 7pm. **EXPECT TO WAIT** Just a few minutes for the next experience to begin. **LENGTH** Varies—generally about 20 minutes for each experience. Some families spend hours, others skip entirely.

Mission: SPACE

RANKING Major attraction. **EMH** Morning, Evening. **FP+** Yes. High priority for Orange (intense), lower priority for Green (less intense). **TYPE** Simulator. **REQUIREMENTS** Must be 44" tall to ride. Mission: SPACE has more warnings than any other ride at Disney World, and is the only ride where you will be handed a card with all of the various warnings on it. Consider skipping if you have suffered motion sickness on any other ride, or are claustrophobic.

WHAT TO EXPECT Mission: SPACE is a space flight simulator, where riders board small four-person capsules that are intended to mimic the inside of a space shuttle. There are two versions of this ride: the Orange Team features a spinning takeoff with G-forces up to 2.5, and is much more thrilling and much more risky for those with physical or motion sickness issues. The Green Team is identical to the Orange Team ride in every way except there is no spinning takeoff, and thus, no G-forces to worry about. After the initial takeoff, the rest of the ride is rather tame with only slight movements by the simulator while you watch a small screen in front of you. On the Orange Team, the intense aspects last for about 15 seconds at takeoff and again for a short amount of time when the spacecraft travels through an asteroid field. **SCARY FACTOR** Medium. The ride itself is not particularly scary, but there are some iffy moments. Mission: SPACE does induce anxiety due to negative hype over people getting sick from the spinning. **CAN WE HANDLE IT?** Apprehensive riders should begin with the Green Team.

WHEN TO GO Before 10:30am, after 7pm, or with FastPass+. **EXPECT TO WAIT** Orange Team peak waits are in the 25–45 minute range, while Green Team waits are usually 15–20 minutes. **LENGTH** 5 minutes. **WHERE TO SIT** Experience is the same from any of the four seats.

Spaceship Earth

RANKING Don't miss. **EMH** Morning, Evening. **FP+** Yes. High Tier 2 priority. **TYPE** Dark ride. **REQUIREMENTS** None.

WHAT TO EXPECT Spaceship Earth is a slow moving, dark omnimover ride that takes guests as high as 16 stories inside Epcot's famous geodesic sphere. Visitors ride past more than 20 Animatronic displays featuring scenes from the past 40,000 years that depict how communication techniques have changed with time. A classic. **SCARY FACTOR** Low. The ride is dark, but there are no startling elements.

WHEN TO GO After 6pm or with FastPass+. **EXPECT TO WAIT** Peak waits of 30 minutes are common. Expect to wait less than 10 minutes after 6pm. **LENGTH** 15 minutes. **WHERE TO SIT** Each row seats two to three people. The view from the left is arguably better.

Sum of All Thrills

RANKING Minor attraction. **EMH** No. **FP+** No. **TYPE** Simulator. **REQUIREMENTS** 48" or taller to ride and 54" or taller to add inversions.

WHAT TO EXPECT Guests first watch a short pre-show video introducing the importance of science. Next is the interactive design stage where riders design the intensity and ride elements, choosing from among a bobsled for a tame ride, or a roller coaster or fighter jet for the most intense experience. Finally, riders board a Kuka Arm simulator and experience their creation. **SCARY FACTOR** Medium. Riders choose how intense their ride is. **CAN WE HANDLE IT?** Probably. The wary can design a slower ride without inversions. Check the example ride vehicle first if claustrophobia is a concern.

WHEN TO GO Immediately after Test Track in the morning or after 6pm. Usually closes at 7pm. **LENGTH** 20 minutes total with about 90 seconds in the simulator. **WHERE TO SIT** In one of the two seats right next to each other.

Test Track

RANKING Don't miss. **EMH** Morning, Evening. **FP+** Yes. Second highest Tier 1 priority behind Soarin'. Test Track is more convenient to get to in the morning and offers a single rider line. **TYPE** Dark/thrill ride. **REQUIREMENTS** 40" or taller.

WHAT TO EXPECT After a 2012 renovation, riders are to imagine themselves to be "inside" a computer simulation of a car being tested. Guests first design their own prototype automobile at a kiosk. The design process takes about three minutes and riders choose what they want their automobile to look like and whether they want to favor capability, efficiency, responsiveness, or power. In a surprise to many, this design step does not affect the ride in any way. Riders then board six-person vehicles with two rows of three seats each and embark on their journey with several sharp turns and increases and decreases in speed before launching outside at speeds up to 65 miles per hour. **SINGLE RIDER**: Test Track offers a single-rider line with the entrance to the left of standby. Waits are usually shorter than standby or FastPass+ because single riders don't go through the design process and the seating arrangement creates more openings. **SCARY FACTOR** Low. Test Track is just a little more intense than normal driving.

WHEN TO GO Immediately after park opening, in the final hour of operation, or with FastPass+. **EXPECT TO WAIT** 60 to 100 minutes in the afternoon. **LENGTH** 5 minutes. **WHERE TO SIT** Request the front row for the best view.

FUTURE WORLD WEST

Three large pavilions make up the bulk of Future World West. Soarin' on the lower level of the Land Pavilion is its headlining attraction and a top morning priority. Most other attractions can safely be saved for the afternoon or early evening. Prior to its 2013 refurbishment, Character Spot was a top priority. Now that it has doubled its capacity, wait times are rarely longer than 20 minutes.

Starbucks is located in the old Fountain View Café building to the right of the fountain. Club Cool, situated behind it, offers free samples of Coca-Cola products from around the world. Sunshine Seasons is arguably the best quick service in any theme park. You'll find it in between Soarin' and Living with the Land in the Land Pavilion. Coral Reef and Garden Grill are the two table service restaurants. Coral Reef receives mixed reviews, but the view of The Seas aquarium is intriguing. Garden Grill is a fun family-style character meal hosted by farmers Mickey, Pluto, Chip, and Dale inside the Land Pavilion.

Retail is light, with small stores and kiosks popping up at most attraction exits.

Captain EO

RANKING Skippable, though the air-conditioned theater is comfortable. **EMH** Evening. **FP+** Yes. Lowest priority. **TYPE** 4D show. **REQUIREMENTS** None.

WHAT TO EXPECT An eight-minute documentary hosted by George Lucas and Francis Ford Coppola precedes the loud 17-minute 3D show. 4D effects are slim, but the theater briefly shakes. The show's plot is both nonsensical and difficult to follow, but *Thriller*-era Michael Jackson has some interest for some. **SCARY FACTOR** EO is dark with aliens, danger, and several unrealistic torture scenes that last a few seconds. It shouldn't upset anyone over the age of ten, but apprehensive youngsters may want to sit it out.

WHEN TO GO For most: never. For the rest: in the afternoon or early evening when waits elsewhere are long. EO usually closes at 7pm. **EXPECT TO WAIT** Only as long as it takes for the next show to start. **LENGTH** 8-minute pre-show, 17-minute show. **WHERE TO SIT** In the middle at least half way from the screen.

Character Spot

RANKING Don't miss for those who wish to meet the characters; skippable for others. **EMH** Evening. **FP+** Yes. High Tier 2 priority. **TYPE** Meet and greet. **REQUIREMENTS** None.

WHAT TO EXPECT Guests line up indoors with televisions playing old cartoon clips. Guests then meet Mickey, Minnie, and Goofy individually in their classic outfits. **SCARY FACTOR** None.

WHEN TO GO As late in the evening as possible—ideally after 7pm. Waits are also short before 10:15am **EXPECT TO WAIT** Peak waits are typically 15–20 minutes. **LENGTH** About five minutes of signing, mingling, and picture taking.

Circle of Life

RANKING Skippable. **EMH** Evening. **FP+** No. **TYPE** Film. **REQUIREMENTS** None.

WHAT TO EXPECT *Circle of Life* is a film starring the *Lion King's* Timon, Pumba, and Simba that focuses on environmental responsibility, and, with no apparent irony, on why building mega-resorts can be bad for the environment. The film features both cartoon and live-action scenes. **SCARY FACTOR** None.

WHEN TO GO Afternoon or early evening. It usually closes at 7pm. **EXPECT TO WAIT** Only as long as it takes for the next show to start. **LENGTH** 15 minutes. **WHERE TO SIT** Near the back for a quick exit.

Innoventions West

RANKING Afternoon diversion. **EMH** No. **FP+** No. **TYPE** Exhibits and interactive experiences. **REQUIREMENTS** None.

WHAT TO EXPECT Mostly a collection of interactive experiences, each exhibit will take 15–30 minutes to complete. The Great Piggy Bank Adventure and Where's the Fire are excellent. **SCARY FACTOR** None.

WHEN TO GO In the afternoon. Usually closes at 7pm. **EXPECT TO WAIT** Just a few minutes for the next experience to begin. **LENGTH** Varies—generally about 20 minutes for each experience. Some families spend hours, others skip entirely.

Journey into Imagination with Figment

RANKING Minor attraction. **EMH** Evening. **FP+** Yes. Low priority. **TYPE** Dark ride. **REQUIREMENTS** None.

WHAT TO EXPECT Narrated by Dr. Nigel Channing with frequent interruptions by Figment the purple dragon, Journey takes riders slowly through a variety of rooms, each designed to stimulate the senses. **SCARY FACTOR** Low. This will only startle the young that are extremely prone to attraction anxiety.

WHEN TO GO In the afternoon or with a shorter child while the rest of the group rides the thrill rides. Usually closes at 7pm. **EXPECT TO WAIT** Less than ten minutes. **LENGTH** 5 minutes. **WHERE TO SIT** Any row is fine.

Living with the Land

RANKING Minor attraction. **EMH** Morning, Evening. **FP+** Yes. Lowest Tier 1 priority. **TYPE** Slow boat ride. **REQUIREMENTS** None.

WHAT TO EXPECT Living with the Land is a meandering, educational boat ride about crop cultivation. It's more fun than it sounds! **SCARY FACTOR** Low, unless you have a fear of genetically modified organisms.

WHEN TO GO By 10:30am or after 5pm is best. Usually closes at 7pm. **EXPECT TO WAIT** Less than ten minutes in most scenarios. **LENGTH** 15 minutes. **WHERE TO SIT** Request the first row for the best view.

Soarin'

RANKING Don't miss. **EMH** Morning, Evening. **FP+** Yes. Highest Tier 1 priority. **TYPE** Simulator. **REQUIREMENTS** Must be 40" tall to ride.

WHAT TO EXPECT Riders are led into a large room with an 80-foot-tall concave movie screen and three ride vehicles, each of which has three rows. Once all riders are seated, the vehicles are lifted into the air so that each row is above the row below it. A series of scenes are projected onto the screen and the ride vehicles move with the scenes to simulate a hang-gliding flight. **SCARY FACTOR** Minimal. The ride takes visitors 40 feet in the air, which may be frightening for those intensely scared of heights. Motion sickness is much less of a problem than "hang glider" might imply. The ride is gentle and there are no significant drops or sharp turns.

WHEN TO GO Immediately after park open, in the final hour of operation, or with FastPass+. **EXPECT TO WAIT** Peak waits of 60–100 minutes are common. **LENGTH** 5 minutes. **WHERE TO SIT** The best seats are in the front row of the middle vehicle because other people's feet won't be dangling in front of your face.

The Seas with Nemo and Friends

RANKING Minor attraction. **EMH** Evening. **FP+** Yes. Low priority. **TYPE** Dark ride. **REQUIREMENTS** None.

WHAT TO EXPECT Nemo & Friends is a slow "clam-mobile" ride through a long *Finding Nemo* themed tunnel. The neatest part of the attraction is when the characters from *Finding Nemo* are shown swimming with real fish inside of the 5.7 million gallon salt-water tank. The ride lets visitors out at The Seas Pavilion, which is full of hands-on activities and places to view the 6,000+ underwater animals that live within one of the largest undersea environments in the world. **SCARY FACTOR** Low. There is a friendly shark Animatronic and it's dark, but that's about it.

WHEN TO GO Before 11am or after 7pm. **EXPECT TO WAIT** Peak waits of 10–20 minutes are common. Expect to wait less than five minutes before 10:30am and after 7pm. **LENGTH** 5 minutes. **WHERE TO SIT** Each clam-mobile seats three across a single row.

Turtle Talk with Crush

RANKING Don't miss for those with young kids, major attraction for everyone else. **EMH** Evening. **FP+** Yes. Medium priority. There are no reserved seats, but FastPass+ guarantees admittance to the next show. **TYPE** Interactive show. **REQUIREMENTS** None.

WHAT TO EXPECT Turtle Talk is a live, interactive show featuring Crush, the turtle from *Finding Nemo*. The theater is small and the kids are asked to sit up front. Crush moves, chats, and fields audience questions in real time, and every show is unique and drop-dead cute. **SCARY FACTOR** Zero.

WHEN TO GO Shows usually begin at 9:40am and run until 8:40pm. Visit before 10:30am or after 7pm. **EXPECT TO WAIT** Up to 30 minutes in the afternoon, but usually just as long as it takes for the next show to begin. **LENGTH** 15 minutes. **WHERE TO SIT** Kids should sit on the floor up front. Adults file into the bleacher-style seating in back.

WORLD SHOWCASE

World Showcase is a collection of 11 individual pavilions, each themed to a country from around the world. The emphasis is undoubtedly on eating, drinking, and shopping, but each pavilion offers authentic entertainment and shows, and two even have rides. Historically, many kids have been bored with the lack of rides, so Disney has installed a variety of interactive experiences designed to engage them. The most popular is Agent P's World Showcase Adventure themed to the popular *Phineas and Ferb* television show. Guests have an opportunity to pick up a handset from several pavilions and embark on a kind of scavenger hunt throughout World Showcase. Kids also have the opportunity to sit down with Cast Members in each pavilion and decorate Duffy or Agent P drawings. With one day at Epcot, try to arrive in Mexico as close to 11am as possible to ride Gran Fiesta Tour before moving on to Maelstrom in Norway. These two rides present the only possible attraction lines later in the day. With two days, consider starting one day in Mexico and touring about half of the pavilions. On the second day, start from the other side. The pavilions on this side have particularly lovely gardens best seen in daylight.

IllumiNations

IllumiNations is the park's nighttime spectacular, scheduled every night, almost always at regular park close, and lasting for about 15 minutes. It takes place on World Showcase Lagoon with viewing available from around World Showcase. Detailed advice on where to see the show is in the Epcot Cheat Sheet at the end of the chapter.
RANKING Don't miss. **EMH** No. **FP+** Yes. Low Tier 1 priority. The FastPass+ viewing location is at the base of World Showcase across from the United States Pavilion in an area called Showcase Plaza. It's a low priority because the show is easy enough to see outside the viewing area and using FastPass+ at Soarin' or Test Track will save more time. **TYPE** Fireworks show. **REQUIREMENTS** None.

WHAT TO EXPECT Guests begin to fill in along the railing as far as two hours in advance, but most guests will find satisfying viewing locations as few as 15 minutes before show time. The action takes place on World Showcase Lagoon as fireworks explode above a massive rotating globe. **SCARY FACTOR** Low. The fireworks are occasionally loud, particularly at the end.
TYPICAL SCHEDULE: Begins at regular park close. **LENGTH** 15 minutes.

Our World Showcase reviews begin in Mexico and run clockwise around World Showcase Lagoon.

Mexico Pavilion

Framed by a giant Mesoamerican pyramid, Mexico is home to a boat ride, two sit-down restaurants, a quick service outlet, a tequila bar, a margarita stand, a Donald Duck meet and greet, and a live mariachi band. Most of what Mexico offers is located inside the dark, air-conditioned pyramid that acts as a cool respite from the heat. Grab a margarita and enjoy the heritage exhibits, stores, ambiance, and music.

Minor attraction: Gran Fiesta Tour is a relaxing, slow-moving boat ride through the world of *The Three Caballeros*. The ride lasts about seven minutes and follows Jose Carioca and Panchito as they hunt down Donald before a big gig. Waits are under five minutes most of the time. On busier days, visit before 12:30pm or after 7pm.

Norway Pavilion

Themed to a Viking-era village, Norway features a replica of the 14th century Akershus Fortress, which the Norwegians originally built to protect Oslo from attack. Disney's version is a bit more sanitized—you'll find a princess-hosted character meal inside. The richly detailed stave church features a *Frozen* tie-in with artwork and artifacts that show how reality influenced the movie. Kringla Bakeri, the pavilion's quick service, offers excellent, inexpensive treats. At the Puffin's Roost, guests can peruse fun Norway-themed merchandise alongside authentic (and expensive) hand-knit apparel, perfume, and toys.

Major attraction: Maelstrom, located in the back of the pavilion on the right, is the best ride in World Showcase. It's basically a Viking-themed boat ride. There is a small backwards drop and it's dark, but it should not upset anyone. The ride lasts about five minutes with an optional film following. Maelstrom is a moderate Tier 2 priority. Ride between 11am and 12pm, after 7pm, or plan to use FastPass+ to minimize waits.

China Pavilion

An intricately detailed triple-arched ceremonial gate welcomes visitors to China. Immediately past the gate is a replica of the Temple of Heaven, inside of which guests can view *Reflections of China*, a 15-minute Circle-Vision 360 film that covers the more positive Chinese traditions and culture (as in all World Showcase shows except the American Adventure, no negative aspects of the culture appear). Visit the air-conditioned, standing-room-only theater at your leisure. While you wait for the next film to begin, check out the cultural exhibit through the door on the left. Chinese acrobats perform most days either in the courtyard or inside the Temple of Heaven in the Hall of Prayer for Good Harvests.

Nine Dragons is the pavilion's table service restaurant, serving up traditional and contemporary Chinese food at prices lower than most other restaurants on property. It has a lousy reputation, but the food has improved in recent memory and the portions are large. Lotus Blossom is the quick service arm, serving Panda Express quality fast food at higher prices. It's best skipped. The Joy of Tea stand on the water is a surprisingly good spot to pick up a strong drink or fruity cocktail depending on the group's mood at the time.

Shopping in China is above average at the expansive House of Good Fortune on the left side of the pavilion. You'll find silk robes, traditional fans, tea sets, jewelry, puppets, and more.

Germany Pavilion

Featuring a statue of Saint George slaying a dragon, and a clock tower with a glockenspiel that chimes on the hour, the architecture in Germany is interesting and varied. The main attraction is Altenmunster Oktoberfest beer on draft—there are no traditional attractions or entertainment here. Still, take a moment to peruse Karamell-Kuche (Caramel Kitchen), in addition to the stores that offer made-in-Germany toys, cuckoo clocks, beer steins, toys, apparel, and other fun items. As you walk toward Italy, pay special attention to the outdoor model train set on the left.

Biergarten is the table service restaurant, featuring a smorgasbord of traditional German salads, roasted meats, pretzel bread, soups, and more. A traditional oompah band plays intermittently throughout the day inside the restaurant. Lunch is priced well. Sommerfest is the pavilion's quick service, offering a variety of bratwurst, frankfurters, and other traditional German foods. Seating for it is scarce.

Italy Pavilion

The focal point of the Italy Pavilion is the 105-foot-tall functioning replica of St Mark's Campanile, the bell tower that looks out over the World Showcase Lagoon. Also prominently featured is a replica of the Doge's Palace, originally built by the Venetians in the early 14th century. In typical Disney fashion, the Palace is full of fine Italian perfume, handmade masks, soccer jerseys, pasta, and other items Italia. Italy is otherwise comprised mostly of restaurants and bars. Best is Via Napoli in the back of the pavilion, serving authentic Neapolitan pizzas. Without a reservation, try Tutto Gusto, the wine bar attached to the Tutto Italia restaurant with hundreds of Italian wines, rare Italian beer on draft, and an appetizer and dessert menu that's hard to beat. Tutto Italia is more formal, but still perfect for families and couples, serving regional Italian fare. Live entertainment is available most days.

United States Pavilion

The United States Pavilion is mostly housed inside of a single Colonial-style mansion that was built using 110,000 hand-made Georgian clay bricks.

Major attraction: *The American Adventure*, a 30-minute theater show blending film and Animatronics, is the principal attraction. The patriotic show briefly retells the history of America and runs on a set schedule with the next show listed on posters outside the pavilion. The theater seats over a thousand in comfortable air-conditioning, making it a perfect respite from the afternoon heat. The show is often preceded in the afternoon by the Voices of Liberty a cappella group inside the mansion and the Fife and Drum Corps outside.

Outside, the America Gardens Theater is home to various free concerts throughout the year with space-available seating, including Flower Power, Sounds like Summer, Eat to the Beat, and the Candlelight Processional.

Liberty Inn is the quick service outlet. Recent menu overhauls have brought a New York Strip Steak for less than $12 and more interesting salad and entrée fare. Seating is plentiful indoors and outdoors. Fife & Drum Tavern outside serves beer, pretzels, turkey legs, popcorn, and an assortment of other snacks.

Japan Pavilion

The red torii gate and the 85-foot-tall Goju-no-to pagoda welcome guests to the Japan Pavilion. These and other buildings are surrounded by beautiful gardens made up of native Japanese plants, bamboo, and evergreen, maple, and monkey puzzle trees. The large courtyard in the middle of the pavilion makes Japan feel more open, relaxed, and less cluttered than other pavilions. Be sure to cross the bridge leading to the White Heron Castle and check out the koi fish below.

While there are no rides or theater shows in Japan, the pavilion is still rich with entertainment and culture. Enjoy the athletic Taiko drummers and the cultural exhibits inside the castle. The Mitsukoshi Department Store on the right side of the pavilion is among the best in Walt Disney World, offering more than 50,000 unique products. Kimonos, Samurai swords, Bonsai trees, chopstick sets, calligraphy brushes, toys, and everything in between are available for purchase. Check out the popular Pick-a-Pearl where guests can pick an oyster and discover what's inside. Hundreds of relatively inexpensive food and drink items are available in the final room, in addition to a sake bar with samples available by the glass.

Dining options are even more plentiful. Teppan Edo and Tokyo Dining are two very different table service restaurants. Teppan Edo, a traditional hibachi-grill experience similar to Benihana, is one of the more consistent restaurants on property, offering grilled meat, fish, and vegetables. Tokyo Dining focuses on sushi and tempura in a contemporary setting. Outside, Katsura Grill serves quick service sushi, teriyaki, and other traditional food. Indoor air-conditioned seating is available, in addition to the beautiful outdoor garden setting. Food at Katsura is merely okay, but it's a relaxing location. A sake bar serving cocktails, beer, and sake is located outside across from Mitsukoshi Department Store. Also outside, Kabuki Café serves kaki gori (snow cones) with traditional toppings, in addition to smoothies, beer, and other snacks.

Morocco

Morocco is represented by architecture and monuments from three famous Moroccan cities: Casablanca, Fez, and Marrakesh. Koutoubia Minaret, the focal point of the pavilion, is a replica of the 12th century Marrakesh prayer tower. Morocco is the only state-sponsored World Showcase pavilion, and the country played an integral part in the design and construction of the buildings, gardens, and Bab Boujeloud arch. The King of Morocco actually sent his personal craftsmen to construct and lay tile in much of the pavilion, making this one of the most authentic areas in Epcot. Because of the religious significance of many of Morocco's buildings, lights are not shined on the pavilion during IllumiNations.

Morocco is the most-passed-over pavilion, which is unfortunate because there is a lot to see and do, despite it not offering a major show or ride. We highly recommend taking 20–30 minutes to explore the marketplace, museum, and art gallery. Mo'Rockin plays Arabic music alongside a belly dancer throughout the afternoon and into the evening.

Restaurant Marrakesh is the under-rated Moroccan restaurant in the pavilion, specializing in couscous and anything with a shank. A belly dancer appears inside the restaurant throughout the day. Spice Road Table opened in late 2013, offering small Mediterranean tapas, wines, cocktails, and desserts. It's a beautiful restaurant that overlooks the picturesque lagoon. Reservations are not required or accepted at Spice Road, and it's rarely busy. Tangierine Café is the quick service, featuring shawarma and falafel. While the food is a bit more expensive, portions are large and the food is freshly prepared. It's our favorite World Showcase quick service.

France Pavilion

The replica of the Eiffel Tower is the most recognizable feature of the France Pavilion. The buildings are themed like those found in Paris between 1870 and 1910, otherwise known as La Belle Epoque, or The Beautiful Time. France features a gorgeous courtyard area with a fountain and immaculately maintained gardens.

France's main attraction is an 18-minute film titled *Impressions de France*. Projected onto five large screens, *Impressions* provides a 200-degree panoramic view of France, its people, and its culture. You'll experience many of France's most popular destinations, including the gardens at Versailles, the Eiffel Tower, and the breathtaking French Alps. Unlike the films at China or Canada, you'll be able to sit and relax during the air-conditioned show. In addition, the fun Serveur Amusant comedy/acrobat show is scheduled throughout the afternoon most days.

France is home to two sit-down restaurants, a quick service boulangerie patisserie (bakery), and an ice cream parlor. Les Chefs de France downstairs is themed to a casual Parisian bistro and serves an excellent, relatively inexpensive three-course lunch in addition to a la carte items. Upstairs is the ritzier Monsieur Paul, serving a more expensive menu catered toward adults. Les Halles Boulangerie Patisserie, located in the back of the pavilion, serves sandwiches, quiche, salads, desserts, and other French specialties. It's an excellent spot to pick up a snack or a meal. Finally, L'Artisan des Glaces serves freshly prepared sorbet and ice cream with the option of a shot of liquor poured on top.

Shopping includes wine, perfume, and fun French-themed Disney merchandise.

United Kingdom Pavilion

The United Kingdom Pavilion is one of the more architecturally diverse World Showcase pavilions, with the Hampton Court Palace, Anne Hathaway's (William Shakespeare's wife) thatched roof cottage, two castles, and a miniature version of Hyde Park represented. You'll see replicas of the red phone booths England is so famous for, as well as a variety of beautiful garden areas.

The British Revolution cover band and World Showcase Players are the entertainment here. The Players are a fun, interactive comedy group, while the Revolution play Led Zeppelin, The Who, and other favorites from famous British artists. Several shops carry a range of British goods, including tea, perfume and makeup, apparel, and a lot of Guinness- and Beatles-related merchandise.

Rose & Crown Dining Room is the pavilion's table service restaurant. It's a casual, low key affair, and your best opportunity to watch IllumiNations from a restaurant while you dine. The Pub next door is an excellent spot to grab a pint. Yorkshire County Fish Co. outside serves excellent fast food fish and chips with limited picturesque seating along the lagoon.

Canada Pavilion

Gorgeous Victoria Gardens and a replica of the Canadian Rockies complete with a 30-foot waterfall lead guests into the Canada Pavilion. The Hotel du Canada, modeled after Ottawa's Fairmont Chateau Laurier, is the pavilion's largest and most magnificently detailed building. Canada features a Circle-Vision 360 film similar to *Reflections of China*. The 18-minute *O' Canada!* show is projected onto nine individual screens that surround the theatre. The film is presented in such a way that each screen shows the view looking out in that particular direction, so you feel like you're right in the middle of the shot. While it's standing-room-only, the theater is large and air-conditioned. Outside, the high energy Off Kilter play throughout the afternoon and evening most days.

Le Cellier is the pavilion's table service restaurant, primarily offering steak. It's a signature restaurant, which means it will set you back two Dining Plan credits or more out of pocket than most restaurants.

Shopping is limited to stuffed animals and other toys, along with apparel items and some food and beverages.

Disney's Hollywood Studios

Disney's Hollywood Studios opened as a combined theme park and working production studio under the name Disney-MGM Studios on May 1, 1989. The name changed to Disney's Hollywood Studios in 2008. While several famous shows and movies were filmed or animated on site, it's been more than ten years since any serious studio work has happened here.

It's now "just" a Disney theme park, but several of Hollywood Studios' rides and shows are among the best Walt Disney World has to offer. With a total of six rides and a dozen shows, its repertoire is thin, but what it does offer will satisfy most guests and fill an entire day.

Touring the Studios is more complicated than one might expect due to long lines at the headliners and several lengthy stage shows that run on a limited schedule. The layout is also a bit confusing for first-time visitors. The Cheat Sheet map at the end of the chapter will make traversing the park significantly easier.

FASTPASS+ AT THE STUDIOS

FastPass+ at the Studios is divided into two tiers. In Tier 1 are Toy Story Mania, Rock 'n' Roller Coaster, Great Movie Ride, Fantasmic!, and Beauty and the Beast: Live on Stage. Guests may initially only select one Tier 1 attraction, which can make it a struggle to visit both Toy Story Mania and Rock 'n' Roller Coaster on a single day without an early arrival. Most guests will want to select Toy Story Mania as their Tier One FastPass+ and ride Rock 'n' Roller Coaster standby early in the morning.

Guests may initially select two of the nine attractions that make up Tier 2. Here's our suggested priority among them—most should pick two of the first four. (There are no reserved seats for FastPass+ users at any of the shows.)

FastPass+ Priority

1.   Tower of Terror
2.   Voyage of the Little Mermaid
3.   Star Tours
4.   Indiana Jones Epic Stunt Spectacular
5.   *Disney Jr. Live on Stage*
6.   Lights, Motors, Action! Extreme Stunt Show
7.   American Idol Experience
8.   Muppet Vision 3D

ARRIVING AT THE STUDIOS

Arriving at least 45 minutes prior to park opening is essential for guests interested in signing up their 4–12 year old for the Jedi Training Academy or riding Toy Story Mania first thing without a significant wait. Arriving closer to regular open will only result in thousands of guests in line in front of you at the priority attractions.

Most guests arrive via Disney bus or their own automobile at one of the Studios' two entrances. The bus stops are just minutes away from the main entrance, while guests driving have the option of walking or taking a tram from the parking lot. Guests staying at the BoardWalk, Yacht Club, Beach Club, Swan, or Dolphin either walk or take the boat that begins service 30 minutes before regular open. Walking or taking the boat both take about 25 minutes, but walking cuts down on the wait for the first boat and allows you to arrive much earlier in the morning.

Guest Services and the primary MyMagic+ service center are located on the left just inside the entrance. Ticket booths in front of the entrance can handle any purchases or upgrades, usually with non-existent lines. Wheelchair and stroller rental are just inside on the right.

HOLLYWOOD BOULEVARD

Hollywood Boulevard, the Studios' main drag, is similar to Main Street, U.S.A. at Magic Kingdom. It consists almost entirely of retail with Mickey's of Hollywood and Keystone Clothiers on the left carrying the widest selection of merchandise. PhotoPass and a couple smaller stores are on the right. Hollywood Brown Derby, a signature restaurant that costs two credits on the Dining Plan, serves the best food in the park on the right near the end of the Boulevard. To the right of it sits Starring Rolls, the best place for a quick croissant or muffin first thing in the morning or a sandwich or cupcake later in the day. Mickey's Sorcerer's Hat, standing over 120 feet tall, serves as the park's central icon at the end of the street. Behind it is Hollywood Boulevard's only attraction, the classic Great Movie Ride.

Great Movie Ride

RANKING Major attraction. **EMH** Morning, Evening. **FP+** Yes. Low Tier 1 priority. **TYPE** Dark ride. **REQUIREMENTS** None.

WHAT TO EXPECT Housed inside of a full-size replica of the famous Grauman's Chinese Theater, Movie Ride's preshow area features movie memorabilia and a large room with a giant movie screen that plays short clips from popular older movies. Riders board 70-person slow-moving vehicles, and a live narrator helps move the story along as you travel through famous movie scenes recreated with the help of Animatronic characters. Movies represented include *Alien, Casablanca, Fantasia, Mary Poppins, Raiders of the Lost Ark*, the *Public Enemy*, and the *Wizard of Oz*. **SCARY FACTOR** Moderate for the very young, low for everyone else. The *Alien* scene is ominous and the *Indiana Jones* section has snakes, skeletons, and snakes.

WHEN TO GO After 5pm or with FastPass+. **EXPECT TO WAIT** Peak afternoon waits of 30 minutes are common. **LENGTH** 25 minutes. **WHERE TO SIT** Rows seat six and the view is best on either the far left or right sides. Request the middle section of the vehicle for the best syncing between the visuals and audio.

ECHO LAKE

Star Tours is the standout in this land, which is also home to American Idol Experience, Indiana Jones Epic Stunt Spectacular, and Jedi Training Academy, in addition to several eateries. 50's Prime Time Café, with its comfort food and fun atmosphere, is Dave's favorite Studios restaurant. Hollywood & Vine next door is a Disney Jr character buffet for breakfast and lunch that is a lot of fun with kids of the appropriate age, but the expensive, usually-characterless dinner is best skipped. Backlot Express is the quick service, largely serving Disney staples like chicken nuggets, hamburgers, hot dogs, and sandwiches. The food at Backlot isn't great, but there's nicely themed air-conditioned seating inside. Min & Bill's Dockside Diner on Echo Lake serves sandwiches, pork shanks, and booze, and is an excellent stop for those in a hurry. Tatooine Traders sits adjacent to Star Tours and is the best location for *Star Wars* merchandise. *Indiana Jones* merchandise is available at the show's exit and to the right of 50's Prime Time.

A Note on Jedi Training Academy: Kids between the ages of 4 and 12 can participate in this show held next to Star Tours that trains them in the arts of the Jedi. Because slots are severely limited in number, sign up your kids first thing. To sign up for a slot, bring the participating child to the building to the left of American Idol Experience, across from Indiana Jones, immediately after the park opens. Ask for an afternoon show to not interfere with morning touring. If they can't accommodate, let others sign up first, and then sign up for a show after 12pm.

Otherwise, with no high priority attractions, Echo Lake is best saved for the late morning or afternoon, particularly with a FastPass+ for Star Tours.

American Idol Experience

RANKING Minor attraction. **EMH** No. **FP+** Yes. Low priority. **TYPE** Musical theater show. **REQUIREMENTS** None.

WHAT TO EXPECT Based on the television show, everything about the lighting and atmosphere is just like it looks on television. As an audience member, you sit in the theater and watch as three (park visitor) contestants sing and receive judge critiques. At the conclusion, you'll vote for your favorite contestant, and the winner will proceed to the finale at the end of the day. The final show crowns the day's champion from among the previous shows' winners. **SCARY FACTOR** None.

WHEN TO GO In the middle of the day as a comfortable, air-conditioned break. The final show is the most fun and features the best talent. **EXPECT TO WAIT** Arrive right before any show other than the last show. Arrive 10–15 minutes early for the finale. **LENGTH** 30 minutes. **WHERE TO SIT** Let about a half of a row fill in to sit in the center at least half way back.

Indiana Jones Epic Stunt Spectacular Show

RANKING Major attraction. **EMH** No. **FP+** Yes. Low priority. **TYPE** Show. **REQUIREMENTS** None.

WHAT TO EXPECT A large theater seats about 2,000 people on bleacher-style seating. In the show, actors perform a series of stunts that mirror those from the movie *Raiders of the Lost Ark*, and the director explains how they are executed so they are safe and seem real. You'll see large explosions, sword fights, car chases, gun battles, and a number of other exciting stunts. **SCARY FACTOR** Low. While there are some thrilling moments on stage, the audience is never in any danger, real or imagined.

WHEN TO GO The first show of the day, usually around 11:15am, is the least crowded. The last show of the day is the second best bet. **EXPECT TO WAIT** Arrive at least 20 minutes early. **LENGTH** 30 minutes. **WHERE TO SIT** At least half way up, in the center section.

Star Tours

RANKING Major attraction. **EMH** Morning, Evening. **FP+** Yes. Moderate priority. **TYPE** Motion simulator show. **REQUIREMENTS** 40" or taller.

WHAT TO EXPECT Riders sit in a 40-person room themed like the inside of a StarSpeeder 1000 spaceship. A 3D movie plays in the front and the ride vehicle tilts, bumps, vibrates, sways, etc., so it feels like you're actually inside of the StarSpeeder making the journey that you see in front of you. **SCARY FACTOR** Low. There is a moderate amount of danger involved, but it isn't realistic enough to be scary. **CAN WE HANDLE IT?** The biggest problems are motion sickness and the jerkiness of the ride. Avoid if similar attractions have caused problems.

WHEN TO GO After the priority attractions, in the last two hours of operation, or with FastPass+. **EXPECT TO WAIT** 20–40 minute afternoon waits are common. **LENGTH** 5 minutes. **WHERE TO SIT** Views are similar from most seats. You'll experience the most motion in the far left or right seat in the back row.

STREETS OF AMERICA

Two shows, a ride, and a playground situate themselves along the Streets of America, the farthest land from the main entrance. None of them build long waits, making the Streets a perfect afternoon destination. Retail is light, with a store specializing in Muppet merchandise sitting across from Muppet Vision 3D's exit.

Dining is more plentiful with Mama Melrose's Ristorante Italiano serving as the Italian-inspired table service restaurant. Pizzas here are significantly better than Pizza Planet next door for not much more money, but the restaurant's pricier fare is inconsistent. Studio Catering Co. is our favorite Studios' quick service, serving above average Panini-style sandwiches, salads, and wraps. High Octane Refreshments next door serves the best mixed drinks and offers the best beer menu of the bars in the park. Finally, Toy Story Pizza Planet is the land's primary quick service, serving up standard Disney pizza that runs about $10 for a personal size pie. It does not resemble Pizza Planet from the film *Toy Story* in any way.

Honey, I Shrunk the Kids Movie Set Adventure

RANKING Great for kids, skippable for everyone else. **EMH** Morning. **FP+** No. **TYPE** Playground. **REQUIREMENTS** None.

WHAT TO EXPECT Movie Set Adventure is a playground area with a soft play surface geared towards kids older than three. The playground features oversized objects since you've been shrunk down to the size of an ant, so you'll naturally run into a 52-foot-long water hose, 40-foot-tall bumblebees, 30-foot-tall blades of grass, and a bunch of slides and other objects to play on. **SCARY FACTOR** None.

WHEN TO GO After 11am. Closes before dusk. **EXPECT TO WAIT** Very rarely any wait. **LENGTH** As long as it takes to pry Junior away.

Lights, Motors, Action! Extreme Stunt Show

RANKING Major attraction. **EMH** No. **FP+** Yes. Low priority. **TYPE** Show. **REQUIREMENTS** None.

WHAT TO EXPECT Lights, Motors, Action is a stunt show spectacular featuring more than 40 vehicles You'll see furious car chases and jet ski escapes, among other stunts that include fireballs, high-speed jumps, and five-story falls. All the while, the director teaches the audience about how the stunts are safely executed, filmed, and edited. The seating section is largely uncovered and gets extremely hot when temperaturs are high. Consider skipping in the summer. **SCARY FACTOR** Low. There are some thrill elements, but the audience is never in any danger.

WHEN TO GO There are usually only two shows scheduled: one around 1:20pm and one around 4:30pm. The 1:20pm show is usually easier to fit into an itinerary. **EXPECT TO WAIT** Arrive at least 15 minutes early. **LENGTH** 35 minutes. **WHERE TO SIT** At least half way up in the center section.

Muppet Vision 3D

RANKING Don't miss. **EMH** Morning, Evening. **FP+** Yes. Low priority. **TYPE** 4D show. **REQUIREMENTS** None.

WHAT TO EXPECT A 12-minute pre-show video in a room full of Muppet gags welcomes viewers. The theater is large, air-conditioned, and comfortable. The 4D film follows the Muppets as they prepare for a show and features a live-action Sweetums character at the end. **SCARY FACTOR** Low. At times the show is loud.

WHEN TO GO Afternoon when crowds have peaked elsewhere. **EXPECT TO WAIT** Only as long as it takes for the next show to start. **LENGTH** 12-minute pre-show, 17-minute show. **WHERE TO SIT** Let guests stream in and fill about half of a row at least half way back from the front before entering in order to sit in the middle.

Studio Backlot Tour

RANKING Minor attraction. **EMH** No. **FP+** No.**TYPE** Effects show, tram tour. **REQUIREMENTS** None.

WHAT TO EXPECT Visitors line up in a large warehouse with a few pieces of movie memorabilia scattered throughout and monitors playing a short video of director Michael Bay talking about *Pearl Harbor's* special effects overhead. Once you complete the first line, you'll move into a live-action theater demonstrating how special effects might be used before moving on to the tram. Once on the tram, you'll be driven around the Hollywood Studios backlot to see a variety of different areas where Disney stores costumes, vehicles, and film sets. **SCARY FACTOR** Low, with one caveat for youngsters (spoilers ahead): the Catastrophe Canyon section at the end is meant to be a little scary. Several large explosions go off, the bridge shakes, and water falls over and around the tram. You may want to forewarn the easily frightened that something like this is going to happen.

WHEN TO GO Between 10:30am and 12pm, or after 4pm is best. It closes before dusk. **EXPECT TO WAIT** 15-minute peak waits are common. **LENGTH** 35 minutes. **WHERE TO SIT** As you're facing the front of the tram, the seats on the far left have the best view of Catastrophe Canyon, but you're more likely to get wet. Sit potentially anxious children on the right.

COMMISSARY LANE

Located behind American Idol Experience, Commissary Lane is home to just ABC Commissary and Sci-Fi Dine-In. ABC Commissary is a decent quick service with an improved menu and plentiful air-conditioned seating, but choices are limited to just a handful of options. Sci-Fi, with its fun drive-in theater theme, is Josh's favorite Studios restaurant, serving reliably good sandwich and burger fare. The more expensive options at Sci-Fi are over-priced considering the quality, and best skipped by those paying cash.

PIXAR PLACE

By far the most congested area in the park, Pixar Place is home to the Studios' most popular attraction: Toy Story Midway Mania! With a severely limited capacity, and with few other things to occupy the time of little kids, Toy Story Mania reliably has the longest waits of any WDW attraction. Expect peak waits in the 60–120 minute range. It is the highest priority ride at the park and must be ridden either first thing in the morning, with FastPass+, or right before close.

Toy Story Midway Mania!

RANKING Don't miss. **EMH** Morning, Evening. **FP+** Yes. Highest Tier 1 priority. **TYPE** Interactive 3D shooting game. **REQUIREMENTS** None.

WHAT TO EXPECT Riders enter slow-moving vehicles and shoot targets to score points with toy guns attached to the front of the ride vehicle. Toy Story Mania is in 3D (with required 3D glasses) and also includes 4D elements. There are five midway style games to play during the ride, none of which are violent. It's a lot more fun to experience than to read about! **SCARY FACTOR** None.

WHEN TO GO Immediately after the park opens, in the last 30 minutes of operation, or with FastPass+. **EXPECT TO WAIT** Afternoon peak waits are 60–120+ minutes. **LENGTH** 5 minutes. **WHERE TO SIT** Pairs of riders sit next to each other and compete with the pair facing the opposite direction in the same vehicle.

MICKEY AVENUE

Mickey Avenue has very little to do with the character, but guests will find two anytime attractions along this narrow corridor that connects Animation Courtyard and Pixar Place behind Mickey's Sorcerer's Hat.

The Legend of Jack Sparrow

RANKING Minor attraction **EMH** Evening. **FP+** No. **TYPE** Effects show. **REQUIREMENTS** None.

WHAT TO EXPECT Guests enter a dark room themed to a pirate's cave and stand while a projection show featuring Jack Sparrow plays all around the room. There's not much to the attraction, but the technology is very cool. **SCARY FACTOR** The theater is dark and there are some startling, loud effects. Consider skipping with anyone scared of similar attractions, or stand on the far right side of the theater for a quick exit if it becomes too much.

WHEN TO GO Disney distributes paper tickets with return times for specific shows in front of the attraction. Grab one in the afternoon for an air-conditioned break when waits peak elsewhere. **LENGTH** 10 minutes. **WHERE TO STAND**: Front right.

Walt Disney: One Man's Dream

RANKING Minor attraction. **EMH** Morning, Evening. **FP+** No. **TYPE** Walk-through exhibit with an optional film. **REQUIREMENTS** None.

WHAT TO EXPECT A sincere, interesting look at the man behind the Walt Disney Company, featuring memorabilia and artifacts from Walt Disney's life and models of Disney park attractions from around the world. The optional

15-minute film at the end is highly recommended. **SCARY FACTOR** None. **WHEN TO GO** See it when waits are long at other rides, or you simply are nearby. **EXPECT TO WAIT** No waits. **LENGTH** As long as you like—most guests spend about 30 minutes, including the film.

ANIMATION COURTYARD

Here you'll find the large Animation Building, which houses The Magic of Disney Animation, the excellent Animation Academy, and several character meet and greets including Sorcerer Mickey. Voyage of the Little Mermaid, an enchanting stage show featuring a live Ariel, is arguably the land's best attraction. Disney Jr. Live on Stage, aimed specifically at preschoolers, is a favorite of most of them. There are no dining options here, but two shops are located on the Voyage of the Little Mermaid side, including one that's almost entirely princess merchandise. The Art of Disney Store to the right of the Magic of Disney Animation entrance sells interesting paintings, Vinylmation, and limited-edition merchandise.

Disney Jr Live on Stage

RANKING Don't miss for young kids, skippable for everyone else. **EMH** No. **FP+** Yes. Low Tier 1 Priority. **TYPE** Musical stage show. **REQUIREMENTS** None.

WHAT TO EXPECT Features characters from *Mickey Mouse Clubhouse, Handy Manny, Little Einsteins,* and *Jake and the Never Land Pirates* in a fun musical stage show. There is no conventional seating in the theater except for in the very back where there are several benches. Parents and kids are expected to sit on the floor throughout the show—at least until the singing, dancing, and clapping starts. There is a lot of audience participation throughout, and little ones really get into it. **SCARY FACTOR** None.

WHEN TO GO Try to see one of the first two or last two shows. **EXPECT TO WAIT** Arrive at least 15 minutes early. **LENGTH** 22 minutes. **WHERE TO SIT** With seating on the floor, there isn't an outstanding place to sit.

The Magic of Disney Animation

RANKING Minor attraction. **EMH** Evening. **FP+** No. **TYPE** Stage show. **REQUIREMENTS** None.

WHAT TO EXPECT The Magic of Disney Animation no longer features a tour of a real animation studio because since 2004 there has been no working studio to show. Instead, this is a brief theater show with a live actor explaining the animation process while a humorous video featuring Mushu the dragon from *Mulan* plays on screen. An optional animation class is located in the same building. It's an excellent way to create a personal, free souvenir. **SCARY FACTOR** None.

WHEN TO GO Sometime in the afternoon—it's located in a nicely air-conditioned theater. **EXPECT TO WAIT** Shows play continuously. Waits are usually less than ten minutes. **LENGTH** 15 minutes. **WHERE TO SIT** At least half way up.

Voyage of the Little Mermaid

RANKING Major attraction. **EMH** Evening. **FP+** Yes. Moderate priority. **TYPE** Musical stage show. **REQUIREMENTS** None.

WHAT TO EXPECT A mixture of puppets, Animatronics, and live actors tell the story of the Little Mermaid inside of a comfortable, relatively small theater. **SCARY FACTOR** Medium for young kids. Ursula, the wicked octopus, may frighten young children. She is 12-feet tall, 10-feet wide, and accompanied by loud effects and darkness. You might want to prepare youngsters by reminding them that she can't leave the stage.

WHEN TO GO The first two or last two shows of the day are least crowded. **EXPECT TO WAIT** Up to 30 minutes in the afternoon. **LENGTH** 15 minutes. **WHERE TO SIT** Let half of a row file in first to be in the center. Sit at least half way back for a full view of the stage.

SUNSET BOULEVARD

Here, you'll find two of Hollywood Studios' best attractions: Rock 'n' Roller Coaster and Tower of Terror. The entrance to the Hollywood Hills Theater, where the night-time spectacular Fantasmic! takes place, is located on the right before Tower of Terror. Nearby *Beauty and the Beast* is an excellent stage show that has been running longer than any other WDW show.

Sunset Boulevard is primarily lined with retail on the left and right side of the street before arriving at the attractions. On the right is a store offering Planet Hollywood merchandise, followed by a store offering mostly apparel and higher-end watches and purses. On the left is Sweet Spells, offering freshly baked treats similar to those found at Main Street Confectionery at Magic Kingdom, in addition to other packaged edibles. Further up is Villains in Vogue, which usually sells *Nightmare Before Christmas* merchandise, in addition to Vinylmation and seasonal items. At the exit to Rock 'n' Roller Coaster is a store selling a smorgasbord of rock 'n' roll-inspired merchandise. The shop at the exit to Tower of Terror features over a hundred items themed to the attraction, including Hollywood Tower Hotel robes and bells.

Sunset Ranch Market is an outdoor collection of six individual stands serving all kinds of food—barbecue, burgers, sandwiches, turkey legs, salads, ice cream, fruit, snacks, and more. The common seating area is outdoors. Hollywood Hills Theater offers snacks and drinks, in addition to a few heartier items like hot dogs and bread cones for about 90 minutes before Fantasmic! starts.

Beauty and the Beast Live on Stage

RANKING Major attraction. **EMH** No. **FP+** Yes. Low priority. **TYPE** Stage show. **REQUIREMENTS** None.

WHAT TO EXPECT This 25-minute Broadway-style musical features characters, music, and scenes from *Beauty and the Beast*. The sets are elaborate, the costumes are first-rate, and the acting is excellent. **SCARY FACTOR** None.

WHEN TO GO The first show of the day, usually around 11:45am, is the least crowded. The last show of the day is the second best bet. **EXPECT TO WAIT** Arrive at least 20 minutes early. **LENGTH** 30 minutes. **WHERE TO SIT** At least half way up in the center section.

Fantasmic!

RANKING Don't miss. **EMH** No. A show may be scheduled to start during or after evening EMH begins, but anyone is welcome to attend. **FP+** Yes. Low Tier 1 Priority. **TYPE** Fireworks and live action show. **REQUIREMENTS** None.

WHAT TO EXPECT The theater seats about 9,000 people on bleacher seating without backs. Mickey is the star of the show as he appears on stage with over 50 live performers as film sequences featuring many best-loved Disney moments and characters, plus Pocahontas, play on screens made of water, fireworks shoot overhead, and fire and magic potions abound. **SCARY FACTOR** Moderate for the young. Mickey is in a considerable amount of danger with a 40-foot-tall dragon and all the villains. Sit near the back with anxious toddlers for a quick escape if it gets to be too much.

TYPICAL SCHEDULE: Presented once or twice per evening almost every evening of the year. Show times vary. The second show, if scheduled, will be less crowded. **LENGTH** 30 minutes. **WHERE TO SIT**: Arrive at least 45 minutes early for the first show. Arriving 20 minutes early is sufficient for the second show. Sit at least half way up, as close to the center as possible.

Rock 'n' Roller Coaster

RANKING Don't miss. **EMH** Morning, Evening. **FP+** Yes. High Tier 1 priority. **TYPE** Roller coaster. **REQUIREMENTS** 44" or taller.

WHAT TO EXPECT An Aerosmith video pre-show explains why you are about to drive really fast. Next you board a limousine-themed roller coaster vehicle that seats 24 people in rows of two. The vehicle will then propel out of the gate with the force of a supersonic jet. **SCARY FACTOR** With max speeds over 60 miles per hour, three inversions, and multiple corkscrews, this is arguably Disney's most intense roller coaster The dark setting may actually ease fears as the track is never fully visible to riders. **CAN WE HANDLE IT?** The initial launch is the most intense part—the rest of the ride is relatively tame compared to any major coaster at Six Flags or Universal. Anyone that made it through Everest or Space Mountain should be fine.

WHEN TO GO First thing or immediately after Toy Story Mania, in the final hour of operation, or with FastPass+. Rock 'n' Roller Coaster offers a single-rider line, but because it's impossible to know how many people are ahead of you in it before you actually get to the indoor pre-show area, it's not recommended. **EXPECT TO WAIT** 50 to 100 minutes in the afternoon. **LENGTH** 90 seconds. **WHERE TO SIT** Request the front row for the best view, the middle if you're apprehensive, or the back to see all the twists and turns.

Twilight Zone Tower of Terror

RANKING Don't miss. **EMH** Morning, Evening. **FP+** Yes. Highest Tier 2 priority. **TYPE** Elevator drop. **REQUIREMENTS** 40" or taller.

WHAT TO EXPECT A pre-show video in the dilapidated hotel's library explains the circumstances surrounding your unfortunate visit. After a tense five- to ten-minute wait in the boiler room, you board your elevator, which will embark on an eerie journey through the hotel. Anyone going down? **SCARY FACTOR** High. The most obviously frightening ride at Disney World, and one of few that puts an emphasis on fear. There are no particularly scary images or scenes, but Disney does an excellent job of building tension up to the final drop. **CAN WE HANDLE IT?** Motion sickness can be an issue, but otherwise walk the nervous past the ride exit and note that almost everyone leaves with a smile on their faces.

WHEN TO GO Immediately after Toy Story Mania and/or Rock 'n' Roller Coaster, in the final hour of operation, or with FastPass+. **EXPECT TO WAIT** 50–100 minutes in the afternoon. **LENGTH** 5 minutes. **WHERE TO SIT** All seats are good, but the view from the front row is the least obscured.

The Magic Kingdom

The original Walt Disney World theme park and the most popular theme park in the world, Magic Kingdom offers more attractions, entertainment, and atmosphere than any of the other theme parks. Its offerings are varied, from elaborate stage shows to classic dark rides to state-of-the-art roller coasters. Magic Kingdom is best toured over two or more days, but guests with limited time still have the opportunity to visit the highlights and take in the fabulous nighttime entertainment.

FASTPASS+ AT MAGIC KINGDOM

There are far more FastPass+ opportunities at Magic Kingdom than at any of the other theme parks, making the decision on which to pick difficult. Visitors who know they want to avoid character meets or the more thrilling rides have an easier set of choices. Otherwise, consider picking three high-priority attractions in a land that you don't plan to visit until the afternoon or evening. For example, if you plan to start your day meeting Tinker Bell and riding Aladdin's Magical Carpets, Jungle Cruise, Big Thunder Mountain, and Splash Mountain, then you may want to use FastPass+ in the afternoon in Fantasyland at Enchanted Tales with Belle, Anna and Elsa, and the Mine Train, or in Tomorrowland at Space Mountain, Tomorrowland Speedway, and Buzz Lightyear.

FastPass+ Priority

1. Anna and Elsa at Princess Fairytale Hall
2. Enchanted Tales with Belle
3. Seven Dwarfs Mine Train
4. Peter Pan's Flight
5. Main Street Electrical Parade (prioritize first/only parade only; second parade on the same night sees light crowds)
6. Space Mountain
7. Splash Mountain (when high temperatures are 80+ degrees)
8. Rapunzel at Princess Fairytale Hall
9. Big Thunder Mountain Railroad
10. Ariel at Ariel's Grotto
11. Tinker Bell at Town Square Theater
12. Buzz Lightyear's Space Ranger Spin
13. Tomorrowland Speedway
14. Haunted Mansion
15. Mickey at Town Square Theater
16. Jungle Cruise
17. Splash Mountain (when high temperatures are less than 80 degrees)
18. Pirates of the Caribbean
19. Barnstormer
20. The Many Adventures of Winnie the Pooh
21. Under the Sea Journey of the Little Mermaid

22. Wishes

23. Disney Festival of Fantasy Parade

24. Dumbo the Flying Elephant

25. it's a small world

26. Magic Carpets of Aladdin

27. Mad Tea Party

28. Monsters Inc. Laugh Floor

29. Mickey's PhilharMagic

ARRIVING AT MAGIC KINGDOM

Magic Kingdom's parking lot is located at the Transportation and Ticket Center (TTC) across Seven Seas Lagoon. Guests arriving via their own automobile or buses from off-site resorts (including Shades of Green) will need to transfer from the TTC to Magic Kingdom via the resort monorail, express monorail, or ferry boat. The express monorail is the fastest because it's a direct route that takes about three minutes. There are also more monorails on the express beam, so a fresh monorail car arrives every three to five minutes. The resort monorail is often less crowded, but the trip takes about 20 minutes with stops at the Polynesian and Grand Floridian resorts first. The five-minute ferry ride is scenic and less cramped because there's more room to spread out. Our preference is the ferry, though the express monorail is often a few minutes faster. Guests traveling from Epcot will also transfer at the Transportation and Ticket Center.

Most guests arriving from Disney resorts and the Swan and Dolphin will arrive via Disney buses, which pick-up and drop-off just a couple minutes walk from the main entrance. Guests from the Contemporary have the option of walking about ten minutes or taking the resort monorail. Guests at the Polynesian and Grand Floridian may take the resort monorail or watercraft. Guests at the Wilderness Lodge and Ft. Wilderness may take a bus or watercraft. Watercraft trips are usually slower, but more scenic.

Guest services is located on the far right outside the entrance and on the left at City Hall inside the entrance. Lines are often shorter inside at City Hall. Wheelchair and ECV rentals are located on the right just inside the entrance. Stroller rental is located underneath the train station.

MAIN STREET, U.S.A.

Main Street, U.S.A. is themed to a small town at the turn of the 20th century. The train station works to block the view of what's inside as guests pass underneath. Once through, the magnificent Cinderella Castle shines in the distance. To the right in Town Square Theater is a Magician Mickey Mouse meet and greet, and the only location where Mickey may talk to guests. Tinker Bell meets separately in the same building. Next door is Tony's Town Square restaurant themed to *Lady and the Tramp*. The relatively inexpensive lunch is recommended, but the pricier dinner steaks are overpriced when paying out of pocket.

On the left is package pickup and Guest Services. Inside the fire station, guests can sign up to play the interactive Sorcerers of the Magic Kingdom game. Five playing cards per person may be picked up daily to help along the game. Next to it is Harmony Barber Shop with surprisingly reasonable prices. Stop in for a fun first haircut or some "pixie dust" for a lot less money than the Bibbidi Bobbidi Boutique in Fantasyland. Also on the left, the Emporium stretches for much of Main Street, offering just about every piece of theme park merchandise from toys and plush to Mickey Crocs.

On the right, The Chapeau offers a wide selection of hats, and Main Street Confectionery is your best spot for handmade treats and cupcakes. Further up on the right is Main Street Bakery, which now hosts the park's Starbucks. Past that is Main Street Cinema, Uptown Jewelers, and Crystal Arts, all offering upscale items like Dooney and Bourke bags and Ray-Ban sunglasses.

At the end of Main Street on the left is Casey's Corner, serving hot dogs with interesting toppings like barbecue pork and coleslaw or a polish sausage with stone-ground mustard and grilled onions. Best are the corn dog nuggets dipped into the gooey hot cheese sauce. Further on the left is Crystal Palace, which hosts a Winnie the Pooh and friends buffet for all three meals. On the right is Plaza Ice Cream Parlor, which is a great spot for a sundae in the afternoon. To the right of it is The Plaza Restaurant, serving the most inexpensive table service sandwich fare on property.

Mickey Mouse at Town Square Theater

RANKING Don't miss for little kids who need to meet Mickey; skippable for others. **EMH** No. **FP+** Yes. Medium priority for guests wanting to meet Mickey. **TYPE** Character meet-and-greet. **REQUIREMENTS** None.

WHAT TO EXPECT Magician Mickey greets guests inside Town Square Theater. At press time, this is the only location where he speaks. The interaction is unique and often times enchanting as kids and adults alike discuss sports, Magic Kingdom rides, birthday buttons, etc. Note that occasionally there are technical difficulties and Mickey will be his traditional silent self. **SCARY FACTOR** None.

WHEN TO GO First two or last two hours of operation, during a parade, or with FastPass+. Skip first thing in the morning for higher priorities. **EXPECT TO WAIT** 35–50 minutes in the afternoon. **LENGTH** 3–4 minutes of chatting, signing, mingling, and picture taking.

The Walt Disney World Railroad

RANKING Minor attraction. **EMH** No. **FP+** No. **TYPE** Steam train tour around the outer perimeter of the park, with additional stops in Frontierland near Splash Mountain and Fantasyland near Barnstormer. **REQUIREMENTS** None.

WHAT TO EXPECT The Disney World Railroad is a relaxing way to see parts of the Magic Kingdom that you might miss by simply walking around in a hurry. Some very minor vignettes are only visible from the train (and the steamboat). You board at any of the three stations and ride for as long as you like around the 1.5 mile track. If you are traveling between areas near two of the stops, the train is a nice break from walking. The strollers Disney rents at the park are not allowed on the train. You will need to remove your belongings, name card, and have your receipt handy to pick up a new stroller at your final destination. Skippable for those on shorter visits. **SCARY FACTOR** None.

WHEN TO GO Anytime attraction. See it when waits are long at other rides, or when you want to use it as transport to save walking. **EXPECT TO WAIT** Only for the next train—7–10 minutes. **LENGTH** A full circle around the Magic Kingdom takes about 20 minutes. **WHERE TO SIT** Views are best from the side where you board.

ADVENTURELAND

Split into two distinct areas—the Arabian Village and Caribbean Plaza—Adventureland is distinctively adventure-y. In the Arabian section, you'll find the majority of the attractions—Tiki Room, Jungle Cruise, Magic Carpets of Aladdin, and Swiss Family Treehouse—in addition to the popular Dole Whips at Aloha Isle. Agrabah Bazaar is the primary, smallish store offering wares perfect for the adventurers among us. To the right of the entrance to Pirates is the signup building for the fun Pirate's Adventure Treasures of the Seven Seas interactive game. It includes a high-quality map that sends players around Adventureland unlocking secrets and setting off surprises. Visit in the afternoon as a fun diversion when waits peak elsewhere.

Arabian Village opens up to Caribbean Plaza on the Frontierland side, hosting the classic Pirates of the Caribbean attraction with an expansive store at its exit offering everything pirate. Tortuga Tavern is the land's quick service, often only open from 11am–3pm and serving taco and nacho fare across from Pirates. It's a nice way to mix up the usual burgers and nuggets found elsewhere. Sunshine Tree Terrace behind Aladdin's Magical Carpets serves soft drinks, ice cream, and the cult favorite Citrus Swirl blend of frozen orange juice and vanilla ice cream.

Enchanted Tiki Room

RANKING Minor attraction. **EMH** Evening. **FP+** No. **TYPE** Audio-Animatronics show. **REQUIREMENTS** None.

WHAT TO EXPECT A groundbreaking ride when it originally opened at Disneyland in the early 60s, the Enchanted Tiki Room entertains with singing Animatronic birds. Today it feels quaint—kids don't enjoy it a lot, and while adults are charmed, it's not a priority. Many Disney fans love it because of its history, but it's ultimately skippable for those immune to nostalgia. **SCARY FACTOR** Not much—just a bit of thunder and lightning.

WHEN TO GO Anytime attraction. See it when waits are long at other rides, or you need to get out of the weather. **EXPECT TO WAIT** 10–15 minutes for the next show. **LENGTH** 10 minutes. **WHERE TO SIT** Sit in the last row, towards the center.

Jungle Cruise

RANKING Don't Miss. **EMH** No. **FP+** Yes. Medium priority. **TYPE** Comedy disguised as a river cruise. **REQUIREMENTS** None.

WHAT TO EXPECT This boat ride takes you through areas themed as several of the world's great rivers, inhabited by Audio-Animatronic people and animals. Your (human) skipper guides the tour, making corny jokes and telling silly puns along the way. The effects are dated, but the skipper can make the ride so much fun that it's not to be missed. **SCARY FACTOR** Low. There is a short section in dark ruins, but that's it.

WHEN TO GO First two or last two hours of operation, or with FastPass+. **EXPECT TO WAIT** 35–70 minutes in the afternoon. **LENGTH** 10 minutes. **WHERE TO SIT** Anywhere along the edge of the boat—avoid the interior seats.

Magic Carpets of Aladdin

RANKING Skippable but fun. **EMH** Evening. **FP+** Yes. Low priority. **TYPE** Spinning ride. **REQUIREMENTS** None.

WHAT TO EXPECT This slow-loading, low capacity ride raises four-person magic-carpet themed vehicles and then spins riders in the air over Adventureland. You can control how high you go. The ride is fun and offers some spectacular views, but most guests won't want to spend more than a few minutes waiting. **SCARY FACTOR** Low. **CAN WE HANDLE IT?** Motion sickness is rarely an issue. A camel may spit water in your general direction.

WHEN TO GO Anytime attraction. See it when waits are long at other rides, or you simply are nearby. **EXPECT TO WAIT** 15–30 minutes in the afternoon. **LENGTH** 2 minutes. **WHERE TO SIT** Cast Members will assign your group a carpet—the experience is the same from all. The front seat controls height, the back seat tilt.

Pirates of the Caribbean

RANKING Don't Miss. **EMH** Evening. **FP+** Yes. Low priority. **TYPE** Boat ride through pirate-themed Audio-Animatronics and settings. **REQUIREMENTS** None.

WHAT TO EXPECT One of the most famous rides at the park, Pirates sends riders floating through a Disneyfied version of a town ransacked by pirates. In a reversal of what usually happens, the Jack Sparrow films were based on the ride, and Jack and others from the films are present in many scenes. This ride is very popular, but because of its high capacity waits usually aren't bad. **SCARY FACTOR** This is a lighthearted, playful ride, yet one with lots of skeletons and implied violence. Skip it if Haunted Mansion was too much. **CAN WE HANDLE IT?** There's a mild drop towards the beginning of a few feet that may result in a bit of water splashing over the first row, but that's it.

WHEN TO GO In the first two or last two hours of the day is best. **EXPECT TO WAIT** 15–40 minutes in the afternoon. **LENGTH** 10 minutes. **WHERE TO SIT** All seats have a similar experience. The front row has slightly better views, and a better chance of getting a little wet.

Swiss Family Treehouse

RANKING Skippable but fun. **EMH** Evening. **FP+** No. **TYPE** Self-guided walking tour. **REQUIREMENTS** There are a lot of stairs up and down.

WHAT TO EXPECT The Treehouse replicates the living conditions from the popular film that few probably remember. While interesting, the attraction is not particularly compelling and guests visiting over one day usually have higher priorities. **SCARY FACTOR** Low. **CAN WE HANDLE IT?** The top of the tree is high; the stairs all the way up and down can be tough on cranky knees or hips.

WHEN TO GO Anytime attraction. See it when waits are long at other rides, or you simply are nearby. **EXPECT TO WAIT** No wait to 5 minutes in the afternoon. **LENGTH** 10 minutes or so.

FRONTIERLAND

Home to Big Thunder Mountain, Splash Mountain, and one of the park's most popular quick services, most guests will spend a considerable amount of time in this land. Fortunately, both rides enjoy hefty capacities that make it possible to visit them in the second hour of operation. You'll also find two anytime attractions in Frontierland: the comfortable serenading of bears in Country Bear Jamboree, and Tom Sawyer Island, where adventures await.

Pecos Bill is the principal quick service, now offering a limited menu primarily of burgers, sandwiches, and salads. Additionally, more expensive items are available beginning at 4pm. Diamond Horseshoe once offered a lively evening show and table service fare, but its current iteration is rarely open and serves below-average sandwiches and salads. Golden Oak Outpost is located at the Pecos' side exit, serving snacks and chicken sandwiches. There's rarely a line, making it a good stop for a Diet Coke. Westward Ho alongside the river serves snacks, in addition to corn dogs. Two to three carts also position themselves along the river across from Diamond Horseshoe, serving turkey legs, churros, and pretzels. Lines are usually shorter at similar stands around the corner in Liberty Square.

Of course, you'll find several merchandise opportunities here, too. Splash Mountain's exit offers some attraction-branded merchandise, in addition to several shops between Pecos Bill and Diamond Horseshoe that offer everything from freshly baked treats to limited-edition pins.

Big Thunder Mountain Railroad

RANKING Don't Miss. **EMH** Evening. **FP+** Yes. High priority. **TYPE** Runaway train-themed roller coaster. **REQUIREMENTS** 40" or taller.

WHAT TO EXPECT Prospective miners board trains consisting of three cars, each with five rows that seat two to three people. With top speeds under 30 miles per hour, Big Thunder is not an intense experience, but the theming is first rate. **SCARY FACTOR** Minimal for a roller coaster—there are two scenes inside caves that are loud and dark, but anyone that made it through any other Disney coaster will be just fine. **CAN WE HANDLE IT?** Some motion sickness issues for the highly susceptible, and jostling.

WHEN TO GO First two or last two hours of operation, or with FastPass+. **EXPECT TO WAIT** 50–80+ minutes in the afternoon. **LENGTH** 4 minutes. **WHERE TO SIT** The back provides the wildest experience. Sit up front for a tamer ride.

Country Bear Jamboree

RANKING Minor attraction. **EMH** Evening. **FP+** No. **TYPE** Audio-Animatronics show. **REQUIREMENTS** None.

WHAT TO EXPECT A musical review and show with country-and-western songs performed by Animatronic bears. Wildly popular when it opened, it is now attended largely by roots/country music fans, diehard Disney fans, and visitors looking for a bit of a rest and some air conditioning. The characters are fun but the jokes are hokey, and the songs, while fun to those with wide musical tastes, aren't everyone's favorite. Skippable for many on shorter visits. **SCARY FACTOR** None. **CAN WE HANDLE IT?** The music is more bluegrass/western than modern country.

WHEN TO GO Anytime attraction. See it when waits are long at other rides, or you need to get out of the weather. **EXPECT TO WAIT** 10–15 minutes for the next show. **LENGTH** 15 minutes. **WHERE TO SIT** Sit in the middle row, towards the center. Wait for 25 people or so to enter a row first, and follow them.

Splash Mountain

RANKING Don't Miss. **EMH** No (surprisingly). **FP+** Yes. High priority on hot days, medium on cool days. **TYPE** Mostly a gentle log ride, with fewer thrills than you'd guess from outside. **REQUIREMENTS** 40" or taller.

WHAT TO EXPECT Splash Mountain is the ride that most showcases all of the best of Disney. You float past brilliantly executed scenes based on the Br'er Rabbit character from Disney's (unavailable) *Song of the South*. And here and there—especially towards the end—there's some thrilling drops. **SCARY FACTOR** The very visible final drop is greatly misleading. Most of this ride is gentle floating through darling settings. But besides the final drop, there are several much shorter drops. **CAN WE HANDLE IT?** You may get wet—especially if you sit in the front, but possibly from any seat. The visible final drop scares many off who would absolutely love this ride. Trust us and give it a chance.

WHEN TO GO First two or last two hours of operation, or with FastPass+. **EXPECT TO WAIT** 15–90+ minutes in the afternoon (the longer waits on crowded hot days, the shorter on cold low-crowd days). **LENGTH** 12 minutes. **WHERE TO SIT** The front seat has the best view, but is most likely to get wet.

Tom Sawyer Island

RANKING Minor attraction. **EMH** No. **FP+** No. **TYPE** Self-guided walking tour and playground. **REQUIREMENTS** None.

WHAT TO EXPECT Tom Sawyer Island is only accessible via motorized rafts that board near the entrance to Big Thunder Mountain Railroad. Once on the island, visitors can explore numerous areas themed to Tom Sawyer and

Huck Finn—caves, a mine, two bridges, a working water wheel, and Fort Langhorn, a play area. Benches are plentiful and the Island is a terrific spot to take a break. Skippable for those without kids, or on a short visit. **SCARY FACTOR** None.

WHEN TO GO Anytime attraction. See it when waits are long at other rides, or you simply are nearby. Afternoons tend to be best, but note that it closes before dusk. **EXPECT TO WAIT** 5–15 minutes to get raft transport in the afternoon. **LENGTH** Allow 30–45 minutes+ including time spent waiting for the rafts, more if your kids really need to run around.

The Walt Disney World Railroad

See the "Main Street" entry on the railroad, which stops in Frontierland near the exit to Splash Mountain.

LIBERTY SQUARE

To the left of Cinderella Castle, Liberty Square offers the fewest attractions and eateries of any land, but what is offered is all above average in terms of quality. Hall of Presidents is a perfect way to spend a hot afternoon, while Haunted Mansion is quintessential Disney.

Columbia Harbour House across from Haunted Mansion is our favorite quick service, offering a delicious fried shrimp platter, in addition to salads, unique sandwiches, grilled salmon, and excellent soups. Sleepy Hollow Refreshments serves excellent waffle sandwiches from 11am–5pm, as well as funnel cakes, waffles, and other ice cream treats. Liberty Tree Tavern is one of our favorite table service restaurants for lunch, when it offers a reasonably priced a la carte menu. The dinner buffet no longer features characters and it's expensive out of pocket.

Across from Hall of Presidents is Ye Olde Christmas Shoppe, which offers primarily Christmas-related merchandise. Yankee Trader Gourmet Shop near Haunted Mansion's exit offers the full line of Haunted Mansion merchandise, along with mostly kitchen-related items.

Hall of Presidents

RANKING Minor attraction. **EMH** No. **FP+** No. **TYPE** Audio-Animatronics show. **REQUIREMENTS** None.

WHAT TO EXPECT A theater show featuring film clips and animatronics of all of the U.S. Presidents. The show is patriotic and expounds on the hardships and triumphs of the United States through the years. The theater is air-conditioned, comfortable, and seats over 700 people, which makes it a nice and easy attraction to enjoy in the afternoon heat. Enjoyed most by adults and patriotic Americans, dull for most kids. Skippable for those on shorter visits. **SCARY FACTOR** None, other than it's full of politicians. **WHEN TO GO** Anytime attraction. See it when waits are long at other rides, or you need to get out of the weather. **EXPECT TO WAIT** Arrive either at 20 or 50 minutes past the hour and your wait should be just ten minutes. **LENGTH** 25 minutes. **WHERE TO SIT** Sit in the middle row, towards the center.

The Haunted Mansion

RANKING Don't miss. **EMH** Evening. **FP+** Yes. Medium priority. **TYPE** Light-hearted, slow-moving ride through a haunted house and its graveyard. **REQUIREMENTS** None.

WHAT TO EXPECT One of the most famous rides at the park, the Haunted Mansion is one of Disney's best and most enduring attractions. Intended to be a fun and goofy ride, not a frightening experience, you won't see anything truly gruesome or disgusting. This is a must-ride for almost all guests. **SCARY FACTOR** Haunted Mansion is much more spooky than it is scary, but a lot of kids are going to be apprehensive about entering the foreboding building. Rest assured that it's a lot of fun. **CAN WE HANDLE IT?** Yes, those brave enough to enter enjoy the experience.

WHEN TO GO First two or last two hours of operation, or with FastPass+. **EXPECT TO WAIT** 20–50 minutes in the afternoon, longer if the Hall of Presidents and Liberty Square Riverboat have just let out guests, as they do every thirty minutes. **LENGTH** 10 minutes. **WHERE TO SIT** Each Doom Buggy seats two to three. Sit apprehensive youngsters (or dads) in the middle.

The Liberty Square Riverboat

RANKING Minor attraction. **EMH** No. **FP+** No. **TYPE** Steamboat tour around the Rivers of America. **REQUIREMENTS** None.

WHAT TO EXPECT The Liberty Square Riverboat is a stately three-tiered paddle-wheel boat that slowly circles Tom Sawyer Island and offers fantastic views of Splash Mountain, Big Thunder Mountain Railroad, and several other popular attractions. Some very minor vignettes otherwise visible only from the Walt Disney World Railroad also appear. The voice of Mark Twain narrates the journey. Skippable for those on short visits. **SCARY FACTOR** None.

WHEN TO GO Anytime attraction. See it when waits are long at other rides, or you need to get out of the weather. **EXPECT TO WAIT** Arrive either at 20 or 50 minutes past the hour and your wait should be just ten minutes. **LENGTH** 17 minutes. **WHERE TO SIT** Bow and stern locations where you can easily see both riverbanks are best. Otherwise sit on the port side. (That's left when facing the bow—the end without the paddlewheel.)

FANTASYLAND

With the longest list of attractions, this is where most guests will spend the majority of their time. Fortunately, most attractions enjoy short durations and healthy capacities, making it relatively easy to bang out the majority of rides in under an hour first thing in the morning or when crowds ease in the late evening. Mickey's PhilharMagic is an outstanding 3D anytime attraction, and Enchanted Tales with Belle is an afternoon FastPass+ priority.

Be Our Guest is a popular quick service lunch option and a nearly-impossible-to-book table service restaurant at dinner. Lunch service typically begins at 10:30am and runs through 4pm. We recommend getting in line at 2pm so as to not waste precious morning touring time in line for lunch. Waits balloon to an hour or more from 11am–1:30pm. On-site guests may be able to book FastPass+, which doesn't count against the initial three FP+ limit. FastPass+ users bypass the standby queue and even have the opportunity to pre-order food, bypassing the line entirely. Dinner is table service with above-average food and the only Magic Kingdom location that serves wine and beer. Cinderella's Royal Table is the popular princess meal inside the Castle.

Pinocchio Village Haus is the primary quick service, located to the left of the entrance to New Fantasyland. The flatbread pizzas and salads are above average and there's plentiful air-conditioned seating in addition to outdoor patio seating. Gaston's Tavern between Be Our Guest and Journey of the Little Mermaid serves pork shanks, cinnamon rolls, and snacks. The pork is surprisingly tender and a nice alternative to the more-difficult-to-eat-than-you-might-expect turkey legs. Indoor seating is minimal, but the theming is exquisite throughout. Friar's Nook, located across from the entrance to Seven Dwarfs Mine Train, serves breakfast daily. Lunch service includes several hearty macaroni-and-cheese dishes with a variety of toppings, including pot roast. Storybook Treats is Fantasyland's version of the Plaza Ice Cream Parlor, serving decadent sundaes and other ice-cream treats. Cheshire Café serves snacks, drinks, and cake cups next to Mad Tea Party, while Prince Eric's Village Market serves drinks, lemonades, sno-cones, and snacks across from the Journey of the Little Mermaid ride in New Fantasyland. Finally, Big Top Souvenirs across from Dumbo is yet another spot to find freshly made treats, including caramel corn, candied apples, and fudge, in addition to the frozen Goofy's Glacier drinks.

Shopping is plentiful in and around Fantasyland. Castle Couture to the left of Mickey's PhilharMagic is one of the best spots for princess merchandise. Across the way is Sir Mickey's, primarily offering toys and apparel. Two great stores are located back in New Fantasyland: Bonjour Gifts, to the right of Gaston's Tavern, offers unique glassware, goblets, and other upscale items, and Storybook Treats also offers a lot of toys and apparel.

Ariel's Grotto

RANKING Don't miss for little kids who need to meet Ariel; skippable for others. **EMH** Morning, Evening. **FP+** Yes. High priority for guests wanting to meet Ariel. **TYPE** Character meet and greet. **REQUIREMENTS** None.

WHAT TO EXPECT After winding through a line themed to undersea rockwork, meet Ariel in her picturesque grotto. **SCARY FACTOR** None.

WHEN TO GO First or last hour of operation, or with FastPass+. **EXPECT TO WAIT** 35–60 minutes in the afternoon. **LENGTH** About a minute with everyone's favorite undersea princess.

The Barnstormer

RANKING Minor attraction. **EMH** Morning, Evening. **FP+** Yes. Low priority. **TYPE** Roller coaster. **REQUIREMENTS** 35" or taller.

WHAT TO EXPECT This slow-loading, low-capacity ride with some light theming around Goofy's stunt plane is the tamest coaster at Disney World, and best thought of as a "starter" roller coaster. Fun, swoopy, and very brief, all of its features are fully visible, so there's no surprises. Great fun for little kids, but skippable for older kids and adults. **SCARY FACTOR** Low. Speeds and heights are mild. **CAN WE HANDLE IT?** If your kids decide after it begins that they aren't ready for coasters, the ride will be over literally within seconds. The ride vehicles are low to the ground with just enough room for two average-size adults to sit side by side.

WHEN TO GO First two or last two hours of operation, or with FastPass+. **EXPECT TO WAIT** 25–40 minutes in the afternoon. **LENGTH** Less than 1 minute. **WHERE TO SIT** The front seat has the best view, but no seats are bad.

Dumbo the Flying Elephant

RANKING Minor attraction. **EMH** Morning, Evening. **FP+** Yes. Low priority. **TYPE** Spinning ride. **REQUIREMENTS** None.

WHAT TO EXPECT Charming Dumbos with two riders side by side rise from their delightfully decorated base and slowly spin. Riders control how high or low their Dumbo flies. A favorite of little kids, but skippable for adults. Those not using FastPass+ have the option to wait in an air-conditioned play area instead of the typical queue. **SCARY FACTOR** Low. The mild heights may trouble the most severely acrophobic. **CAN WE HANDLE IT?** Spinning is too slow to affect motion sickness. Little kids can't ride alone.

WHEN TO GO First two or last two hours of operation, or with FastPass+. **EXPECT TO WAIT** 30–50 minutes in the afternoon. **LENGTH** Less than 2 minutes. **WHERE TO SIT** All seats are good.

Enchanted Tales with Belle

RANKING Major attraction. **EMH** Morning, Evening. **FP+** Yes. High priority. **TYPE** Combined walk-through tour, Audio-Animatronic show, interactive show, and character photo op. **REQUIREMENTS** None.

WHAT TO EXPECT This experience starts as a tour of Maurice's cottage, magically shifts to the Beast's Mansion where audience volunteers are recruited by Madame Wardrobe for a show, moves to the Beast's Library where under Lumiere's direction the volunteers act the show out for Belle, and ends with the show volunteers getting a chance to meet and have pictures with Belle. Only show volunteers get photos by default, so if your kids aren't picked for a part, have them volunteer at the last "anybody else?" casting call. Drop dead cute, it's Disney at its best. **SCARY FACTOR** None.

WHEN TO GO During the afternoon parade, in the final hour of operation, or with FastPass+. **EXPECT TO WAIT** 30–50 minutes+ in the afternoon. **LENGTH** 25 minutes.

it's a small world

RANKING Minor attraction. **EMH** Morning, Evening. **FP+** Yes. Low priority. **TYPE** Boat ride. **REQUIREMENTS** None.

WHAT TO EXPECT Boats seating 20 or so float past miniatures of singing children from around the world, colorfully attired and accompanied by toys and representations of their cultures. A world-famous tour-de-force of design, song writing, and artistic unity. **SCARY FACTOR** None.

WHEN TO GO Before 11am, in the final two hours of operation, or with FastPass+. **EXPECT TO WAIT** 20–35 minutes in the afternoon. **LENGTH** 11 minutes. **WHERE TO SIT** Seats at the sides of the boat have the best view.

Mad Tea Party

RANKING Minor attraction. **EMH** Morning, Evening. **FP+** Yes. Low priority. **TYPE** Spinning ride. **REQUIREMENTS** None.

WHAT TO EXPECT Spinning tea cups lightly themed to *Alice in Wonderland* delight kids, annoy most adults. Skippable for those on shorter visits. **SCARY FACTOR** None. **CAN WE HANDLE IT?** There's three simultaneous spins: the whole ride, a group of cups, and individual cups. Don't ride if you are subject to motion sickness.

WHEN TO GO Anytime attraction. See it when waits are long at other rides, or you simply are nearby. **EXPECT TO WAIT** 5–15 minutes in the afternoon. **LENGTH** 90 seconds. **WHERE TO SIT** In a different cup than your children, who will wish to spin much more than you do.

The Many Adventures of Winnie the Pooh

RANKING Minor attraction. **EMH** Morning, Evening. **FP+** Yes. Low priority. **TYPE** Dark ride. **REQUIREMENTS** None.

WHAT TO EXPECT Four-person "honey pots" make their way through multiple, richly-detailed Winnie the Pooh-themed scenes featuring Pooh, Eeyore, Piglet, Owl, Tigger, and others. **SCARY FACTOR** Low—a briefly blustery day where the ride vehicle tips up and down slightly for a few seconds.

WHEN TO GO First two or last two hours of operation, or with FastPass+. **EXPECT TO WAIT** 30–40 minutes in the afternoon. **LENGTH** 3 minutes. **WHERE TO SIT** All seats are good.

Mickey's PhilharMagic

RANKING Don't miss. **EMH** Morning, Evening. **FP+** Yes. Lowest priority. **TYPE** 4D show. **REQUIREMENTS** None.

WHAT TO EXPECT This 3D film (supplemented by in-theater effects—hence 4D) tells the tale of Donald getting in trouble, with Mickey ultimately to the rescue. Interwoven between are some of the best bits from some of Disney's most popular films: *Peter Pan, Aladdin, Little Mermaid, Lion King*, and more. It's a must-see because of its fun and diabolically creative celebration of some of Disney's best-loved animation. **SCARY FACTOR** Low. 3D effects and typical cartoon mayhem spook some little ones. Take off their 3D glasses if this happens.

WHEN TO GO Anytime attraction. See it when waits are long at other rides, or you simply are nearby. **EXPECT TO WAIT** Up to 15 minutes for the next show. **LENGTH** 12 minutes. **WHERE TO SIT** Sit in a middle row, towards the center. Wait for 25 people or so to enter a row first, and follow them.

Peter Pan's Flight

RANKING Don't miss. **EMH** Morning, Evening. **FP+** Yes. High priority. **TYPE** Dark ride. **REQUIREMENTS** None.

WHAT TO EXPECT Pirate ships seating 2–3 people fly through scenes from *Peter Pan*. Kids love it, but teens and adults are mixed. For some, the flight over London instantly makes it among their favorite rides at Disney World; others find it pedestrian, a little dull—especially the middle section—and overrated. It's a "Don't miss" so that you can discover for yourself where you stand. **SCARY FACTOR** Dark, but not scary.

WHEN TO GO At park open, in the final hour of operation, or with FastPass+. **EXPECT TO WAIT** 50–70+ minutes in the afternoon. **LENGTH** 3 minutes. **WHERE TO SIT** All seats are good.

Pete's Silly Sideshow: Goofy and Donald

RANKING Don't miss for little kids who need to meet Goofy or Donald; skippable for others. **EMH** No. **FP+** No. **TYPE** Character meet and greet. **REQUIREMENTS** None.

WHAT TO EXPECT Goofy and Donald in elaborate circus costumes greet guests in a tent at Pete's Silly Sideshow. Minnie and Daisy greet in the same tent, but their line is separate. **SCARY FACTOR** None.

WHEN TO GO Anytime attraction. See it when waits are long at other rides, or you simply are nearby. **EXPECT TO WAIT** 10–20 minutes in the afternoon. **LENGTH** About a minute with each character individually.

Pete's Silly Sideshow: Minnie and Daisy

RANKING Don't-miss for little kids who need to meet Minnie or Daisy; skippable for others. **EMH** No. **FP+** No. **TYPE** Character meet and greet. **REQUIREMENTS** None.

WHAT TO EXPECT Minnie and Daisy in elaborate circus costumes greet guests in a tent at Pete's Silly Sideshow. Goofy and Donald greet in the same tent, but their line is separate. **SCARY FACTOR** None.

WHEN TO GO Anytime attraction. See it when waits are long at other rides, or you simply are nearby. **EXPECT TO WAIT** 20–30 minutes in the afternoon. **LENGTH** About a minute with each character individually.

Prince Charming Regal Carrousel

RANKING Minor attraction. **EMH** Morning, Evening. **FP+** No. **TYPE** Slowly spinning carousel. **REQUIREMENTS** None.

WHAT TO EXPECT As stately and lovely a carousel as you will ever see, the essence of this ride is obvious from simply looking at it. Ride it if you have kids that wish to; just watch it otherwise. **SCARY FACTOR** None, other than getting the spelling right (two r's in carrousel). **CAN WE HANDLE IT?** Spins too slowly to bother most.

WHEN TO GO Anytime attraction. See it when waits are long at other rides, or you simply are nearby. **EXPECT TO WAIT** 5–10 minutes in the afternoon. **LENGTH** 2 minutes. **WHERE TO SIT** Along the outside for the best photo opportunities.

Princess Fairytale Hall: Anna, Elsa, and a Visiting Princess

RANKING Don't miss for little kids who need to meet Anna and Elsa; skippable for others. **EMH** Morning, Evening. **FP+** Yes. High priority for those who want to greet these characters. **TYPE** Character meet and greet. **REQUIREMENTS** None.

WHAT TO EXPECT Anna, Elsa, and another princess greet guests in Princess Fairytale Hall. Cinderella and Rapunzel greet in the same building, but their line (and FastPass+) is entirely separate. **SCARY FACTOR** None.

WHEN TO GO Immediately at park open, or with FastPass+. At press time, Anna and Elsa meet through 30 minutes before park close. **EXPECT TO WAIT** Waits of two or more hours develop within ten minutes of park open and stay that long all day. **LENGTH** 3–5 minutes of signing, mingling, and picture taking.

Princess Fairytale Hall: Cinderella and Rapunzel

RANKING Don't miss for little kids who need to meet Cinderella and Rapunzel; skippable for others. **EMH** No. **FP+** Yes. High priority for those who want to greet these characters. **TYPE** Character meet and greet. **REQUIREMENTS** None.

WHAT TO EXPECT Cinderella and Rapunzel greet guests in Princess Fairytale Hall. Anna and Elsa greet in the same building, but their line (and FastPass+) is entirely separate. **SCARY FACTOR** None.

WHEN TO GO At park open, in the final hour of operation, or with FastPass+. **EXPECT TO WAIT** 30–60 minutes in the afternoon. **LENGTH** 3–5 minutes of signing, mingling, and picture taking.

Seven Dwarfs Mine Train

RANKING Don't miss. **EMH** Morning, Evening. **FP+** Yes. High priority. **TYPE** Combined roller coaster and dark ride. **REQUIREMENTS** 38" or taller.

WHAT TO EXPECT This ride combines the swoops and curves of a moderate roller coaster with richly detailed scenes from *Snow White*, focusing especially on the Dwarfs. The vehicles are small and seating may be uncomfortable for guests over six feet tall. **SCARY FACTOR** Low—the roller coaster parts are mild and the dark scenes brief. **CAN WE HANDLE IT?** A new ride system (cars that swing side to side) increases the impressions of speed and make the ride more comfortable for those with motion sickness. However, it will add side-to-side jostling to typical coaster back-and-forth jostling, making the ride rough on those with back and neck issues.

WHEN TO GO At park open, in the final hour of operation, or with FastPass+. **EXPECT TO WAIT** 30–70+ minutes in the afternoon. **LENGTH** 3 minutes. **WHERE TO SIT** The front row provides the best views while the back row offers the wildest ride.

Under the Sea ~ Journey of the Little Mermaid

RANKING Major attraction. **EMH** Morning, Evening. **FP+** Yes. Low priority. **TYPE** Dark ride. **REQUIREMENTS** None.

WHAT TO EXPECT Two-to three person "clamshells" take you under the sea into a fairly literal re-telling of the *Little Mermaid*. There's much color and movement, and the party scene is particularly well-done, but those who are not Little Mermaid fans may find it dull. If just one Little Mermaid attraction is enough for you, see the one at Disney's Hollywood Studios instead. **SCARY FACTOR** Low. It has its moments shrouded in darkness, but it's not in any way scary.

WHEN TO GO First two or last two hours of operation, or with FastPass+. **EXPECT TO WAIT** 30–40 minutes in the afternoon. **LENGTH** 5 minutes. **WHERE TO SIT** All seats are good.

The Walt Disney World Railroad

See the "Main Street" entry on the railroad for more details. The Fantasyland stop is near the entrance to The Barnstormer.

TOMORROWLAND

One of the most popular lands, and the one located just off the Hub to the right, Tomorrowland is home to several of Magic Kingdom's most popular attractions, including the venerable Space Mountain and Buzz Lightyear's Space Ranger Spin. Several anytime attractions are also situated here, including the Carousel of Progress, Tomorrowland PeopleMover, and Monsters Inc. Laugh Floor.

Tomorrowland is host to no table service restaurants, but Cosmic Ray's Starlight Café is one of Magic Kingdom's most popular quick services. Offering rotisserie chicken, ribs (only after 4pm), burgers, sandwiches, hot dogs, chicken nuggets, and salads, you'll find a wider selection of food here than at most other quick service locations. Tomorrowland Terrace is another major quick service, located closer to the Plaza Restaurant on Main Street than the rest of Tomorrowland, but it's only open when Magic Kingdom is particularly crowded. If it is open, the salad, sandwich, and pasta fare may be worth checking out. Lunching Pad is located underneath Astro Orbiter in the center of Tomorrowland, serving a couple of forgettable hot dogs, in addition to sweet cream-cheese pretzels, frozen beverages, and other snacks. Also near Astro Orbiter, Cool Ship serves beverages and snacks. Rounding out the choices is Auntie Gravity's Galactic Goodies, serving smoothies, snacks, and ice cream treats.

Mickey's StarTraders and Merchant of Venus near Stitch's Great Escape are the two primary stores, though most everything sold here is available elsewhere. There are small shops at the exits to Buzz Lightyear and Space Mountain as well.

Astro Orbiter

RANKING Skippable but fun. **EMH** Morning, Evening. **FP+** No. **TYPE** Spinning ride. **REQUIREMENTS** None.

WHAT TO EXPECT This slow-loading, low capacity ride spins riders high over Tomorrowland. Twelve "rocket ships" load from an elevated platform (two to a vehicle), raise up, and spin. You can control how high you go. Views are nice, and being high is bit of a thrill, but not worth long waits. **SCARY FACTOR** Medium. This is the most intense spinner attraction at WDW, with the high altitude and rocket ships that slant inward. **CAN WE HANDLE IT?** Put a parent with each kid to help with any fears about height. Those with severe fear of heights should sit this out. Motion sickness is rarely an issue. Note that the seating situation is different than other spinner rides. Riders sit one in front of the other with their legs spread out to the sides. Two adults may want to split up as parties of one for a more comfortable ride. The brief elevator ride before and after the ride is packed full and cramped.

WHEN TO GO At park open or in the final hour of operation. **EXPECT TO WAIT** 20–40 minutes in the afternoon. **LENGTH** 2 minutes. **WHERE TO SIT** Seat adults in back with the kids up front.

Buzz Lightyear's Space Ranger Spin

RANKING Don't Miss. **EMH** Morning, Evening. **FP+** Yes. Medium priority. **TYPE** Dark ride shooting gallery. **REQUIREMENTS** None.

WHAT TO EXPECT In this slow-moving ride, prospective space rangers protect the universe by turning their ride vehicle and shooting an "ion cannon" at targets as they traverse a series of *Toy Story*-themed spaces. Vehicles hold more than two, but have only two cannons. Scores are tallied, so you compete with your ride-mate. The simple concept—being inside a *Toy Story*-themed video game—delights almost everyone. **SCARY FACTOR** None. **CAN WE HANDLE IT?** A joystick controls much of the spinning. Keep youngsters away to enjoy a ride with less motion.

WHEN TO GO First two or last two hours of operation, or with FastPass+. **EXPECT TO WAIT** 25–80 minutes in the afternoon. **LENGTH** 5 minutes. **WHERE TO SIT** All vehicles and seats give the same experience.

Monsters Inc. Laugh Floor

RANKING Minor attraction. **EMH** Evening (usually first hour only). **FP+** Yes. Low priority. **TYPE** Interactive show. **REQUIREMENTS** None.

WHAT TO EXPECT Mike Wazowski, the one-eyed green monster from *Monsters Inc.*, puts on a comedy show to collect laughs from the audience to power Monstropolis. Cool technology allows the monsters to directly interact with the audience. The laughs typically are weak—though often fun for kids. Turtle Talk with Crush at Epcot uses similar technology much, much better. Those on shorter visits may elect to skip. **SCARY FACTOR** None, if your kids have seen the movies. **CAN WE HANDLE IT?** Avoid if you already have had enough Billy Crystal in your life.

WHEN TO GO Anytime attraction. See it when waits are long at other rides, or you need to get out of the weather. **EXPECT TO WAIT** 10–20 minutes in the afternoon. **LENGTH** 10 minutes. **WHERE TO SIT** As in most shows, the center of the theater seating, midway back, give the best views.

Space Mountain

RANKING Don't miss. **EMH** Morning, Evening. **FP+** Yes. High priority. **TYPE** Roller coaster in the dark. **REQUIREMENTS** 44" or taller.

WHAT TO EXPECT In one of the park's most popular rides, small three-person rockets, coupled together in flights of two, blast into the darkness of space, and traverse sharp curves and minor dips past planets, stars, moons, and meteors before returning to the launch facility. **SCARY FACTOR** Moderate. Because the ride is in the dark, speed seems much higher than it is, and everything that happens is unexpected. This scares some. But otherwise it's a very mild coaster. **CAN WE HANDLE IT?** Motion sickness typically is not an issue, but the ride's jerkiness can aggravate (or create, Josh says) back/neck/shoulder pain.

WHEN TO GO At park open, in the final hour of operation, or with FastPass+. **EXPECT TO WAIT** 45–120+ minutes in the afternoon. **LENGTH** 3 minutes. **WHERE TO SIT** The six seats in each coupled-together ride vehicle are single file. Front seats are the most fun. If you are concerned a kid might panic, sit behind them so you can comfort them by touch. The third and fourth seats are the least jerky.

Stitch's Great Escape!

RANKING Skippable. **EMH** Morning, Evening. **FP+** No. **TYPE** Audio-Animatronics show. **REQUIREMENTS** 40" or taller.

WHAT TO EXPECT Stitch's Great Escape replaces a prior show that was great, but far too scary to be in the Magic Kingdom—or perhaps anywhere at Disney World. However, Stitch's Great Escape replaced only one of the many scary elements of the old show, added the annoyances of Stitch—Animatronic belching, anyone? —and now scares kids and bores adults. **SCARY FACTOR** High. Guests are trapped in separated individual seats while scary things happen around them, often in the dark. This attraction has the highest potential to scare kids tall enough for it of any Disney World attraction, and because of the seat design, parents can't comfort kids until the end of the "show". **CAN WE HANDLE IT?** Don't go if your kids have been scared by anything else at Disney World.

WHEN TO GO Anytime attraction. See it when waits are long at other rides, or you need to get out of the weather. **EXPECT TO WAIT** 5–10 minutes in the afternoon. **LENGTH** 10 minutes. **WHERE TO SIT** On a different ride.

Tomorrowland Speedway

RANKING For little kids: don't miss. For everyone else: skippable. **EMH** Morning, Evening. **FP+** Yes. High priority only if you have little kids. **TYPE** Slow, go-cart-style ride on a highly constrained track. **REQUIREMENTS** 32" or taller to ride, 54" or taller to drive.

WHAT TO EXPECT An opportunity for kids to drive or ride along a speedway-themed track in a small two-seater car, at speeds of less than 8 miles an hour and along a guide rail that prevents getting out of their lane. Go-cart-style rides can be fun for adults, but this largely isn't. Young kids tall enough to drive love it, and waits can be long. **SCARY FACTOR** A reminder that Junior is turning 16 far too soon. **CAN WE HANDLE IT?** Both the queue and the ride reek of exhaust and are largely unprotected from the sun. Getting rear-ended by a gleeful 6 year old is common, which can be rough on your back and neck.

WHEN TO GO At park open, in the final hour of operation, or with FastPass+. **EXPECT TO WAIT** 20–40 minutes in the afternoon. **LENGTH** 5 minutes. **WHERE TO SIT** All vehicles give the same experience. If the kids are tall enough (54"+), let them drive. Then keep whining at them, "Are we there yet?"

Tomorrowland Transit Authority PeopleMover

RANKING Minor attraction. **EMH** Morning, Evening. **FP+** No. **TYPE** Tour above and through Tomorrowland. **REQUIREMENTS** None.

WHAT TO EXPECT This slow-moving elevated attraction sends four-person magnetically powered vehicles around Tomorrowland and through parts of several rides, providing a bit of a tour of the land's attractions, and a rest for weary feet. Skippable for those on short visits. **SCARY FACTOR** None.

WHEN TO GO Anytime attraction. See it when waits are long at other rides, or you need to get out of the weather. **EXPECT TO WAIT** No wait to 10 minutes in the afternoon. **LENGTH** 10 minutes. **WHERE TO SIT** All vehicles and seats give the same experience.

Walt Disney's Carousel of Progress

RANKING Minor attraction. **EMH** Morning, Evening. **FP+** No. **TYPE** Audio-Animatronics show. **REQUIREMENTS** None.

WHAT TO EXPECT The theater-style seating area rotates through four charming scenes of American family life, highlighting changes in home technology from the turn of the last century until the mid-90s. Designed for, and an enormous hit at, the New York World's Fair of 64/65, the ride suffers from the lack of a recent update and is dull for many kids. Many diehard Disney fans love it—and it's the only ride in the park that Walt Disney touched. Unlike most theater shows, leaving midway through is not allowed due to the theater's movement. **SCARY FACTOR** None.

WHEN TO GO Anytime attraction. See it when waits are long at other rides, or you need to get out of the weather. **EXPECT TO WAIT** 10–15 minutes in the afternoon. **LENGTH** 20 minutes. **WHERE TO SIT** As in most shows, the center of the theater seating, midway back, give the best views.

PARADES, FIREWORKS, AND SHOWS

Afternoon Festival of Fantasy Parade

RANKING Don't miss. **EMH** No. **FP+** Yes. Low priority. The viewing area is in the Hub in front of the Castle. **TYPE** Parade. **REQUIREMENTS** None.

WHAT TO EXPECT Featuring astonishing floats, a great mix of characters, and wonderful walking entertainers, this parade (which debuted in early 2014) is a don't miss. **SCARY FACTOR** None.

TYPICAL SCHEDULE: Begins at 3pm most days of the year. Unusual events, e.g., tapings of shows on Main Street, may result in different times. The busiest days of the year often see two parades: one around noon, the other at 3pm or 3:30pm. Heavy rain may lead to the parade being scaled back, or even cancelled. **LENGTH** 15 minutes once it arrives.

WHERE TO SEE IT: The parade begins in Frontierland to the left of Splash Mountain, takes a turn near Hall of Presidents, and continues down Main Street, exiting in between the Firehouse and Emporium. People begin staking out spots on Main Street more than an hour before showtime, but most days of the year there are great spots still available in Frontierland just 15–30 minutes before the parade. The height of the floats means that even little kids don't need to be right in front, but the great entertainers and walking characters will be hard for them to see from farther back. Plan to see it across from Pecos Bill where crowds are lighter and you can be on your way sooner.

Evening Main Street Electrical Parade

RANKING Major entertainment. **EMH** No. A parade may be scheduled at the beginning of an evening EMH, but everyone is welcome to stay and watch. **FP+** Yes. High priority, as your parade FP+ locates you well for the two events that typically follow the parade: the Celebrate the Magic castle show and the Wishes fireworks show. Viewing is in the Hub directly in front of the castle. **TYPE** Parade. **REQUIREMENTS** None.

WHAT TO EXPECT Disney's World's current evening parade has been around in some form for decades. Some view it as a worthy classic, others as an offering that was dated more than a decade ago. **SCARY FACTOR** While the repetitive music and some of the floats may seem like they're straight out of a Stanley Kubrick movie, the parade isn't overtly scary.

TYPICAL SCHEDULE: Runs twice most nights during busier weeks, and as rarely as 2–3 nights a week during quieter weeks and during periods when the park frequently closes for evening parties. Heavy rain may lead to the parade being scaled back, or even cancelled. **LENGTH** 15 minutes once it arrives.

WHERE TO SEE IT: The parade begins on Main Street between the Emporium and the Firehouse, and exits to the left of Splash Mountain. If you are seeing the parade before Wishes, pick your spot based on where you want to view Wishes from. Otherwise, pick a spot in Frontierland 15–45 minutes before the parade, depending on how crowded the park is. Floats are low compared to the afternoon parade, so getting your kids at the front pays off. On nights with two parades, the second parade is much less crowded.

Evening Castle Show: Celebrate the Magic

RANKING Don't miss. **EMH** No. **FP+** No, but see the Evening Parade Fast-Pass+ discussion. **TYPE** Projection show. **REQUIREMENTS** None.

WHAT TO EXPECT Astonishing visual projections transform Cinderella Castle in many fun and breathtaking ways. Hard to describe in words, it's one of Disney World's best offerings. **SCARY FACTOR** None.

TYPICAL SCHEDULE: Runs twice most nights during busier weeks, and as rarely as 2–3 nights a week during quieter weeks and during periods when the park frequently closes for evening parties. When both Wishes and the evening parade are on, Celebrate the Magic most commonly has a show prior to Wishes with the potential for a second after. **LENGTH** 10 minutes.

WHERE TO SEE IT: The show is best seen from near the castle, in a location from which you can see the entire castle with no obstructions. The evening parade FastPass+ location fits this, as do many spots in the nearer parts of the hub on the Main Street side of the castle, Fantasyland, Liberty Square, and Tomorrowland. On nights with two shows, the second is much less crowded.

Wishes: Evening Fireworks

RANKING Don't miss. **EMH** No. **FP+** Yes. Low priority, The viewing location is on the grass near the rose garden. **TYPE** Fireworks show. **REQUIRE-MENTS** None.

WHAT TO EXPECT A great fireworks display, lightly tied to a narrated story, with some affecting music. **SCARY FACTOR** Too loud for some little kids.

TYPICAL SCHEDULE: Runs almost every night most of the year, but as few as 3 nights a week during the early-September to mid-December period when the park frequently closes at 7pm for evening parties. Wishes may begin as early as 8pm or as late as 10pm. The Electrical Parade is usually scheduled one hour before Wishes, with Celebrate the Magic beginning 15 minutes before Wishes. Thunderstorms with lightning will delay the show. **LENGTH** 15 minutes.

WHERE TO SEE IT: Wishes was designed to be seen on Main Street in front of Cinderella Castle, but the fireworks are visible from parts of Adventure-land, Fantasyland, Liberty Square, and Tomorrowland. We like to see the show from around Casey's Corner, which is far enough back that crowding is less of a concern and the fireworks are centered above the Castle.

The Cheat Sheets

The Cheat Sheets that follow are designed to break down all of our touring advice and principles into an easy guide that can be brought along to the theme parks. Print out the newest versions in color at EASYWDW.COM/EASY-GUIDE.

Each Cheat Sheet covers one park, and includes:

- Coded maps
- Touring overviews
- General FastPass+ priorities
- Daily touring plans that include specific FastPass+ suggestions

The maps are shaded based on the best time to visit the various attractions:

- The dark gray attractions are your top morning priorities, or best saved for the very end of the day or FastPass+.
- Medium gray attractions are best visited in the first/second hour of operation, or in the last two hours the park is open. They're a lower priority than the dark attractions because waits build slower and peak lower.
- Light gray attractions are designated "anytime", which is another way of saying they're best saved for the afternoon when waits at

the higher priority attractions are longer. Most shows are designated "light gray" because you want to save them for the afternoon or evening when waits are longer at the major attractions.

Attractions that offer FastPass+ are followed by a +. FastPass+ kiosks are noted with the FP+ symbol. Also included are bathrooms, quick services, restaurants, and the larger stores.

Several touring plans are included with each Cheat Sheet. You may need to make changes based on the previous reviews (which is why we offer them), particularly with kids too short or too easily scared to experience certain attractions. For example, you may want to avoid roller coasters, character meets (at press time, no rides include both), or motion simulators, etc. Once you've picked your plan, it's easiest to simply cross off attractions the group isn't interested in experiencing. That will only result in shorter waits at the next attraction. Also consider substituting attractions coded the same. For example, you may want to substitute a second ride on Great Movie Ride over Star Tours because motion simulators may prove problematic.

Animal Kingdom Cheat Sheet

PARK MAP

TOURING AT THE ANIMAL KINGDOM

GENERAL TOURING PHILOSOPHY Because it has so few attractions, touring Animal Kingdom is fairly straightforward. It can be done with or without FastPass+(doing without saves the FastPass+ for the evening at another park) and even with a late arrival. You'll find short to non-existent waits through lunch if you follow the morning plans below. After lunch, relax and visit the less crowded attractions and stage shows when temperatures and humidity peak. Animal Kingdom typically empties out by 4:15pm because there's no night-time entertainment to keep guests at the Park. Stay through close (usually between 5pm and 8pm) and you'll find low crowds in the last 60–120 minutes of operation.

CHARACTERS Mickey and Minnie in Adventurers Outpost are the only major priority, and they are FastPass+ enabled. Meet them in the first 30 minutes or last hour of operation to reduce waits, or use FastPass+. Russell and Dug next to It's Tough to Be a Bug, and Pocahontas on the walkway between Africa and Asia, are also priorities, and see 15–30 minute waits.

ROPE DROP Animal Kingdom usually begins letting guests inside the Park 15 minutes prior to official open. Guests are free to head to the attraction of their choice, but only Kilimanjaro Safaris, Expedition Everest, and TriceraTop Spin usually operate before official open.

WARNINGS Depending on time of year (particularly November–February), even on nights the park is open later, Kilimanjaro Safaris and the animal exhibits and trails may close early due to darkness (typically around 5pm). Check your *Times Guide* to verify. Most quick service venues close an hour before park close. Restaurantosaurus, Pizzafari, and the sit-down restaurants should continue serving through close. Consider a dinner reservation at Tusker House or Yak & Yeti, and you'll be able to walk out of the park in the dark with very few other people around.

FASTPASS+ AT THE ANIMAL KINGDOM

It's relatively easy to tour Animal Kingdom without FastPass+ if you tour efficiently in the first or last two hours the park is open. Doing so will give you an opportunity to use FastPass+ elsewhere. Here, FastPass+ is best used at Kali River Rapids in the afternoon when waits are longest and temperatures highest. The Adventurers Outpost Meet and Greet has a limited capacity and is another priority. A third use is best at Kilimanjaro Safaris or Expedition Everest.

FastPass+ Priority

1. Kali River Rapids (when highs are 80+ degrees)
2. Adventurers Outpost Mickey and Minnie Meet
3. Kilimanjaro Safaris
4. Expedition Everest
5. Kali River Rapids (when highs are less than 80 degrees)
6. Primeval Whirl
7. DINOSAUR
8. *Finding Nemo the Musical*
9. *Festival of the Lion King*
10. It's Tough To Be A Bug

MORNING TOURING PLAN WITH FASTPASS+

Use FastPass+ at Adventurers Outpost Mickey/Minnie Meet (10:30am–11:30am), Kali River Rapids (11:30am–12:30pm), and a third attraction of your choice sometime in the afternoon.

1. Ride Kilimanjaro Safaris: 8:55am–9:25am.
2. Ride Expedition Everest: 9:40am–9:55am.
3. Ride Primeval Whirl: 10:05am–10:15am.
4. Ride TriceraTop Spin: 10:17am–10:25am.
5. Ride DINOSAUR: 10:30am–10:50am.
6. Meet Mickey and Minnie at Adventurers Outpost with Fast-Pass+: 11am–11:15am.
7. Have lunch. Flame Tree Barbecue and Yak & Yeti are nearby, very good, and a little different. Pizzafari and Restauranto-saurus offer ample air-conditioned seating. Tusker House is a character meal in Africa that offers a wide variety of options, most familiar and a few exotic. It's usually much more relaxed than other character buffets.
8. Ride Kali River Rapids with FastPass+: 12:15pm–12:30pm.
9. Then follow the afternoon plan, below.

MORNING TOURING PLAN WITHOUT FASTPASS+

1. Ride Kilimanjaro Safaris: 8:55am– 9:25am.
2. Meet Mickey and Minnie at Adventurers Outpost: 9:35am–9:55am.

3. Ride Kali River Rapids: 10am–10:20am.

4. Ride Expedition Everest: 10:30am–10:50am.

5. Ride Primeval Whirl: 10:55am–11:10am.

6. Ride TriceraTop Spin: 11:12am–11:25am.

7. Ride DINOSAUR: 11:30am–12pm.

8. Have lunch. Restaurantosaurus and Flame Tree Barbecue are nearby.

9. Then follow the afternoon plan, below.

AFTERNOON TOURING PLAN

12:30PM–3:30PM Take it easy. Do It's Tough to be a Bug, Wilderness Explorers, Maharajah Jungle Trek, Flights of Wonder, *Finding Nemo the Musical*, *Festival of the Lion King*, Rafiki's Planet Watch, and Boneyard.

3:45PM PARADE VIEWING Parade viewing is easiest outside of Yak & Yeti in Asia or Tamu Tamu Refreshments in Africa. The parade begins and ends to the right of Pizzafari in Discovery Island. *Note:* Parade is scheduled to end May 31, 2014, with no announced replacement.

INSTEAD OF THE PARADE The parade cuts off most traffic to the Africa section from 3:40pm–4:15pm. If you don't mind skipping the parade, walk Pangani Forest Exploration Trail from 3:30pm–4pm. Then get in line for Kilimanjaro Safaris where the wait will be short.

AFTER THE PARADE Crowds diminish and wait times shorten as park close approaches. With a 7pm or later close, you'll have two to three more excellent hours of park touring with much shorter waits than in the afternoon. Visit DinoLand with about two hours to park close. Return to Asia for Kali River Rapids and Expedition Everest in the final hour of operation.

LATE ARRIVAL TOURING PLAN (WITH 6PM OR LATER CLOSE AND FASTPASS+)

1. Arrive between 10:30am and 11am. Schedule FP+ at Expedition Everest (12:30pm–1:30pm), Adventurers Outpost Mickey and Minnie Meet (1:30pm–2:30pm), and Kali River Rapids (2:30pm–3:30pm).

2. Visit Oasis Exhibits until 11:15am.

3. See It's Tough to be a Bug: 11:15am–11:30am.

4. See Finding Nemo the Musical: 12pm–12:45pm.

5. Ride Expedition Everest with FastPass+: 12:50pm–1:05pm.

6. Have lunch. Yak & Yeti and Flame Tree Barbecue are closest.

7. Meet Mickey and Minnie at Adventurers Outpost with Fast-Pass+: 2pm–2:15pm.

8. Walk Maharajah Jungle Trek: 2:20pm–2:45pm.

9. Ride Kali River Rapids with FastPass+: 2:50pm–3:10pm.

10. Ride Kilimanjaro Safaris: 3:20pm–3:50pm.

11. See Mickey's Jungle Parade in front of Tamu Tamu Refreshments in Africa or walk Pangani Forest Exploration Trail: 3:50pm–4:25pm.

12. Ride Primeval Whirl: 4:40pm–5pm.

13. Ride TriceraTop Spin: 5:02pm–5:15pm.

14. Ride DINOSAUR: 5:20pm–5:40pm.

15. Ride Expedition Everest: 5:50pm–6pm.

TYPICAL ANIMAL KINGDOM WAIT TIMES IN MINUTES

Low Crowds, 5pm Close

	9:30am	10am	11am	12pm	1pm	2pm	3pm	4pm	5pm
DINOSAUR	10	10	10	15	15	15	10	10	5
Expedition Everest	10	10	15	15	20	20	20	15	10
It's Tough to be a Bug	5	5	5	5	5	5	5	5	5
Kali River Rapids (hot)	10	10	20	25	30	30	20	15	15
Kali River Rapids (cool)	5	5	10	15	15	15	15	10	5
Kilimanjaro Safaris	10	20	20	20	20	20	15	10	10
Primeval Whirl	10	10	10	15	15	10	10	10	5
TriceraTop Spin	5	5	10	10	10	10	10	5	5

Moderate Crowds, 6pm Close

	9:30am	10am	11am	12pm	1pm	2pm	3pm	4pm	5pm	6pm
DINOSAUR	10	10	20	30	30	30	30	20	10	10
Expedition Everest	10	20	25	30	35	30	25	20	10	5
It's Tough to be a Bug	5	5	5	10	10	10	10	5	5	5
Kali River Rapids (hot)	10	15	30	40	50	60	50	40	30	20
Kali River Rapids (cool)	5	10	15	20	20	20	15	15	10	5
Kilimanjaro Safaris	20	30	40	40	30	30	30	20	10	5
Primeval Whirl	10	10	15	15	15	20	15	10	5	5
TriceraTop Spin	5	10	10	15	15	15	15	10	5	5

Heavy Crowds, 8pm Close

	9:30am	10am	11am	12pm	1pm	2pm	3pm	4pm	5pm	6pm	7pm	8pm
DINOSAUR	20	30	45	60	60	60	50	40	30	20	20	10
Expedition Everest	25	35	45	50	60	60	45	40	30	25	15	10
It's Tough to be a Bug	5	10	15	15	20	20	20	15	10	10	5	5
Kali River Rapids (hot)	20	20	60	70	80	80	70	50	40	25	15	5
Kali River Rapids (cool)	5	5	15	15	20	20	15	15	10	5	5	5
Kilimanjaro Safaris	30	40	60	60	70	80	70	30	40	35	20	10
Primeval Whirl	15	15	25	30	30	30	25	20	20	10	5	5
TriceraTop Spin	5	5	15	20	20	15	15	10	10	5	5	5

Epcot Cheat Sheet

PARK MAP

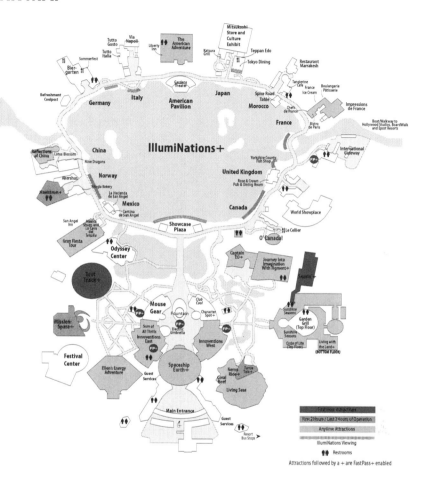

Mitsukoshi Store and Culture Exhibit

The American Adventure

Teppan Edo

Tokyo Dining

Restaurant Marrakesh

Tutto Gusto

Via Napoli

Liberty Inn

Katsura Grill

Tutto Italia

Sommerfest

Bier-garten

Tangierine Café

France

Boulangerie Pâtisserie

Ice Cream

Refreshment Coolpost

Gardens Theater

Spice Road Table

Chefs de France

Impressions de France

Germany

Italy

American Pavilion

Japan

Morocco

France

Bistro de Paris

Boat/Walkway to Hollywood Studios, BoardWalk and Epcot Resorts

Reflections of China

Lotus Blossom

China

IllumiNations+

Yorkshire County Fish Shop

International Gateway

Nine Dragons

United Kingdom

Akershus

Norway

Rose & Crown Pub & Dining Room

Kringla Bakery

La Hacienda de San Angel

Mexico

Canada

World Showplace

San Angel Inn

Mexico Shops and La Cava del Tequila

Cantina de San Angel

Showcase Plaza

Le Cellier

Gran Fiesta Tour

O' Canada!

Odyssey Center

Captain EO+

Journey Into Imagination With Figment+

Test Track+

Mouse Gear

Club Cool

Character Spot+

Sunshine Seasons

Garden Grill (Top Floor)

Mission: Space+

Sum of All Thrills

Fountain

Electric Umbrella

Innoventions East

Innoventions West

Sunshine Seasons

Circle of Life (Top Floor)

Living with the Land+ (BOTTOM FLOOR)

Festival Center

Ellen's Energy Adventure

Guest Services

Spaceship Earth+

Nemo Ride+

Turtle Talk+

Coral Reef

Living Seas

Main Entrance

Guest Services

Resort Bus Stops

First Hour Attractions

First 2 Hours / Last 2 Hours of Operation

Anytime Attractions

IllumiNations Viewing

Restrooms

Attractions followed by a + are FastPass+ enabled

TOURING AT EPCOT

GENERAL TOURING PHILOSOPHY Because of its massive size and the length of many of its attractions, Epcot is best experienced over two days. There are exactly two morning or FastPass+ priorities: Soarin' and Test Track. Each builds lines quickly, only one can be pre-booked using FastPass+ per day, and because they are about ten minutes away from each other and each takes about 20 minutes to experience, even with a minimal initial wait, it's best to focus on one or the other over two separate days. This way, you won't run into waits longer than a few minutes all day. On your Test Track day, visit Future World East and the World Showcase Pavilions from Mexico through the U.S. On your Soarin' day, hit Future World West and the Pavilions from Canada through Japan.

If you have only one day, things are a bit more complicated. There are a few ways to make it work. First, you can experience Test Track via its single-rider line with waits that are often shorter than standby or FastPass+. However, your group won't ride together, and you won't be able to design a car in the regular pre-show. You can enter the single-rider line later in the day and find waits of 10 to 20 minutes. Second, you could use FastPass+ at Soarin' or Test Track, seeing the other first thing in the morning. Third, if you're skipping IllumiNations, you could visit either Soarin' or Test Track in the morning, and then the other right before park close. Waits will be relatively short at the end of the night, and as long as you're in line before official park close, you'll ride, regardless of the posted wait.

In World Showcase, the only attraction that sees waits is Maelstrom in Norway. It's best to ride before 12pm or after 7:30pm. You may need to wait a few minutes for the next show to begin in China, France, and Canada. They are all worth seeing. You generally get out of World Showcase what you put in—spend some time exploring and you'll get much more out of it than someone who simply walks past the pavilions.

CHARACTERS The princesses in World Showcase can see substantial waits. Mickey, Minnie, and Goofy at Character Spot can also see 20–40 minute waits. If you're skipping Soarin' and Test Track in the morning, visit Character Spot right after park open. Otherwise, it's best to do Character Spot near park close to avoid long waits. Most other characters will have 5–15 minute waits. Atypical characters may also appear. Check for them between the Canada and United Kingdom Pavilions, and to the left of Liberty Inn in the United States Pavilion in the afternoon.

ROPE DROP Epcot has two entrances. At the main entrance, a brief welcome spiel will play over the speakers beginning at 8:45am. At 8:47am, Disney will begin letting guests into the park. If things aren't quite ready, the welcome spiel may be delayed by a few minutes. There are no ropes inside and guests are free to head to the Future World attraction of their choice. From the International Gateway, there is no welcome spiel, but Disney admits guests at the same time as the main entrance. It is a slightly longer walk from the International Gateway, but with fewer people entering, Gateway visitors should arrive at Soarin' or Test Track alongside most guests entering from the main entrance. At the main entrance, arrive by 8:15am to ensure the shortest waits possible throughout the morning. At the International Gateway, arrive by 8:30am.

FASTPASS+ AT EPCOT

FastPass+ at Epcot is divided into two tiers.

In Tier 1 are Soarin', Test Track, IllumiNations, and Living with the Land. Guests may initially select only one Tier 1 experience. We recommend Soarin' because its location makes it more convenient to visit in the afternoon with FastPass+, and Test Track offers a single rider line that reduces waits.

There are eight options for Tier 2 and you may initially select two of them. Most guests will want to initially select two of the top four choices.

FastPass+ Priority

Tier 1 (choose one)
1. Soarin'
2. Test Track
3. IllumiNations (not available every night)
4. Living with the Land

Tier 2 (choose two):
1. Mission: SPACE Orange
2. Spaceship Earth
3. Character Spot
4. Maelstrom
5. Mission: SPACE Green
6. Turtle Talk with Crush
7. The Seas with Nemo and Friends
8. Journey into Imagination with Figment
9. Captain EO

TWO DAY TOURING PLAN

Two Day Plan, Morning Day 1

Use FastPass+ at Soarin' and your choice of two Tier 2 attractions.
1. Ride Soarin': 9am–9:25am.
2. Ride Living with the Land: 9:30am–9:45am.
3. Ride The Seas with Nemo and Friends at The Seas: 9:55am–10:05am.
4. See Turtle Talk with Crush and look around The Seas: 10:10am–10:40am.

5. Ride Soarin' again with FastPass+: 10:50am–11:10am.

6. Have lunch at Sunshine Seasons in the Land, or at a restaurant in World Showcase.

Two Day Plan, Afternoon and Evening Day 1

You have a lot of options depending on what you want to do and where you plan to have dinner. You won't find any waits at the attractions in Innoventions West or the Imagination Pavilion (Captain EO and Journey into Imagination with Figment) if you want to do those now. We like to head up to World Showcase beginning with the Canada Pavilion. Most people arrive around 10am and linger in Future World until the afternoon. Even though there aren't waits at the attractions in Canada, France, etc., touring the area in low crowds means you'll have an easier time perusing the shops and fewer people in front of you at the various acts. Consider returning to Future World around 5pm. You'll be exiting World Showcase when crowds peak there, and returning to Future World when waits will be short for everything other than Soarin' and Test Track. Head back down to Spaceship Earth in the evening on one of your days. Also plan to see IllumiNations one of your evenings—see the note on it at the end of this Cheat Sheet.

Two Day Plan, Morning Day 2

Use FastPass+ at Test Track, Spaceship Earth, and one other Tier 2 attraction.

1. Ride Test Track: 8:55am–9:20am.

2. Ride Sum of All Thrills in Innoventions East: 9:25am–9:45am.

3. Ride Mission: SPACE: 9:55am–10:15am.

4. Ride Test Track with FastPass+: 10:20am–10:40am.

Two-Day Plan, Late Morning and Afternoon Day 2

You have some options depending on what you plan to do in World Showcase and whether you're planning to head back to Future World. Now would be a fine time to visit Ellen's Energy Adventure or anything in Innoventions East other than Sum of All Thrills. But those are lengthy attractions that could be kept for a 5pm return. Consider heading up to World Showcase beginning with the Gran Fiesta Tour in the Mexico Pavilion. Then it's up to Maelstrom in Norway and the rest of the World Showcase. You can stay in World Showcase or take the boat in Germany back to Future World around 5pm when crowds thin. Standby waits will be short for anything other than Test Track, which has the single rider line, and Soarin'.

TWO DAY LATE ARRIVAL TOURING PLAN

A late arrival is relatively straightforward over two days by using FastPass+ at the priority attractions on one side of the park each day. Future World crowds thin after 5pm as most people move up to World Showcase for shopping, dinner, and IllumiNations. Most nights, Captain EO, Journey into Imagination, Innoventions West, Innoventions East, Living with the Land, and Circle of Life close at 7pm. Evening waits are typically much shorter than afternoon waits at the attractions that remain open through close.

Two Day Late Arrival Plan, Day 1

Use FastPass+ at Spaceship Earth (10:30am–11:30am), Mission: SPACE (4:30pm–5:30pm), Test Track (5:30pm–6:30pm).
1. Arrive between 10:30am and 11am.
2. Ride Spaceship Earth with FastPass+: 11am–11:20am.
3. Ride Gran Fiesta Tour: 11:35am–11:50am.
4. Ride Maelstrom: 12pm–12:15pm.
5. Have lunch. There are lots of options in World Showcase.
6. Explore Mexico through Italy and take boat in Germany or walk back to Future World by 5pm.
7. Ride Mission: SPACE with FastPass+: 5:15pm–5:40pm.
8. Ride Test Track with FastPass+: 5:45pm–6:10pm.
9. Ride Ellen's Energy Adventure or explore Innoventions East: 6:15pm–6:55pm.
10. Ride Sum of All Thrills: 6:55pm–7:15pm.
11. Have dinner. Electric Umbrella is nearby in Future World, or head up to World Showcase.
12. See IllumiNations or get in line for Test Track at 8:55pm (see the note on IllumiNations at the end of this Cheat Sheet).

Two Day Late Arrival Plan, Day 2

Use FastPass+ at Turtle Talk with Crush (11am–12pm), Character Spot (12pm–1pm), and Soarin' (1pm–2pm).
1. Arrive between 10:30am and 11am.
2. Ride The Seas with Nemo and Friends: 11:10am–11:25am.
3. See Turtle Talk with Crush with FastPass+ and look around Seas Pavilion: 11:25am–12pm.
4. Visit Character Spot with FastPass+: 12:20pm–12:30pm.

5. Have lunch at Sunshine Seasons: 12:30pm–1:30pm.
6. Ride Soarin' with FastPass+: 1:35pm–2pm.
7. Ride Living with the Land: 2:05pm–2:25pm.
8. Ride Journey into Imagination with Figment: 2:35pm–2:50pm.
9. See Captain EO and/or explore Innoventions West: 3pm–3:30pm.
10. Tour World Showcase from Canada to the United States.
11. If desired, return to Future World and visit Character Spot after 8pm.
12. See IllumiNations or get in line for Soarin' at 8:55pm.

ONE DAY TOURING PLAN

Use FastPass+ at Turtle Talk with Crush (11am–12pm), Soarin (12pm–1pm), and Spaceship Earth (1pm–2pm).

Morning and Early Afternoon Plan

1. Ride Test Track: 8:55am–9:20am.
2. Ride Sum of All Thrills: 9:25am–9:45am.
3. Ride Mission: SPACE Green or Orange: 9:50am–10:10am.
4. Ride The Seas with Nemo and Friends: 10:25am–10:35am.
5. See Turtle Talk with Crush with FastPass+: 10:35am–11am.
6. Ride Living with the Land: 11:10am–11:30am.
7. Have lunch at Sunshine Seasons: 11:30am–12:15pm.
8. Ride Soarin' with FastPass+: 12:20pm–12:55pm.
9. Ride Spaceship Earth with FastPass+: 1:10pm–1:30pm.
10. Ride Journey into Imagination with Figment: 1:40pm–1:55pm.
11. See Captain EO if desired: 2pm–2:20pm.

Later Afternoon and Evening Plan

Visit World Showcase beginning with Canada. Finish by riding Maelstrom in Norway and Gran Fiesta Tour in Mexico after 7:30pm, if possible. Visit Character Spot as late in the evening as possible. See "IllumiNations", next.

ILLUMINATIONS

IllumiNations is the nightly entertainment at Epcot, scheduled at 9pm most nights. For the best experience, pick a viewing spot 30–45 minutes before the start of the show. Target several spots—certain sections may be roped off for private parties, so you need a backup plan.

Best Spots

1. Base of the World Showcase near Future World directly across from the United States Pavilion. This "front of house" view is elevated with a direct view of the globe and fireworks. This area may be partially reserved for FastPass+.

2. The bridge connecting the UK and France.

3. The Italy Isola, or raised section across from Italy. Parts can be reserved, but the viewing location behind the seated guests is almost as good.

4. The stretch from Mexico to Norway. Areas closer to Norway have fewer people.

5. Other options: there's limited space outside Tokyo Dining on the second level in Japan; limited viewing is available along Canada into the U.K.; there are areas to the right of the U.K. downstairs that are good locations, but they may be reserved for private events.

6. Rose & Crown has patio seating and a reserved platform for those dining inside prior to the show. La Hacienda de San Angel also has indoor viewing, but only some of the tables face the windows. It isn't a great choice if you're looking for a guaranteed view. Consider a meal that begins after 7:45pm.

After IllumiNations, hang out for 20–45 minutes and let others exit in front of you. It's a great opportunity to walk around World Showcase at night and take in the sights with fewer people around.

TYPICAL EPCOT WAIT TIMES IN MINUTES

Low Crowds

	9:30am	10am	11am	12pm	1pm	2pm	3pm	4pm	5pm	6pm	7pm	8pm
Ellen's Energy Adventure	5	5	5	5	5	5	5	5	5	5	n/a	n/a
Gran Fiesta Tour	n/a	n/a	5	5	5	5	5	5	5	5	5	5
Journey into Imagination	5	5	5	5	5	5	5	5	5	5	n/a	n/a
Living with the Land	5	5	5	5	5	5	5	5	5	5	n/a	n/a
Maelstrom	n/a	n/a	5	10	15	15	20	15	10	10	5	5
Mission: Space Green	5	5	10	10	10	10	10	10	10	10	5	5
Mission: Space Orange	10	10	15	15	15	15	15	15	15	15	10	10
Seas with Nemo	5	5	5	5	5	5	5	5	5	5	5	5
Soarin'	20	30	30	40	40	30	30	25	25	20	15	10
Spaceship Earth	5	10	10	10	10	10	10	10	5	5	5	5
Sum of All Thrills	5	10	15	20	20	20	20	20	10	10	n/a	n/a
Test Track	20	30	40	40	40	40	30	30	30	30	20	20

Moderate Crowds

	9:30am	10am	11am	12pm	1pm	2pm	3pm	4pm	5pm	6pm	7pm	8pm
Ellen's Energy Adventure	5	5	5	5	5	5	5	5	5	5	n/a	n/a
Gran Fiesta Tour	n/a	n/a	5	5	10	10	10	5	5	5	5	5
Journey into Imagination	5	5	10	10	15	10	10	10	10	5	n/a	n/a
Living with the Land	5	10	10	10	15	15	15	10	10	5	n/a	n/a
Maelstrom	n/a	n/a	5	20	30	35	35	30	25	20	15	10
Mission: Space Green	5	10	20	20	25	25	20	20	15	10	10	5
Mission: Space Orange	10	15	25	25	30	30	30	25	20	15	15	10
Seas with Nemo	5	10	10	15	15	15	10	10	10	10	5	5
Soarin'	30	40	50	60	70	70	70	60	60	50	40	20
Spaceship Earth	5	15	20	20	15	15	15	15	15	10	5	5
Sum of All Thrills	5	20	20	20	20	20	20	20	20	20	n/a	n/a
Test Track	30	50	60	70	70	70	60	60	50	45	30	20

Heavy Crowds

	9:30am	10am	11am	12pm	1pm	2pm	3pm	4pm	5pm	6pm	7pm	8pm
Ellen's Energy Adventure	5	5	5	5	5	5	5	5	5	5	n/a	n/a
Gran Fiesta Tour	n/a	n/a	5	10	15	15	15	10	10	5	5	5
Journey into Imagination	5	10	15	15	20	20	20	15	15	10	n/a	n/a
Living with the Land	5	10	15	20	20	20	20	20	15	10	n/a	n/a
Maelstrom	n/a	n/a	10	30	40	45	40	30	30	20	15	10
Mission: Space Green	5	15	30	35	45	45	45	45	35	30	20	15
Mission: Space Orange	10	20	60	60	60	70	60	60	40	35	30	25
Seas with Nemo	5	10	15	20	25	25	20	20	20	15	10	5
Soarin'	45	70	90	100	120	120	110	100	90	70	60	50
Spaceship Earth	10	15	30	30	30	30	30	25	25	20	15	5
Sum of All Thrills	5	20	20	30	30	30	30	20	20	20	n/a	n/a
Test Track	50	70	90	120	120	120	100	100	80	80	70	60

Hollywood Studios Cheat Sheet

PARK MAP

TOURING AT DISNEY'S HOLLYWOOD STUDIOS

GENERAL TOURING PHILOSOPHY Toy Story Mania is the highest priority and should be most guests' first stop. It's also the top FastPass+ priority. Rock 'n' Roller Coaster and Tower of Terror are the other two ride priorities. Star Tours and Great Movie Ride are the only other rides that often have posted waits longer than 15 minutes. A challenge most people run into is trying to see the various scheduled shows, all of which take 40–60 minutes. With a one day visit, you may need to prioritize several of the lengthy attractions that appeal to your group while skipping others—there just isn't enough time. FastPass+ allows those willing to miss some of these shows to have a good visit even with a late arrival.

CHARACTERS The *Toy Story* characters across from Toy Story Mania are the highest priority and see 30–50 minute afternoon waits. Sorcerer Mickey, Sofia, and Phineas/Ferb also see 20–40 minute waits. Classic characters like Goofy, Donald, Daisy, Stitch, and Pluto greet at the Sorcerer's Hat through the early afternoon.

JEDI TRAINING ACADEMY Kids between the ages of 4–12 can participate in this show held next to Star Tours. You must bring the participating child to the old Sounds Dangerous building to the left of American Idol Experience and across from Indiana Jones Epic Stunt Spectacular immediately after the park opens to guarantee a slot. There are usually 12–15 shows scheduled throughout the day. Ask for a show in the afternoon so it doesn't interfere with morning touring. If they can't accommodate, let others sign up first and sign up for a show after 12pm.

ROPE DROP Hollywood Studios may be the most essential rope drop to hit due to how fast Toy Story Mania wait times skyrocket. If you're not among the first 200–300 people inside the park, you can expect to wait 25–40 minutes at Toy Story Mania even if you hurry straight there. Disney usually begins letting guests into the Studios 10 minutes before official Park open, but it may be earlier (30–40 minutes) if crowds are expected to be well above average. In order to be among the first to enter the park, plan to be at the entrance no later than 45 minutes prior to open. Once the park opens, guests are free to head to the attraction of their choice with no internal ropes, though Toy Story Mania is often the only attraction actually operating until official open.

FASTPASS+ AT THE STUDIOS

Guests may initially select only one Tier 1 attraction, which can make it a struggle for those arriving late to visit both Toy Story Mania and Rock 'n' Roller Coaster without long waits. Most guests will want to select Toy Story

Mania and ride Rock 'n' Roller Coaster standby early in the morning. Rock 'n' Roller Coaster also offers a single rider line, though waits are usually in the 20–30 minute range due to the way the vehicles are loaded, and it's impossible to gauge how many people are in line until the final loading area.

FastPass+ Priority:

Tier 1 (choose one):

1. Toy Story Mania
2. Rock 'n' Roller Coaster
3. Fantasmic!
4. Great Movie Ride
5. Beauty and the Beast Live on Stage

Tier 2 (choose two):

1. Tower of Terror
2. Voyage of the Little Mermaid
3. Star Tours
4. Indiana Jones Epic Stunt Spectacular
5. Disney Jr. Live on Stage
6. Lights, Motors, Action! Extreme Stunt Show
7. American Idol Experience
8. Muppet Vision 3D

TOURING PLAN

Morning Plan

Use FastPass+ at Tower of Terror (9am–10am), Toy Story Mania (10am–11am), and Star Tours (11am –12pm).

1. Ride Toy Story Mania: 8:55am–9:10am.
2. Ride Rock 'n' Roller Coaster: 9:20am–9:35am.
3. Ride Tower of Terror with FastPass+: 9:40am–10:05am.
4. Ride Toy Story Mania with FastPass+: 10:15am–10:35am.
5. See Voyage of the Little Mermaid: 10:45am–11:10am.
6. Ride Star Tours with FastPass+: 11:20am–11:40am.
7. Visit a FastPass+ kiosk and select The Great Movie Ride for after lunch.
8. Have lunch: Studios Catering Co., Backlot Express, and ABC

Commissary are nearby. Sci-Fi Dine-In and 50's Prime Time are nearby inexpensive table service restaurants.

9. Ride Great Movie Ride with FastPass+: 12:30pm – 1pm.

Alternative: If you'd only like to ride Toy Story once and prefer to ride Rock 'n' Roller Coaster and Tower of Terror multiple times, head to the thrill rides first and rely on FP+ at Toy Story Mania later in the day. Waits won't build at Rock 'n' Coaster or Tower of Terror until 10am.

Afternoon and Evening Plan

It's time for the Studios' scheduled stage shows and low-wait attractions like Backlot Tour, the Magic of Disney Animation, One Man's Dream, and Muppet Vision 3D. For good seats at Beauty and the Beast and Indiana Jones, arrive 15–25 minutes before show time—earlier always results in better seats. For American Idol Experience, Disney Jr. Live on Stage, Jedi Training Academy, and Lights Motors Action Extreme Stunt Show, arriving 5–15 minutes early will suffice. Visit desired characters in the last 60–90 minutes that they're scheduled to appear. See Fantasmic! in the evening (there's more on Fantasmic! later in this Cheat Sheet).

CHARACTER-CENTRIC TOURING PLAN

Morning Plan

Use FP+ at Toy Story Mania (10am–11am), Disney Jr. Live on Stage (11am–12pm), and Star Tours (12pm–1pm).

1. If desired, sign the kids ages 4–12 up for Jedi Training Academy. If you're not signing up kids, you may be able to ride Toy Story Mania standby with a short wait before meeting the characters. Long waits may develop if you take the time to sign kids up for Jedi Training.

2. Visit Toy Story Characters: 9:05am–9:15am.

3. Visit Sofia the First/Jake the Pirate in Animation Courtyard: 9:20am–9:45am.

4. Meet characters at the Sorcerer's Hat: 9:45am–10:10am.

5. See Voyage of the Little Mermaid: 10:15am–10:40am.

6. Ride Toy Story Mania with FastPass+: 10:45am–11:05am.

7. See Disney Jr. Live on Stage with FastPass+: 11:10am – 11:45am

8. Have lunch. ABC Commissary, Starring Rolls, and Min & Bill's Dockside Diner are nearby.

9. Ride Star Tours with FastPass+ or visit Honey I Shrunk the Kids Movie Adventure: 11:15am–11:30am.

10. Ride Star Tours with FastPass+: 12:45pm – 1pm

11. Visit a FastPass+ kiosk and schedule Great Movie Ride for later in the day. Ride when applicable.

Afternoon Plan

Same as the "Afternoon and Evening Plan", above.

LATE-ARRIVAL TOURING WITH FASTPASS+

Use FastPass+ at Toy Story Mania or Rock 'n' Roller Coaster, and for two of the attractions from Tier 2 that you would like to experience. Most people will want to select Tower of Terror and Star Tours.

Visit the anytime attractions in the afternoon when crowds are heaviest, prioritizing the shows that run on a set schedule and Studio Backlot Tour, which often closes early due to darkness. Visit characters in the last 60–90 minutes they're scheduled to appear. End the evening with Fantasmic!, or visit Rock 'n' Roller Coaster, Tower of Terror, and Toy Story Mania (in that order) in the final hour when waits are shorter. Disney will allow guests to enter the line and ride any operating attraction right up until official park close, regardless of posted wait time. Posted wait times are usually exaggerated at the end of the night. Ask a Cast Member at the entrance for the actual expected wait time. Hollywood Boulevard shops operate for an hour after official park close, and Disney will have plenty of buses waiting.

EVENING ENTERTAINMENT: FANTASMIC!

Hollywood Studios' nighttime spectacular Fantasmic! is now scheduled at least once almost every night. During busier times, a second show is often scheduled 90 minutes after the start of the first, and the most crowded days of the year can see three shows. Shows can start as early as 6:30pm or as late as 10:30 pm. If two shows are scheduled, the second will always be less crowded, especially if that show begins at 9pm or later, due to the number of families that will opt for the earlier show. If you're headed to the first or only Fantasmic!, plan to arrive 45–75 minutes early to secure good seats together. For the second show, an arrival 15–30 minutes early should suffice. Seating is bleacher-style, uncomfortable, and without backs. The best seats are at least half way up in the middle section. Any closer and you risk getting wet and won't be able to see everything. The Fantasmic Dining Package, a fixed-price meal at Hollywood Brown Derby, Hollywood & Vine, or Mama Melrose, guarantees a seat for the show and a three-course meal. Reserved seats are now in the middle section. Arrive at least 20 minutes early. There is no reserved section with FastPass+ and users will find seats in the standby section. The only time FastPass+ is beneficial is if the standby section is filling to capacity and only FastPass+ users are guaranteed admittance.

TYPICAL HOLLYWOOD STUDIOS WAIT TIMES IN MINUTES

Low Crowds, 7pm Close

	9:30am	10am	11am	12pm	1pm	2pm	3pm	4pm	5pm	6pm	7pm
Backlot Tour	5	5	5	10	10	10	10	5	5	5	5
Great Movie Ride	5	10	10	10	10	10	10	10	10	5	5
Muppet Vision 3D	5	5	5	5	5	5	5	5	5	5	5
Rock 'n' Roller Coaster	20	20	20	25	30	35	30	30	20	20	20
Star Tours	5	10	10	10	10	10	10	10	10	5	5
Tower of Terror	10	20	30	30	30	40	30	30	30	30	20
Toy Story Mania	30	40	40	50	50	50	50	40	40	30	30
Voyage of the Little Mermaid	10	10	10	10	10	10	10	10	10	10	10

Moderate Crowds, 9pm Close

	9:30am	10am	11am	12pm	1pm	2pm	3pm	4pm	5pm	6pm	7pm	8pm	9pm
Backlot Tour	5	10	15	15	15	15	15	15	10	10	10	n/a	n/a
Great Movie Ride	10	15	20	20	20	20	20	20	15	10	10	10	5
Muppet Vision 3D	5	5	5	5	5	5	5	5	5	5	5	5	5
Rock 'n' Roller Coaster	30	40	50	60	60	60	60	50	40	40	30	20	20
Star Tours	5	10	20	20	20	20	20	20	20	20	10	5	5
Tower of Terror	20	40	50	60	60	60	60	60	50	45	40	30	20
Toy Story Mania	50	60	70	70	70	70	70	70	70	60	50	45	30
Voyage of the Little Mermaid	10	10	10	10	10	10	10	10	10	10	10	10	10

Heavy Crowds, 9pm Close

	9:30am	10am	11am	12pm	1pm	2pm	3pm	4pm	5pm	6pm	7pm	8pm	9pm
Backlot Tour	5	15	20	20	20	20	20	20	20	20	10	n/a	n/a
Great Movie Ride	10	20	30	40	40	40	30	30	25	20	15	10	5
Muppet Vision 3D	5	5	5	5	5	5	5	5	5	5	5	5	5
Rock 'n' Roller Coaster	40	70	80	90	90	90	100	90	80	70	60	40	30
Star Tours	10	20	40	40	50	50	50	50	40	40	30	20	20
Tower of Terror	30	60	70	90	90	90	80	70	60	60	60	40	30
Toy Story Mania	50	70	90	120	120	100	100	90	90	80	70	60	50
Voyage of the Little Mermaid	10	10	20	20	20	20	20	20	20	20	10	10	10

Magic Kingdom Cheat Sheet

PARK MAP

TOURING AT MAGIC KINGDOM

GENERAL TOURING PHILOSOPHY With 60+ attractions, Magic Kingdom is best toured over two or more days. The best plans compartmentalize the park by visiting two or three lands each day. Visit the character and attraction priorities in one land before moving on to the next. Have lunch and then continue in the same lands visiting the "anytime attractions". This minimizes both waiting and walking. One-day touring will require more walking and more choices. You can still accomplish a lot in one day by touring intelligently, but some attractions will need to be skipped.

CHARACTERS Unlike the other three parks, there are characters that (because of fast-building long lines) need to be prioritized ahead of even the priority attractions. If you'd like to visit Anna and Elsa, Enchanted Tales with Belle, Merida, Tinker Bell, or Rapunzel, you need to visit first thing in the morning, in the last hour they're scheduled to appear, or use FastPass+ (where applicable) to avoid 30–75 minute waits.

ROPE DROP Magic Kingdom ordinarily opens its gates 75 minutes before official park open. Guests are held just inside the entrance in the courtyard in front of the train station. The opening show, which features Mickey and the gang arriving via steam train, begins 10–15 minutes prior to park open and lasts about six minutes. At the conclusion of the show, the park is opened. The best viewing area for the show is front and center, but this puts you at a disadvantage entering the park as everyone off to the sides will enter before you. To minimize morning waits, instead make your way to the far left or right of the courtyard in front of one of the entrances and watch the opening show from there..

FASTPASS+ AT THE MAGIC KINGDOM

There are far more FastPass+ opportunities at Magic Kingdom than at any of the other theme parks, making the decision on which to pick difficult. Visitors who know they want to avoid characters meets or the more thrilling rides have an easier set of choices. Otherwise, consider picking three high-priority attractions in a land that you don't plan to visit until the afternoon or evening. For example, if you plan to start your day meeting Tinker Bell and riding Aladdin's Magical Carpets, Jungle Cruise, Big Thunder Mountain, and Splash Mountain, then you may want to use FastPass+ in the afternoon in Fantasyland at Enchanted Tales with Belle, Anna and Elsa, and the Mine Train, or in Tomorrowland at Space Mountain, Tomorrowland Speedway, and Buzz Lightyear.

FastPass+ Priority

1. Anna and Elsa at Princess Fairytale Hall
2. Enchanted Tales with Belle
3. Seven Dwarfs Mine Train
4. Peter Pan's Flight
5. Main Street Electrical Parade (prioritize first/only parade only; second parade on the same night sees light crowds)
6. Space Mountain
7. Splash Mountain (when high temperatures are 80+ degrees)

8. Rapunzel at Princess Fairytale Hall

9. Big Thunder Mountain Railroad

10. Ariel at Ariel's Grotto

11. Tinker Bell at Town Square Theater

12. Buzz Lightyear's Space Ranger Spin

13. Tomorrowland Speedway

14. Haunted Mansion

15. Mickey at Town Square Theater

16. Jungle Cruise

17. Splash Mountain (when high temperatures are less than 80 degrees)

18. Pirates of the Caribbean

19. Barnstormer

20. The Many Adventures of Winnie the Pooh

21. Under the Sea Journey of the Little Mermaid

22. Wishes

23. Disney Festival of Fantasy Parade

24. Dumbo the Flying Elephant

25. it's a small world

26. Magic Carpets of Aladdin

27. Mad Tea Party

28. Monsters Inc. Laugh Floor

29. Mickey's PhilharMagic

TWO DAY TOURING PLAN

Two-Day Plan, Morning Day 1

Use FastPass+ at Mine Train (12pm-1pm), Enchanted Tales with Belle (1pm-2pm), Anna and Elsa at Fairytale Hall or an alternate (2pm–3pm).

1. Ride Space Mountain: 9am–9:20am.

2. Ride Buzz Lightyear's Space Ranger Spin: 9:25am–9:35am.

3. Ride Astro Orbiter: 9:37am–9:55am.

4. Ride Tomorrowland Speedway (if desired): 10am–10:20am.

5. Ride The Many Adventures of Winnie the Pooh: 10:25am–10:40am.

6. Ride Dumbo: 10:45am–11am.

7. Ride The Barnstormer: 11:03am–11:15am.

8. Ride Journey of the Little Mermaid: 11:20am–11:40am.

9. Have lunch. If available, use FastPass+ (not a charge against your three-attraction FastPass+) at Be Our Guest Restaurant. Otherwise, Pinocchio Village Haus is closest. Cosmic Ray's is relatively close.

10. Ride Seven Dwarfs Mine Train with FastPass+: 12:45pm–1pm.

11. Visit Enchanted Tales with Belle with FastPass+: 1pm–1:30pm.

12. See Mickey's PhilharMagic and/or Prince Regal Royal Carrousel: 1:35pm–2pm.

13. Visit Anna and Elsa at Princess Fairytale Hall with FastPass+: 2pm–3pm.

Two Day Plan, Afternoon and Evening Day 1

Consider an afternoon break or visit the anytime attractions in Fantasyland and Tomorrowland like Mickey's PhilharMagic, Prince Regal Carrousel, Monsters Inc. Laugh Floor, Tomorrowland PeopleMover, Carousel of Progress, and Stitch's Great Escape. Plan to see the evening entertainment (see the end of this Cheat Sheet) tonight or the evening of your second day.

Two-Day Plan, Morning Day 2

Use FastPass+ at Peter Pan's Flight (10am-11am), Jungle Cruise (11am-12pm), and a third attraction.

1. Ride Big Thunder Mountain Railroad: 9:10am–9:20am. Ride again if desired.

2. Ride Splash Mountain: 9:23am–9:45am (won't get too wet but can return later w/ FP+).

3. Ride Haunted Mansion: 9:55am–10:15am.

4. Ride it's a small world: 10:17am–10:40am.

5. Ride Peter Pan's Flight with FastPass+: 10:42am–10:55am.

6. Ride Jungle Cruise with FastPass+: 11:05am–11:25am.

7. Ride Aladdin's Magical Carpets: 11:30am–11:45am.

8. Ride Pirates of the Caribbean: 11:50am–12:15pm or in the late evening, if waits are already long.

9. Have lunch. Tortuga Tavern and Pecos Bill are closest. Columbia Harbour House, Liberty Tree Tavern, and Casey's Corner are relatively close.

Two Day Plan, Afternoon and Evening Day 2

Consider an afternoon break or visit the anytime attractions like Tom Sawyer Island, Hall of Presidents, Liberty Square Riverboat, Country Bear Jamboree, Enchanted Tiki Room, and Swiss Family Treehouse.

CHARACTER-CENTRIC TWO DAY TOURING PLAN

Two Day Character-Centric Plan, Morning Day 1

Use FastPass+ at Seven Dwarfs Mine Train (11:30am–12.:30pm) Enchanted Tales with Belle (12:30pm–1:30pm), Anna and Elsa at Fairytale Hall (1:30pm–2:30pm). Meet Rapunzel and Cinderella at Princess Fairytale Hall: 9am–9:15am.

1. Ride Peter Pan's Flight: 9:18am–9:30am.
2. Meet Ariel at Ariel's Grotto: 9:35am–9:50am.
3. Ride Journey of the Little Mermaid: 9:52am–10:05am.
4. Meet Gaston outside Gaston's Tavern in New Fantasyland: 10:07am–10:15am.
5. Meet Daisy and Minnie at Pete's Silly Sideshow: 10:20am–10:30am.
6. Meet Donald and Goofy at Pete's Silly Sideshow: 10:31am–10:40am.
7. Ride The Barnstormer: 10:42am–10:55am.
8. Ride Dumbo the Flying Elephant: 11am–11:15am.
9. Ride The Many Adventures of Winnie the Pooh: 11:20am–11:40am.
10. Ride Seven Dwarfs Mine Train with FastPass+: 11:42am–11:55am.
11. Have lunch. Pinocchio Village Haus is closest. Cosmic Ray's is nearby. Use FastPass+ at Be Our Guest Restaurant, if possible.
12. Experience Enchanted Tales with Belle with FastPass+: 12:50pm–1:20pm.
13. Meet Anna and Elsa in Princess Fairytale Hall with FastPass+: 1:30pm–1:45pm.

Two Day Character-Centric Plan, Afternoon and Evening Day 1

Consider an afternoon break or visit the anytime attractions in Fantasyland and Tomorrowland like Mickey's PhilharMagic, Prince Regal Carrousel, Monsters Inc. Laugh Floor, Tomorrowland PeopleMover, Carousel of Progress, and Stitch's Great Escape. Plan to see the evening entertainment (see the end of this Cheat Sheet) tonight or the evening of your second day.

Two Day Character-Centric Plan, Morning Day 2

Use FastPass+ at Buzz Lightyear (12:15pm–1:15pm), Space Mountain (1:15pm–2:15pm), and Town Square Mickey Meet (either on the way out or after a break).

1. Meet Tinker Bell in Town Square Theater or Merida in Fairytale Garden: 9am–9:25am.

2. Meet Aladdin and Jasmine at Agrabah Bazaar: 9:30am–9:45am.

3. Ride Jungle Cruise: 9:50am–10:15am.

4. Ride Big Thunder Mountain Railroad: 10:25am–10:45am.

5. Ride Splash Mountain: 10:47am–11:15am.

6. Meet Chip and Dale in Liberty Square across from Diamond Horseshoe: 11:20am–11:35am.

7. Ride Pirates of the Caribbean: 11:40am–12pm.

8. Have lunch. Pecos Bill and Tortuga Tavern are closest. Columbia Harbour House and Liberty Tree Tavern are nearby.

9. Ride Buzz Lightyear's Space Ranger Spin with FastPass+: 1pm–1:15pm.

10. Meet Buzz Lightyear at the exit to Space Ranger Spin: 1:17pm–1:40pm.

11. Ride Space Mountain with FastPass+: 1:45pm–2:05pm.

12. Meet Stitch in Tomorrowland near Space Mountain: 2:10pm–2:30pm.

13. See Festival of Fantasy Parade in Frontierland or Liberty Square: 3pm–3:20pm.

Two Day Character-Centric Plan, Afternoon and Evening Day 2:

Consider an afternoon break or visit the anytime attractions like Tom Sawyer Island, Hall of Presidents, Liberty Square Riverboat, Country Bear Jamboree, Enchanted Tiki Room, and Swiss Family Treehouse. Visit it's a small world, Haunted Mansion, and any other skipped attractions as late in the evening as possible. Check *Times Guide* for missed characters (Tiana and Prince Naveen, in particular) and visit them in the last hour they're scheduled to appear.

ONE DAY TOURING PLAN

One Day Plan, Morning and Afternoon:

Use FastPass+ at Buzz Lightyear (12pm–1pm), Space Mountain (1pm–2pm), and Tomorrowland Speedway (2pm–3pm).

1. Ride Seven Dwarfs Mine: 9am–9:10am.
2. Ride The Many Adventures of Winnie the Pooh: 9:12am–9:20am.
3. Ride Peter Pan's Flight: 9:25am–9:40am.
4. Ride Big Thunder Mountain Railroad: 9:55am–10:15am.
5. Ride Splash Mountain 10:17am–10:40am.
6. Ride Jungle Cruise: 10:50am–11:15am.
7. Ride Pirates of the Caribbean: 11:20am–11:40am.
8. Have lunch. Pecos Bill is closest. Tortuga Tavern and Columbia Harbour House are nearby.
9. Ride Buzz Lightyear's Space Ranger Spin with FastPass+: 12:55pm–1:10pm.
10. Ride Space Mountain with FastPass+: 1:15pm–1:35pm.
11. Ride PeopleMover: 1:40pm–2pm.
12. Ride Tomorrowland Speedway with FastPass+ or see Monsters Inc Laugh Floor: 2:05pm–:20pm.
13. Grab snacks and see Disney Festival of Fantasy Parade from Frontierland: 2:30pm–3:15pm.
14. See Enchanted Tiki Room: 3:25pm–3:45pm.
15. Walk Swiss Family Robinson Treehouse: 3:50pm–4:10pm.
16. See Country Bear Jamboree: 4:15pm–4:35pm.
17. See Mickey's PhilharMagic: 4:45pm–5:05pm.
18. Ride Prince Regal Royal Carrousel: 5:07pm–5:20pm.
19. Have dinner. Pinocchio Village Haus is closest. Be Our Guest Restaurant would be perfect if you've snagged reservations. Cosmic Ray's is relatively close.
20. Ride it's a small world: 6:30pm–6:50pm.
21. Ride Haunted Mansion: 6:53pm–7:20pm.

One Day Plan, Evening

Your evening depends greatly on how late the park is open, if and when Wishes and the Electrical Parade are scheduled, and how long you want to stay. If only one parade is scheduled and you want to see it, visit attractions marked "anytime" on the map until about 30 minutes before the parade, find a spot near Main Street, and then move closer to the Castle for Celebrate the Magic and Wishes. If two parades are scheduled, and you have the stamina, start with Celebrate the Magic and Wishes, and then see the much less crowded second parade. Return to the priority attractions, particularly in Fantasyland, in the final hour.

LATE ARRIVAL

LATE ARRIVAL AND NIGHTTIME CROWDS Most nights after Wishes crowds diminish as the worn-out and families with small children leave early. The later it gets, the lower wait times will be, particularly if close is 11pm or later. Use FastPass+ when you arrive when wait times are longest. Visit the light gray "anytime" attractions until two to three hours before close. Then move on to the medium gray attractions like Buzz Lightyear and Big Thunder Mountain and finish the night with the highest priority attractions like Peter Pan's Flight, Mine Train, and Space Mountain.

EVENING ENTERTAINMENT AND EXIT

MAIN STREET ELECTRICAL PARADE The Electrical Parade is scheduled between three and seven nights per week, usually between 7pm and 11pm. It typically begins on Main Street and exits to the left of Splash Mountain. The best viewing locations are near Pecos Bill and outside Hall of Presidents in Liberty Square. Two parades are often scheduled the same night, with the second beginning two hours after the first. If this is the case, see the later parade as it will be far less crowded. Arrive 20–30 minutes early if there's one parade, or 10–15 minutes early for the second parade. The parade FastPass+ viewing location is in the Hub in front of the Castle. It's a great location and you won't need to be as concerned with people arriving late and pushing their way in front of you.

CELEBRATE THE MAGIC AND WISHES The Castle projection show Celebrate the Magic, which is a don't-miss, usually begins 15 minutes before Wishes. Position yourself on Main Street just in front of Casey's Corner for the best view of the show, which is almost immediately followed by Wishes fireworks. Arrive 30 minutes before Wishes is scheduled to start. The Wishes FastPass+ viewing area is in the Rose Garden in front of the Castle on the right. It's a decent spot, but trees block the area and it's off-center. Wishes is easy enough to see that FastPass+ isn't necessary.

INSTEAD OF THE NIGHTTIME ENTERTAINMENT The Electrical Parade and Wishes pull a ton of people away from the attractions. It's a great opportunity to visit Tomorrowland and Fantasyland.

EXIT As usual, you can enter the queue for any operating attraction up until the official close. Consider getting in line for Mine Train, Peter Pan's Flight, Space Mountain, or another attraction with a few minutes until close. Main Street stores will remain open for about an hour after park close. This is the best time to shop. Linger a bit while others exit in front of you. The Express Monorail is the fastest way to the Transportation and Ticket Center (parking lot) unless the line is significantly backed up. The ferry is often a more comfortable ride with more room to spread out, particularly up the stairs on the second level.

TYPICAL MAGIC KINGDOM WAIT TIMES IN MINUTES

Low Crowds, 8pm Close

	9:30am	10am	11am	12pm	1pm	2pm	3pm	4pm	5pm	6pm	7pm	8pm
Ariel's Grotto	10	20	30	30	30	30	30	25	25	20	15	15
Astro Orbiter	10	15	20	20	20	20	20	15	15	15	10	10
Barnstormer	5	5	10	20	20	20	15	15	10	10	10	10
Big Thunder Mountain	10	20	25	25	30	30	30	20	15	15	10	10
Buzz Lightyear Spin	5	10	15	20	20	20	20	15	15	15	10	10
Dumbo	10	15	20	20	20	20	15	15	15	15	15	10
Enchanted Tales w/ Belle	20	30	40	40	30	30	30	30	30	30	20	20
Haunted Mansion	5	10	15	15	20	20	15	15	15	15	10	5
it's a small world	5	10	15	15	15	15	15	15	15	10	10	5
Jungle Cruise	10	15	20	25	30	20	20	20	15	15	10	10
Mad Tea Party	5	5	5	10	10	10	10	10	10	5	5	5
Magic Carpets of Aladdin	5	10	10	15	20	15	15	15	15	10	10	5
Many Adventures of Pooh	10	15	15	20	25	20	20	20	20	15	15	10
Monster's Inc Laugh Floor	10	10	10	10	10	10	10	10	10	10	10	10
Peter Pan's Flight	15	20	25	35	45	45	45	30	25	25	20	15
Pirates of the Caribbean	5	10	10	15	15	15	10	10	10	10	5	5
Prince Regal Carrousel	5	5	5	5	5	5	5	5	5	5	5	5
Princess Fairytale Anna/Elsa*	120	150	180	180	180	120	120	120	120	120	120	n/a
Princess F. Cinderella/Rapunzel	15	20	30	35	35	35	30	30	30	25	20	20
Seven Dwarfs Mine Train*	40	60	60	75	80	70	60	50	40	40	40	30
Space Mountain	10	15	20	25	30	25	20	20	20	20	15	10
Splash Mountain (Hot)	10	10	20	25	30	25	25	20	20	20	10	10
Splash Mountain (Cold)	5	5	10	10	15	15	10	10	10	5	5	5
Stitch's Great Escape	5	5	5	5	5	5	5	5	5	5	5	5
Swiss Family Treehouse	0	0	0	0	0	0	0	0	0	0	0	0
Tomorrowland Speedway	5	15	20	20	20	20	20	20	20	20	15	10
Tomorrowland PeopleMover	0	0	0	0	0	0	0	0	0	0	0	0
Town Square Mickey	10	20	25	25	30	25	20	20	20	20	15	10
Under the Sea	20	20	20	30	30	30	20	20	20	20	20	20

*Projected

Moderate Crowds, 10pm Close

	9:30am	10am	11am	12pm	1pm	2pm	3pm	4pm	5pm	6pm	7pm	8pm	9pm	10pm
Ariel's Grotto	10	20	40	50	50	50	50	40	40	30	25	20	20	10
Astro Orbiter	10	15	20	20	20	20	20	20	20	20	20	20	20	15
Barnstormer	5	10	15	25	35	35	30	30	25	25	20	20	15	10
Big Thunder Mountain	10	20	30	45	45	50	50	40	40	35	30	25	20	15
Buzz Lightyear Spin	5	15	25	35	40	40	40	35	35	30	30	30	20	15
Dumbo	10	15	15	25	30	30	30	30	25	25	25	20	15	15
Enchanted Tales w/ Belle	30	40	50	50	50	40	40	40	40	40	30	30	20	20
Haunted Mansion	5	10	20	25	30	30	30	30	25	25	20	15	15	10
It's a small world	5	10	20	25	30	30	30	25	25	25	20	15	10	10
Jungle Cruise	10	20	35	45	45	40	40	40	30	30	30	25	20	15
Mad Tea Party	5	5	10	15	15	10	10	10	10	10	10	10	10	5
Magic Carpets of Aladdin	5	15	15	20	20	20	20	20	20	15	15	15	10	5
Many Adventures of Pooh	10	15	20	25	30	30	30	30	25	20	20	20	15	10
Monster's Inc Laugh Floor	10	10	10	10	10	10	10	10	10	10	10	10	10	10
Peter Pan's Flight	20	30	40	50	60	60	60	50	50	50	45	30	20	20
Pirates of the Caribbean	5	10	15	25	30	30	30	25	25	20	15	10	10	5
Prince Regal Carrousel	5	5	5	5	5	5	5	5	5	5	5	5	5	5
Princess Fairytale Anna/Elsa*	120	180	240	240	240	180	180	180	120	120	120	120	120	n/a
Princess F. Cinderella/Rapunzel	25	40	50	60	60	60	60	60	50	50	40	30	20	15
Seven Dwarfs Mine Train*	60	70	80	80	80	80	70	60	50	50	40	40	40	30
Space Mountain	15	25	40	50	60	60	60	60	50	45	45	40	30	20
Splash Mountain (Hot)	10	15	30	50	60	60	60	50	50	40	30	30	20	15
Splash Mountain (Cold)	5	10	15	20	20	20	20	20	15	15	15	15	10	10
Stitch's Great Escape	5	5	5	5	5	5	5	5	5	5	5	5	5	5
Swiss Family Treehouse	0	0	0	0	0	0	0	0	0	0	0	0	0	0
Tomorrowland Speedway	10	20	30	30	30	30	30	30	30	20	20	20	15	10
Tomorrowland PeopleMover	0	0	0	5	5	5	5	5	5	5	5	5	0	0
Town Square Mickey	15	30	40	40	40	40	40	35	30	30	25	25	15	10
Under the Sea	20	20	30	30	40	40	30	30	30	30	20	20	20	20

*Projected

Heavy Crowds, 12MN Close

	9:30am	10am	11am	12pm	1pm	2pm	3pm	4pm	5pm	6pm	7pm	8pm	9pm	10pm	11pm	12am
Ariel's Grotto	15	30	50	60	70	70	60	60	50	40	40	30	30	20	10	10
Astro Orbiter	10	20	20	30	30	30	30	30	30	25	25	25	25	20	10	10
Barnstormer	10	15	25	35	50	50	40	40	40	40	35	25	20	15	10	10
Big Thunder Mountain	15	20	40	60	60	60	60	60	50	45	45	35	30	25	20	15
Buzz Lightyear Spin	10	20	40	50	60	60	60	55	50	45	40	40	35	30	30	30
Dumbo	10	25	30	45	50	60	60	50	50	50	35	30	30	20	15	15
Enchanted Tales w/ Belle	30	50	60	70	70	70	60	60	50	50	40	40	30	30	20	20
Haunted Mansion	5	15	30	45	50	50	50	40	40	30	30	25	20	15	10	5
it's a small world	5	15	30	45	50	50	50	40	40	35	30	30	20	15	10	10
Jungle Cruise	10	20	40	50	60	60	60	50	50	45	40	40	30	20	20	15
Mad Tea Party	5	10	10	15	15	15	15	15	15	15	15	15	10	5	5	5
Magic Carpets of Aladdin	5	15	20	25	25	25	25	25	20	20	15	15	15	15	10	10
Many Adventures of Pooh	10	15	30	40	40	40	40	35	35	30	20	20	20	20	15	10
Monster's Inc Laugh Floor	10	10	10	20	20	20	20	20	20	20	20	10	10	10	10	10
Peter Pan's Flight	20	45	60	70	80	80	70	70	60	60	50	50	40	30	30	20
Pirates of the Caribbean	5	10	25	45	50	50	50	45	45	40	40	30	25	20	10	5
Prince Regal Carrousel	5	5	5	10	10	10	10	10	10	10	10	5	5	5	5	5
Princess Fairytale Anna/Elsa*	180	180	240	240	240	240	240	240	180	180	180	180	120	120	120	n/a
Princess F. Cinderella/Rapunzel	25	45	60	75	75	75	70	70	60	60	50	40	35	30	20	15
Seven Dwarfs Mine Train*	60	90	120	120	120	90	90	90	80	80	70	70	70	60	50	40
Space Mountain	15	40	60	75	90	90	80	80	80	70	70	60	50	45	40	20
Splash Mountain (Hot)	15	25	50	70	80	90	90	90	70	60	60	50	50	30	30	20
Splash Mountain (Cold)	10	15	25	25	25	30	30	30	25	20	20	15	15	15	10	10
Stitch's Great Escape	5	5	5	10	10	10	10	10	10	10	10	10	5	5	5	5
Swiss Family Treehouse	0	0	0	5	5	5	5	5	5	5	5	5	0	0	0	0
Tomorrowland Speedway	10	20	30	40	40	40	40	40	30	30	30	20	20	20	10	10
Tomorrowland PeopleMover	0	0	5	5	10	10	10	0	10	10	10	5	5	0	0	0
Town Square Mickey	20	40	50	50	60	60	60	50	50	40	30	30	25	20	15	10
Under the Sea	20	30	40	40	50	50	40	40	40	30	30	30	20	20	20	20

*Projected

9am - 7pm Party Night

	9:30am	10am	11am	12pm	1pm	2pm	3pm	4pm	5pm	6pm	7pm
Ariel's Grotto	10	20	30	30	30	30	30	25	25	20	15
Astro Orbiter	10	15	20	20	20	20	20	15	15	15	10
Barnstormer	5	5	10	20	20	20	15	15	10	10	10
Big Thunder Mountain	10	20	25	25	30	30	30	20	15	10	10
Buzz Lightyear Spin	5	10	15	20	20	20	20	15	10	10	10
Dumbo	10	15	15	20	20	20	15	15	15	15	10
Enchanted Tales w/ Belle	20	30	40	40	30	30	30	30	30	20	20
Haunted Mansion	5	10	15	15	20	20	15	15	10	10	5
it's a small world	5	10	15	15	15	15	15	15	15	10	5
Jungle Cruise	10	15	15	25	30	20	20	20	15	10	10
Mad Tea Party	5	5	5	10	10	10	10	10	5	5	5
Magic Carpets of Aladdin	5	10	10	15	20	15	15	10	10	10	5
Many Adventures of Pooh	10	15	15	20	25	20	20	20	15	15	10
Monster's Inc Laugh Floor	10	10	10	10	10	10	10	10	10	10	10
Peter Pan's Flight	15	20	25	35	45	45	45	30	20	20	15
Pirates of the Caribbean	5	10	10	15	15	15	10	10	10	10	5
Prince Regal Carrousel	5	5	5	5	5	5	5	5	5	5	5
Princess Fairytale Anna/Elsa*	120	120	180	180	120	120	120	120	120	120	n/a
Princess F. Cinderella/Rapunzel	15	20	30	35	35	35	30	30	25	25	20
Seven Dwarfs Mine Train*	30	50	60	60	60	50	40	40	40	30	30
Space Mountain	10	15	20	25	30	25	20	20	15	15	10
Splash Mountain (Hot)	10	10	20	25	30	25	25	20	15	15	10
Splash Mountain (Cold)	5	5	10	10	15	15	10	10	5	5	5
Stitch's Great Escape	5	5	5	5	5	5	5	5	5	5	5
Swiss Family Treehouse	0	0	0	0	0	0	0	0	0	0	0
Tomorrowland Speedway	5	15	20	20	20	20	20	20	20	15	10
Tomorrowland PeopleMover	0	0	0	0	0	0	0	0	0	0	0
Town Square Mickey	10	20	25	25	30	25	20	20	15	15	10
Under the Sea	20	20	20	30	30	30	20	20	20	20	20

*Projected

Where to Eat

First-time family visitors to Walt Disney World need to know three things about dining:

1. Several dining venues are among the most memorable and delightful experiences Walt Disney Word has to offer. Options range from dining in the banquet hall inside Cinderella Castle with the Disney Princesses to sharing sushi and filet mignon on the 15th floor of the Contemporary to joining Mickey and the Gang for lunch in an exotic African marketplace.

2. Table service reservations open 180 days in advance, and availability at the most sought-after restaurants is gobbled up almost immediately. A list of the hardest restaurants to reserve follows later.

3. Disney World dining is expensive. Expect to pay 25–40% more on-property than you would for comparable meals off-property, whether we're talking about a fast food hamburger at Pecos Bill's or a 28-ounce Porterhouse at Yachtsman Steakhouse. In effect, most of the upcharge is a convenience fee, but the Disney restaurants offer a reliably consistent experience, many times in unique settings.

The rest of this chapter:

- Offers suggestions on where to eat
- Explains how to reserve meals at Disney World—and why starting to do so 180 days before your visit is crucial
- Introduces and compares the various Disney Dining Plans
- Shares some thoughts on saving money

The chapter ends with overviews of dining at the parks and brief reviews of all the Disney World table service dining options.

Where to Eat at Walt Disney World

Service, food quality, and atmosphere vary immensely among the Disney World restaurants, even those inside the same park with similar price points. The information and reviews that follow will help identify restaurants that are the perfect fit for your group's budget and preferences. Disney World dining locations come in several shapes and sizes:

QUICK OR COUNTER SERVICE Basically a fancy name for fast food, quick service locations don't accept reservations and food is usually ordered at a register and then available for pickup several minutes later. Quick service is usually cheaper and faster than table service. Menus, food quality, and atmosphere vary wildly among the various options, making your choices more important than you might expect.

TABLE SERVICE These venues are typical restaurant experiences, where a host will seat your party and a server will take your order and deliver the food to the table. Most require reservations, particularly for dinner. Prices range from $12 sandwiches at The Plaza Restaurant in Magic Kingdom to $135+ for a seven-course meal at Victoria & Albert's. Buffets are generally lumped into this category, even when guests typically serve themselves.

DINNER SHOWS Spirit of Aloha at the Polynesian and Hoop-Dee-Doo Revue at Fort Wilderness offer all-you-care-to-enjoy family-style dining accompanied by two-hour shows. Mickey's Backyard Barbecue, also located at Ft. Wilderness, is an all-you-care-to-enjoy buffet amidst fun line dancing and live music.

FAVORITE FAMILY DINING

In addition to the food, the most fun and best-loved family dining contains some or all of the following:

- A fun setting
- Some kind of show and/or interactive play-along elements
- Visits by Disney characters like Mickey, Tigger, or the Disney Princesses.

On almost every family's list of the best among these are:

- The Hoop-Dee-Doo Musical Revue, a silly, energetic dinner show with interactive elements and plenty of audience participation at Disney's Fort Wilderness Resort.

- The Princess meals: Cinderella's Royal Table in the Magic Kingdom and Akershus Royal Banquet Hall in Epcot. The first has the better setting, the second is much less expensive.
- Dining with Tigger, Pooh, and friends at the Crystal Palace in the Magic Kingdom.
- Dining with Mickey and friends at Chef Mickey's at Disney's Contemporary Resort and 'Ohana breakfast at Disney's Polynesian Resort.
- Dining in the Beast's Castle at Be Our Guest Restaurant in the Magic Kingdom.
- Various degrees of wait-staff induced silliness at 50's Prime Time Café in Disney's Hollywood Studios and Whispering Canyon at Disney's Wilderness Lodge.
- Exotic settings in the local versions of national chain restaurants like the Rainforest Café, in both Disney's Animal Kingdom and Downtown Disney, and T-Rex in Downtown Disney.

SELECTING CHARACTER MEALS

Character meals are table service meals or dinner shows where the group has the opportunity to interact and take pictures with the characters during the dining experience. There are several benefits to these meals. First, they replace the lengthy waits to meet the characters inside the theme parks. At Magic Kingdom, meeting Mickey, Minnie, Goofy, Donald, and Pluto might take 90 or more minutes standing in line, often outdoors and unprotected from the heat and rain. At Chef Mickey's, you can enjoy your ice cream sundae while they all come to you. In addition, several characters don't ordinarily meet outside of character meals, including Piglet, Beast, and Prince Charming.

When deciding on a character meal, first identify which characters you'd like to meet. Then narrow down the potential choices by cost, setting, and convenience via the reviews that follow.

Character meal options include:

Animal Kingdom:

- Tusker House (breakfast and lunch only): Mickey, Donald, Daisy, Goofy in safari gear.

Epcot:

- Garden Grill (dinner only): Mickey, Pluto, Chip, Dale in farming apparel.

- Akershus Royal Banquet Hall: Belle, in her yellow gown, joins diners for a picture before they're seated. Ariel, Aurora, Jasmine, and Snow White usually greet tableside.

Hollywood Studios:

- Hollywood & Vine (breakfast and lunch only): Sofia, Doc McStuffins, Jake, Handy Manny.

Magic Kingdom:

- Be Our Guest Restaurant (dinner only): While not a "character meal" per se, guests have the opportunity to meet and take pictures with Beast after the meal.
- Cinderella's Royal Table: Pictures with Cinderella before the meal, with Ariel, Aurora, Jasmine, and Snow White usually meeting tableside.
- Crystal Palace: Pooh, Tigger, Eeyore, and Piglet.

Resorts:

- 1900 Park Fare Breakfast at Grand Floridian: Mary Poppins, Alice, the Mad Hatter, Tigger, and Winnie the Pooh.
- 1900 Park Fare Dinner at Grand Floridian: Cinderella and Prince Charming, Lady Tremaine, Anastasia, Drizella, and the Fairy Godmother.
- Cape May Café at Beach Club Resort (breakfast only): Goofy, Minnie, and Donald in ridiculous beach outfits.
- Chef Mickey's at Contemporary Resort: Mickey, Chip, Dale, and Goofy in culinary outfits.
- 'Ohana (breakfast only): Mickey, Pluto, Lilo, Stitch in Hawaiian outfits.
- Mickey's Backyard Barbecue at Fort Wilderness: Mickey, Minnie, and "friends"—typically Goofy, Chip, and Dale, in cowboy outfits.
- Goofy and friends will meet select days for breakfast at the Four Seasons after its late summer 2014 open.

For the princesses, we prefer Cinderella's Royal Table, which is also the only opportunity to see inside the beautiful castle. Absurdly expensive? Yes, but it's a special experience that can't be duplicated elsewhere.

For Mickey, we like Garden Grill at Epcot, and Tusker House lunch at Animal Kingdom. Both are conveniently located inside the theme parks, making them easy to access while you're visiting those parks. For Mickey at the resorts, Chef Mickey's is a family favorite, as is breakfast at 'Ohana.

DINING FOR COUPLES

For couples looking for the most romantic atmosphere and the best food, we suggest:

- **California Grill**: Located on the 15th floor of the Contemporary Resort, California Grill offers breathtaking views of Magic Kingdom during the evening fireworks, in addition to a great menu focused on fresh ingredients, sushi, and contemporary cocktails.
- **Artist Point**: Nestled inside Wilderness Lodge, this romantic rendezvous is themed to the restaurants found in the great National Park lodges of the west. Buffalo, salmon, and a terrific mushroom soup and berry cobbler are menu mainstays.
- **Victoria & Albert's**: For a truly special occasion; astonishing dining.

WHAT ABOUT EARLY BREAKFAST AT THE PARKS?

Tusker House at Animal Kingdom, Akershus at Epcot, Hollywood & Vine at Hollywood Studios, and Cinderella's Royal Table and Crystal Palace at Magic Kingdom all routinely open at 8am for breakfast, which is often a full hour before the rest of the park. Many people recommend these 8am breakfasts because they afford an opportunity to get pictures in the park "when nobody else is around". Unfortunately, and particularly at Magic Kingdom and Hollywood Studios, this is not usually the case because hundreds of other people have the same idea. 8am reservations are also awfully early and awfully expensive. Transportation from the resorts is also dodgier and less consistent so early. With the parks routinely opening at 15 minutes prior to the officially stated time, an 8am reservation either means rushing through the meal and hoping the characters arrive in time for a hasty exit, or wasting precious morning touring time eating. Instead, we recommend a late breakfast or early lunch, which allows you to sleep in an extra hour and hit the priority attractions when crowds are lowest before taking a restful, air-conditioned break with the characters.

RECOMMENDED DINING

Families using the 9-day itineraries introduced in Chapter 6 will find recommended dining at the top of each day in the graphic of the itinerary. The associated To-Do Lists for these itineraries have instructions on when and how to book the reservable table service meals, in addition to walking you through each step of the planning process. Each of the park "Cheat Sheets" in the previous chapter has recommended counter-service options.

Our recommendations are not set in stone. Families with much younger kids may wish to cut some of the non-character meals and replace them with character meals. Families with teens might want to do the opposite. Substitutions can be based on the graphic below—which ranks the Disney World theme park and resort table service options based on kid and adult appeal—or on the capsule reviews that follow at the end of this chapter.

In the graphic, high adult appeal is based on "date night" criteria: a restaurant having fine dining, fine service, and a lovely setting. High kid appeal means that a restaurant has the elements that make the rest of Disney World a joy for kids—playful action, characters, and a fun setting—and also has a menu suited to picky eaters. By these criteria, it's hard for a restaurant to appeal to both. Be Our Guest in the Magic Kingdom comes closest, and if it had a better kids menu for picky eaters, would be ranked with high appeal for both groups.

Because kids and adults vary, it's best to use the chart and the reviews at the end of this chapter together.

Guide to Disney World Dining

Bold=Character Meal   Underline=Require 2 Dining Plan Credits   (paren)=which meal, if ratings differ
Italic= Resort Casual dress code   CAPS=Location (see key below)

KID APPEAL:		Adult Appeal: Low	Medium	High
	High	Chef Mickey's C, 50's Prime Time Café S	Akershus E, Beaches & Cream BC, Biergarten E, <u>Cinderella's Royal Table</u> MK, **The Crystal Palace** MK, <u>Hoop-Dee-Doo Revue</u> FW, **Mickey's Backyard Barbecue** FW, 'Ohana P (b), Rainforest Cafe AK DTD, San Angel Inn E, Sci-Fi Dine in Theater S, **Tusker House** AK {b, l} Whispering Canyon Cafe WL	
	Medium	Hollywood and Vine* S	Cape May Café BC {b}, Cape May Cafe BC {d} Coral Reef E, ESPN Club BW, **Garden Grille** E, La Hacienda de San Angel E, Liberty Tree Tavern MK, Mama Melrose's S, Nine Dragons E, 1900 Park Fare GF {b, d}, 'Ohana P (d), Olivia's OKW, Plaza MK, Restaurant Marrakesh E, Rose & Crown E, Sanaa KAKL, Tony's Town Square MK, Turf Club SS, Tusker House AK {d}, Tutto Italia E, Via Napoli E, Yak and Yeti AK	Be Our Guest MK {d}, *California Grill* C, Boma AKL, Hollywood Brown Derby S, <u>Le Collier</u> E, Teppan Edo E,
	Low	<u>Spirit of Aloha Polynesian Luau</u> P	Big River Grille BW, Captain's Grille YC, Grand Floridian Café GF, Kona Café P, Kouzzina BW, Les Chefs de France E, Spice Road Table E	*Artist Point* WL, <u>Monsieur Paul's</u> E, *Citricos* GF, *Flying Fish Café* BW, *Jiko* AKL, *Narcoossee's* GF, Queen Victoria's Room** GF, Tokyo Dining E, Victoria and Albert** GF, The Wave C, <u>Yachtsman Steakhouse</u> YC,
		Low	Medium	High

Locations: AK=Animal Kingdom; AKL=Animal Kingdom Lodge; BC=Beach Club; BW=BoardWalk; C=Contemporary; DTD=Downtown Disney E=Epcot; FW=Fort Wilderness; GF=Grand Floridian; KAKL=Kidani Village at AKL; MK=Magic Kingdom; OKW=Old Key West; S= Hollywood Studios; SS=Saratoga Springs; WL=Wilderness Lodge; YC=Yacht Club

*Though a character meal, low kid appeal except for fans of Playhouse Disney--for them the appeal is off the charts
**Not on dining plan; jacket required; no kids under 10

Advance Dining Reservations

Make Advance Dining Reservations (ADRs) beginning 180 days before your first planned table service meal.

The best Disney World dining options have limited capacity and are wildly popular. Because of this, these restaurants can be filled almost as soon as reservations open for them—180 days before the dining date.

One topic that surprises first-time visitors is the importance and fun of dining experiences. Because quality and price vary so much between restaurants in the same vicinity, researching your options and booking the best restaurants far in advance puts you in the best possible position to have a fun, stress-free vacation. Identify your table service dining favorites as soon as possible and then make your ADRs as soon as reservations open.

Note that ADRs are not "reservations" in the traditional sense. With the exception of Victoria & Albert's and the dinner shows, the restaurant does not actually reserve a table. Instead, your party will receive the next available table that opens up. This can lead to the occasional long wait, particularly at the popular buffets that are often overbooked. To help mitigate this, book a meal right after the restaurant starts service or near the end of service when empty tables are more common.

MAKING YOUR RESERVATIONS

Reservations currently open 180 days before the date of dining—online at 6 a.m. and over the phone at 7 a.m. Moreover, if you are staying at a Disney World hotel, once 180 days from your hotel arrival date rolls around, you can make ADRs for not just that day, but also for the first ten days of your visit. You'll sometimes see this referred to as 180+10. Input your arrival date into HTTP://PSCALCULATOR.NET/PSCALC.PHP to identify the first day you can make reservations. As an example, let's say you're visiting from December 1–8 and staying on property at Art of Animation. According to the calculator, the first day you can make reservations is June 4. Not only could you make reservations for December 1, the first day of our hypothetical vacation, but you can also make reservations for up to ten additional days because you're staying at a Disney-owned resort. Off-site guests visiting on the same dates would also be able to make their reservations for December 1 on June 4, but they would need to call or go online again on June 5 to book December 2, June 6 to book December 3, and so forth.

Most table service reservations require prospective diners to put a credit card on file. A $10 per person fee will be assessed if the group does not show up within 15 minutes of the reservation time. To avoid this fee, cancel the reservation no later than the day before. Same-day cancellations will be charged the no-show fee. Note that only one person needs to show up regardless of how many people are on the reservation. So if you have a reservation for six and only three show up, your party will not be assessed any fees. If weather, transportation delays, or something else cause you to miss your reservation, visit Guest Services and explain your case. Disney will likely waive the charge for good stories.

The hardest reservations to get, and which you should book as soon as you can, are:

- Be Our Guest Restaurant [Magic Kingdom]
- Cinderella's Royal Table [Magic Kingdom]
- Chef Mickey's [Contemporary Resort]
- 'Ohana [Polynesian Resort]
- Akershus Royal Banquet Hall [Epcot]
- 1900 Park Fare Dinner [Grand Floridian Resort]
- California Grill [Contemporary Resort]
- Crystal Palace [Magic Kingdom]
- T-Rex [Downtown Disney]

Typically, over 40 restaurants will have same-day reservations available at some point during the day. It's always best to secure reservations via 407-WDW-Dine, DISNEYWORLD.COM, the My Disney Experience mobile app, or in person at Guest Services or the restaurant itself. It's not uncommon for a restaurant to entirely turn guests away without reservations, particularly at peak dinner times. Make reservations as soon as you know where you want to eat.

The Disney Dining Plan

Disney World dining is expensive. For some guests, it may even be the priciest component of the vacation, eclipsing the cost of lodging and theme park tickets. The three versions of the Disney Dining Plan (Quick Service, Regular, and Deluxe) are a way to prepay some of these dining expenses.

Years ago, when the Regular Dining Plan included appetizer and tip at sit-down restaurants, you could actually save some money by using these plans. These days it's hard for us to recommend them:

- The Quick Service Dining Plan is priced so high that it's only possible to break even or come out ahead if you use the credits solely for lunch and dinner. From there, you'll need to order only the most expensive items to eke out a potential savings of a dollar or two per day.

- At a cost north of $64 per adult per day, the Regular Dining Plan is expensive and saving money with it requires planning only the most expensive meals.
- The Deluxe Dining Plan comes with three quick or table service meals per day at a cost of more than $115 per day per adult. Users either spend three or more hours per day eating table service meals or use their credits on faster quick service meals, in turn reducing the value of each credit.

With only a couple of exceptions, we suggest skipping the dining plans. Exceptions include:

- If you take comfort in pre-paying some of your dining expenses as a budgeting tool (even if this means you spend more money), the Quick Service or Regular plans may make sense for you—the cash loss may be worth the budget comfort. It's nice knowing that food is pre-paid and users are free to order whatever entrees and desserts that they like, even if those prices are higher than they're accustomed to paying. As an alternative, consider loading a Disney gift card with the amount of money you plan to pay for meals.
- Pricing on the Regular Plan is advantageous for groups with kids under the age of ten that plan multiple buffets and character meals. The cost of a child buffet at many character meals exceeds their cost of the Regular Dining Plan for that day.

With or without a dining plan, the typical family eating their meals on property should budget $35-$60+ per adult per day for dining, and somewhere between $15 and $40/day for the kids—depending on their ages and appetites.

DINING PLAN CREDITS AND WHAT THEY COVER

The Dining Plans are only available to guests staying at Disney owned and operated resorts. All guests on a single reservation (except children under three—not covered on any plan) must opt for the same Dining Plan if you elect to purchase it. There's no such thing as having four people on a room reservation and only three people on the Deluxe Plan. And it isn't possible for one person to purchase Deluxe, while the other chooses Regular. Everyone over the age of nine must pay the adult rate, regardless of how much they plan to eat. And kids three to nine must order from the Kids' Menu if the dining location has one.

Those on the Dining Plan receive a number of credits based on the number of nights they're staying. The Dining Plan and credits are not connected to theme park tickets or anything else—just the number of nights on the reservation. The credits are usable as soon as the guest checks in through midnight on the checkout day. Credits can be used in any order on any of these days. On a three-night stay, a guest could conceivably use all their credits on the first day, the last day, or space them out.

Quick service meals generally consist of one entrée or combo meal, one dessert, and one non-alcoholic beverage. Virtually every quick service on property participates in the Dining Plan, and all quick service meals cost one credit.

Table service meals, including one entrée, one dessert, and one non-alcoholic beverage, cost one or two credits. Two credit meals are signature experiences at the most expensive dinner shows, buffets, and restaurants like Hoop-Dee-Doo Revue, Cinderella's Royal Table, and California Grill. The Deluxe Dining Plan credits also include an appetizer, in addition to the entrée, dessert, and non-alcoholic beverage. Snack credits can be used on most food items under $5.49. Examples include ice cream bars, pastries, and bottles of water and soda.

The credits don't always cover everything you might want at a meal and no credits cover alcohol (except beer and wine at the dinner shows) or tips. Most guests have some additional dining expenses, in addition to the cost of the Dining Plan.

THE QUICK SERVICE DINING PLAN

The Quick Service Dining Plan includes per person, per night:

- Two quick service meals
- One snack

In addition, each guest receives a refillable mug for use at their resort's quick service, and, if available, pools.

So a family of four staying for five nights would receive ten quick service meals, five snacks, and a refillable mug each. At press time, after-tax pricing is:

- $44.72 per night for those ten and older
- $17.07 per night for kids ages three to nine

Adult quick service entrees are typically $8–$11 in the theme parks. Add a $3 fountain beverage and a $4 carrot cake and your average meal comes to around $17. Eat two of those, in addition to a $4 Mickey Ice Cream Bar, and add about $2.50 for a day's worth of the refillable mug, and you've come out just about even. Kids' Picks generally come in around $7 each. Eat two and add a $3 popsicle and the use of the refillable mug, and you've covered the day's cost.

While technically possible to eke out a savings of a dollar or two per day, those savings evaporate whenever you eat breakfast, when prices are usually lower and dessert isn't included, or whenever someone is forced to order something they ordinarily wouldn't. It also makes it difficult to schedule a table service meal or character buffet since they aren't included on the Plan. You can pay cash for such meals, but if doing so pushes you to using a credit for breakfast—or worse, ending your vacation with unused credits—the Quick Service plan will cost you money.

THE "REGULAR" DINING PLAN

The "Regular" Dining Plan—often known simply as the Disney Dining Plan—includes per person, per night:

- One quick service meal
- One table service meal
- One snack

In addition, each guest receives a refillable mug for the duration of the stay. At press time, after-tax pricing is:

- $64.58 per night for those ten and older
- $20.48 per night for kids ages three to nine

Child pricing is advantageous with a cost just $3.50 more than the Quick Service Plan. With several character buffets priced over $20, it's relatively easy for kids to come out ten dollars or more ahead each day they dine at such a venue. For those older than 9, the price of $20/per day more than the Quick Service is harder to justify. There are meals where you do well—Akershus for dinner, after tax, is around $50. A day for family members older than 9 with a typical counter service lunch, a snack, and Akershus for dinner will cost less under the Dining Plan than cash. Dinner at Crystal Palace approaches this cost, as does Chef Mickey's.

Outside of buffets, it's difficult to find restaurants with average entrée and dessert prices high enough to cover the cost of the Plan. Let's assume you're spending the day at Hollywood Studios and select 50's Prime Time Café for dinner. You select the second most expensive entrée, the $22 pork chop, in addition to the most expensive dessert (Traditional Warm Apple Crisp a la Mode for $7.49) and order a $5 milkshake as your beverage. With tax, the meal comes out to $36.75. That puts you $27.83 away from covering the cost of the Dining Plan with just a quick service meal and snack to go. At our recommended Studios' quick service, Studio Catering Co., the most expensive quick service meal you could put together is $19 with tax. Add a $4 Mickey Ice Cream Bar as a snack and you're still $5 away from covering the cost of the Dining Plan after already ordering the most expensive items.

The economics of two-credit meals are even worse. Signature restaurant prices generally are about 1.5x the cost of regular restaurants, but cost twice the number of credits, resulting in a lower per-credit value. For example, the most expensive meal you could put together on the Dining Plan at California Grill is a $49 Bone-In Veal Chop, $13 Pudding Cake, and $4 Coke. That's $66, or just $33 per credit for the most expensive meal at one of the most expensive restaurants on property. To compare, Teppan Edo in the Japan Pavilion at Epcot offers several entrees for $28–$32. Add dessert and a drink and your single credit has a value of about $10 more than California Grill.

THE DELUXE DINING PLAN

The Deluxe Dining Plan includes per person, per day:

- Three meals per day—either quick service or table service. Table service meals include an appetizer where applicable.
- Two snacks

In addition, each guest receives a refillable mug for the duration of the stay. At press time, after-tax pricing is:

- $116.65 per night for adults
- $31.19 per night for kids ages three to nine

On paper, there is a lot of value potential here, particularly for kids under the age of ten. To maximize that value, however, you could be spending more than three hours a day dining—even more if you avoid two-credit meals—and building an itinerary largely around being at specific restaurants at specific times. And let's not forget the actual cost. A family of two adults, a 15-year old, and a 7-year old would cost a whopping $380 per day. For that, Josh and Dave will cook and serve your family of four both lunch and dinner, while intermittently breaking out into song and dance. (A word to the wise though: Josh's specialty is Hot Pockets and Dave's favorite ingredient is Sriracha.)

Saving Money on Dining

Purchasing ingredients and preparing meals where you're staying is the easiest way to slash a food budget. This works best for quick breakfasts in the room. Pack or purchase a dozen bagels or donuts, fruit, cereal and milk, and some protein bars and you can easily eliminate busy breakfasts at the resort food court, in addition to cutting meal time down to a few minutes from 30+.

Unfortunately, Disney doesn't make purchasing these items economical at its resort gift shops, for reasons you might be able to guess. Other than Fort Wilderness and the Disney Vacation Club properties, pickings can be slim and prices are high. On top of that, only Ft. Wilderness cabins and the villas in the DVC resorts have kitchens, making even simple prep work difficult in most situations. If you have a car and the time to shop, we recommend the Hess stores on property for convenience. One is located across the street from the BoardWalk Inn near Epcot, another after the exit to Magic Kingdom parking, and the third is across the street from the Marketplace section of Downtown Disney. For a better selection, visit the Winn-Dixie (and nearby liquor store) at 1957 S Apopka Vineland Rd, in Orlando, or the Publix (and nearby liquor store) at 2925 International Drive, in Kissimmee. The nearest to your hotel will be about a 10–15 minute drive.

Without transportation or the wherewithal to venture out to a supermarket on vacation, consider a grocery delivery service. We like GARDENGROCER.COM and WEGOSHOP.COM. Garden Grocer is the most popular, but you're limited to what you can order based on their web store. We Go Shop will visit whatever area store you specify for whatever specific products you want, but the delivery fee is higher. Both deliver beer and wine.

Dining Reviews: Introduction

Brief reviews of the table service restaurants in the parks, Downtown Disney, and the Disney resorts follow.

First, you'll find reviews of the restaurants inside each theme park, in alphabetical order. Next, you'll find an alphabetized list of the resorts, with reviews of all restaurants located at that resort.

We start with the venue name and location within its area, indicating also whether a meal is a character meal or a dinner show. We then note cuisine, operating hours, and whether or not it is on the Disney Dining Plan (abbreviated as DDP)—note that some DDP meals require two credits and are so indicated. Next we give typical prices and any available discounts for Disney Vacation Club point owners ("DVC"), those who have purchased Tables in Wonderland discount cards* ("TiW"), Annual Passholders ("AP"), and holders of Disney Visa cards ("DV"). We then get into the food and ambiance of the restaurants themselves. This material is necessarily brief—for more, see Josh's EASYWDW.COM. Prices, menus, hours, required credits, discounts etc., are all subject to change.

We also throw some Disney jargon around:

- Signature Restaurant: two credit venues usually aimed at adults—that is, thin on kid appeal, but with finer and more elegant dining. Most have a mild dress code, e.g., on men, pants are preferred, nice shorts are OK, but no tank tops.
- Family Style: food for the entire table is served on platters and shared amongst the table.
- Walk-up: trying to get a seating without having a reservation.

Note also that some venues will require full pre-payment—at press time, Hoop-Dee-Doo, Spirit of Aloha, Mickey's Backyard Barbecue, and Cinderella's Royal Table—and most others will require a credit card so that a no-show fee can be charged. To avoid no-show fees, cancel no later than 11:59pm on the day before the reservation.

*Only Annual Pass holders, DVC owners, and Florida residents are eligible to buy the Tables in Wonderland card. Visit TABLESINWONDERLAND. COM for more information on availability and blackout dates.

Dining Reviews: The Theme Parks and Downtown Disney

DINING AT DISNEY'S ANIMAL KINGDOM

Disney's Animal Kingdom offers a nice variety of consistently high-quality restaurants and quick services, and we like each for different reasons. The Rainforest Café at the front of the park is much less crowded than the Downtown Disney iteration, and offers the same fun atmosphere fueled by Animatronics and a vast menu. Theme park admission is not required to dine there. Tusker House in Africa is a low-key character meal featuring Donald and Mickey for breakfast and lunch. The expansive buffet area makes sampling the 30+ items easy, and the characters have more time to spend with guests than at the more crowded resort meals. Yak & Yeti serves up fantastic Pan-Asian food in a restaurant full of authentic artifacts from India, China, and elsewhere.

Quick service options at Animal Kingdom are above average as well. Pizzafari serves up standard Disney pizza in a colorful, air-conditioned space. Pizza is serviceable, but expect to pay about $10 each for a personal pan. Restaurantosaurus in DinoLand USA is your burger and nugget option. You'll find plenty of air-conditioned seating, in addition to outdoor patio tables. Better is Yak & Yeti Local Food Cafes, which serves up Asian specialties like Beef Lo Mein and Honey Chicken. Unfortunately, all seating is outdoors, and it can be uncomfortably hot and wet in the summer. Best is Flame Tree Barbecue, where you'll find Disney's best quick service ribs, pork sandwiches, and half chickens. Even the Smoked Chicken Salad is one of the best on property. While seating is outdoors, it's better covered with fans overhead. Walk all the way down to the water for expansive views of Asia and Expedition Everest.

Rainforest Café

Front of park; theme park admission not required to dine

CUISINE American. **HOURS** 8:30am–park close. **DDP** Yes. **DISCOUNTS** No TiW; DVC: 10% on entrees; AP: 10%.

PRICES Breakfast: $10–$14. Lunch/Dinner Appetizers: $7–$19. Entrées: $13–$26. Kids: $6–$7.

OVERVIEW Part of a chain of 25+ restaurants sprinkled around the world, Rainforest Cafe blends an immersive environment with a laundry list of a menu. Dine on steaks, pastas, salads, burgers, or one of 50+ other items, all while Animatronic gorillas pound their chests, birds sing, and thunder booms from the starry night-time sky. The food is unlikely to impress, but it's all serviceable and portions are huge. The restaurant is extremely loud and the atmosphere may startle young children apprehensive about rides like DINOSAUR and Haunted Mansion, although older children love the atmosphere. Because it's located at the front of the park, plan to eat when you're near the entrance/exit.

Tusker House

Character meal (breakfast and lunch, only), in Africa

CUISINE African-inspired. **DDP** Yes. **DISCOUNTS** 20% TiW.

HOURS AND PRICES *Breakfast* (8am–10:55am): $26–$30 adults, $15–$17 kids. *Lunch* (11am–3:30pm): $29–$32 adults, $16–$18 kids. *Dinner* (4:30pm–15 minutes before park close; no characters): $28–$33 adults, $15–$17 kids. *Pricing may vary depending on the season.*

OVERVIEW Donald, Daisy, Mickey, and Goofy greet guests tableside for breakfast and lunch inside this vibrant African marketplace. Some of the 30+ items at each meal retain touches of African flair and spice, but Disney is careful to cater to the typical American palate. Character interaction is among the best, with the characters leading parades around the restaurant and playing games with guests. No characters for dinner, but the restaurant offers high quality food in a relaxed environment. Schedule a meal right before close and enjoy exiting with virtually nobody else around.

Yak & Yeti

Asia, between Flights of Wonder and Kali River Rapids

CUISINE Asian. **HOURS** 11am–park close. **DDP** Yes. **DISCOUNTS** No TiW; DVC: 10%; AP: 10%.

PRICES Lunch/Dinner Appetizers: $5–$16. Entrées: $17–$26. Kids: $8–$10.

OVERVIEW Located in Asia, this air-conditioned respite is appropriately themed to a rural countryside sanctuary set in the heart of the Himalayan Mountains. The menu is reminiscent of P.F. Chang's and features such favorites as Lettuce Wraps, Crispy Honey Chicken, and Sweet-and-Sour Pork, in addition to Shaoxing Steak & Shrimp and a Kobe Beef Burger. Portions are large and service is friendly as guests dine amongst hundreds of authentic artifacts from all over Asia. Request a window table upstairs for a great view.

DINING AT EPCOT

Epcot offers an overwhelming number of dining options, predominantly located in World Showcase with national cuisines tied into the respective pavilions. You could very easily visit Epcot every day for a month and dine in a different venue each day. We present reviews of all the table service options below, but our recommended restaurants are Biergarten in Germany, Via Napoli in Italy, Akershus Banquet Hall in Norway, and San Angel Inn in Mexico.

Biergarten is a richly themed buffet restaurant with a cornucopia of authentic German items like beer cheese soup, sauerbraten, spaetzle, veal sausage, mini frankfurters, and a whole lot more. A live oompah band plays intermittently with guests invited up to the dance floor to sing and dance along.

Via Napoli is an authentic Neapolitan pizzeria serving the best pizza (by far) on property. A large mezzo-metro pizza is plenty to feed a family of four for about $11 per person, making it a great value. Stay conservative with a signature pepperoni pie or try something like the Prosciutto e Melone Signature Pie (fontina, mozzarella, prosciutto, and cantaloupe).

Akershus is the part-buffet, part-table service character meal in Norway. While pricey, it's significantly less expensive than Cinderella's Royal Table at the Magic Kingdom, and the price includes a picture with Belle in her yellow gown, along with four other princesses meeting tableside. The cold buffet guarantees everyone will have plenty to eat, and the entrees are varied and above average as well.

At San Angel Inn, guests dine underneath perpetual twilight as the boats from the Gran Fiesta Tour next door glide by. Food quality is a bit lower than at our other three picks, but the unique atmosphere can't be replicated elsewhere.

Quick service options at Epcot are even more abundant.

Of the Future World options, Sunshine Seasons near Soarin' in the Land Pavilion receives nearly universal acclaim. Serving freshly grilled pork chops, rotisserie chicken, salmon, salads, sandwiches, Asian entrees, and more, with plentiful air-conditioned seating, it's a great choice for a convenient Future World lunch. Electric Umbrella is your Future World spot for the usual Disney hamburgers and chicken nuggets, in addition to a great vegetarian flatbread.

In World Showcase, you may pick a quick service based on the mood—or location—of the group at the time. We both highly recommend Tangierine Café in Morocco. While the menu of shawarma, falafel, kefta, and tabouleh might initially seem exotic, the typical Mediterranean flavors are more familiar than you might expect. Food is also higher quality and portions are larger than at just about any other quick service. Josh likes the U.K.'s Fish and Chips, particularly when a table overlooking the lagoon is available. Liberty Inn in the U.S. serves a surprisingly good New York Strip Steak for less than $11, in addition to the excellent Southwest Chicken Salad. With plenty of air-conditioned and outdoor seating, the only thing keeping it from being highly recommended is the fact that it's all American, and it seems like World Showcase should be an opportunity to try something a little different. Dave wishes that Liberty Inn would shift to an all-barbecue theme, highlighting all the different U.S. barbecue variants and their regional fixin's. Sommerfest in Germany is quite good, but the seating section consists of only a handful of tables, and there's rarely anywhere comfortable to sit.

We don't care much for La Cantina de San Angel in Mexico or Lotus Blossom Café in China. La Cantina is expensive and serves lower quality food than just about any other Mexican restaurant, for more money. Panda Express serves better food than Lotus Blossom. Katsura Grill in Japan doesn't live up to its potential, but the udon and chicken cutlet curry are quite good and the outdoor garden seating area is among the most peaceful you'll find. The sushi largely disappoints. Boulangerie Patisserie in France offers some unique quiche, sandwich, and salad fare, but the ordering process is confusing and the seating section is small, loud, and often chaotic.

Overall, visiting Tangierine Café or Sunshine Seasons for lunch and one of our recommended table service restaurants for dinner is your best bet. But most guests are satisfied no matter where they choose to dine.

Akershus Royal Banquet Hall

Princess character meal, in Norway

CUISINE Norwegian/American. **DDP** Yes. **DISCOUNTS** 20% TiW.

HOURS AND PRICES *Breakfast* (8am–11:10am): $42 adults, $24 kids. *Lunch* (11:45am–3:30pm): $43 adults, $25 kids. *Dinner* (4:55pm–park close): $49 adults, $26 kids.

OVERVIEW Themed to a 14th century Scandinavian castle, Akershus is Epcot's much less expensive version of Cinderella's Royal Table. A picture with Belle is included in the price, and four other princesses meet tableside—usually Ariel, Aurora, Cinderella, and Snow White. For breakfast, guests are brought platters of hot breakfast foods like scrambled eggs, potato casserole, sausage, and bacon. Lunch and dinner feature a set menu of Norwegian and American favorites like Norwegian Meatballs with Lingonberry Sauce, Salmon, and Chicken Breast. All meals include unlimited access to the cold bar, which includes bread, salads, sliced meats, cheeses, fish, and a variety of other chilled foods, including traditional Scandinavian items. Kids' meals include pizza, salmon, pasta, and meatballs. Breakfast is the most consistent and least expensive meal.

Biergarten

Germany

CUISINE German. **HOURS** 12pm–park close. **DDP** Yes. **DISCOUNTS** 20% TiW.

PRICES Lunch: $26-$30 adults, $14-16, kids. Dinner: $37–$41 adults, $18–$20 kids.

OVERVIEW Be transported to a quaint Bavarian village in the heart of Oktoberfest at this German buffet that features live oompah music throughout the day. Selections include bratwurst, rotisserie chicken, pork schnitzel, and a variety of seasonal salads. Dessert includes Apple Strudel and Black Forest Cake. The selection and food quality are both outstanding. Service is genuinely friendly and the music is a lot of fun. Tables seat eight and smaller parties will be seated with others. There is no dedicated buffet section for kids, though most will be happy loading up on macaroni and cheese, chicken, pretzel rolls, and dessert. The liters of beer are the best price on property.

Coral Reef

To the right of The Seas with Nemo and Friends

CUISINE American. **HOURS** 11:30am–park close. **DDP** Yes. **DISCOUNTS** 20% TiW.

PRICES Lunch/Dinner Appetizers: $7–$17. Entrées: $19–$33. Kids: $9–$11.

OVERVIEW More than 4,000 creatures, including sharks, rays, and turtles, join diners seated in front of the 5.7 million gallon aquarium glass here at Coral Reef. Food is average table service quality and the menu skews towards fish and beef with the salmon and trout standing out as excellent. Kids love the aquarium view and their menu features fried shrimp, steak, cheesy shells, and a burger. Request a lower-level aquarium view at check-in. Note that Coral Reef typically receives the worst reviews of any Epcot restaurant.

Garden Grill

Character meal, upper floor of the Land Pavilion

CUISINE American. **HOURS** 4pm–8pm. **DDP** Yes. **DISCOUNTS** 20% TiW. **PRICES** Dinner: $38 adults, $20 kids.

OVERVIEW Join Chip, Dale, Mickey, and Pluto at this fun restaurant featuring views of the Living with the Land ride below. Dinner is served family-style and includes filet of beef, turkey breast, sustainable fish of the day, vegetables, mashed potatoes, and non-alcoholic beverages (alcohol is available for an additional cost). Kids receive chicken drumsticks, macaroni-and-cheese, broccoli, and sweet potato fries. Dessert is cupcakes for the kids, and bread pudding and a baked pie for adults. Food is quite good, and this is one of the more laid-back character meals, with excellent character interaction.

La Hacienda de San Angel

Mexico, outside on the water

CUISINE Mexican. **HOURS** 4pm–park close. **DDP** Yes. **DISCOUNTS** No TiW. 10% DVC.

PRICES Dinner Appetizers: $7–$13. Entrées: $24–$27. Kids: $8–$10.

OVERVIEW This restaurant on the Lagoon features floor-to-ceiling windows with the potential for grand views of World Showcase Lagoon. The limited menu (five individual entrée choices averaging $26) skews away from typical Tex-Mex and towards grilled and marinated meats and seafood. Parties of two or more should stick to one of the two combination skillets for $49 each, which are plenty of food for up to three people to share. Kids' meals include cheese quesadillas, steak or chicken tacos, and grilled chicken. Food quality and service range from below average to average. The atmosphere at the nearby San Angel Inn is more charming.

Le Cellier Steakhouse

Canada (look for the walkway down to the O Canada! show)

CUISINE Steak and fish, mostly. **HOURS** 12pm–park close. **DDP** 2 Credits. **DISCOUNTS** 20% TiW.

PRICES Lunch/Dinner Appetizers: $10–$17. Entrées: $27–$64. Kids: $8–$15.

OVERVIEW Now a two-credit signature meal on the Dining Plan, this dark, wine-cellar-themed restaurant that focuses on Canadian beef is an expensive proposition. Sirloin steak starts at $40 and the Bone-In Rib-Eye is well over $60. While cozy, tables are virtually on top of each other, creating a less-than-intimate atmosphere. Food quality is high and service is typically above average, but it's hard to justify these prices. On the plus side, the $10 cheese soup is excellent, the complimentary pretzel bread is out of this world, and the Unibroue beer on draft is world-class. Kids, who are unlikely to be enthralled by the restaurant, can get in on the action with a grilled sirloin steak, seared salmon, and a kids' portion of the cheese soup.

Les Chefs de France

France, ground level

CUISINE French. **HOURS** 12pm–park close. **DDP** Yes. **DISCOUNTS** 20% TiW; 15% DVC lunch only.

PRICES Lunch/Dinner Appetizers: $7–$15. Lunch Entrées: $15–$30. Dinner Entrées: $19–$35. Kids: $8–$10.

OVERVIEW This family-friendly Parisian café provides a casual atmosphere for guests to sample French cuisine like Quiche Lorraine, Casserole of Burgundian Escargots, and Duck Breast and Leg Confit. Steaks, roasted chicken, and broiled salmon are also available. The charming French service is perhaps a bit too authentic at times, but meals at this busy brasserie are a lot of fun. The three-course lunch for under $30 is an excellent value. The kids' menu may be limiting, with just Chicken Strips, Ground Beef Steak on a Brioche Bun, and Grilled Fish typically available.

Monsieur Paul

France, above Les Chefs de France

CUISINE French. **HOURS** 5:30pm–park close. **DDP** 2 credits. **DISCOUNTS** 20% TiW.

PRICES Dinner Appetizers: $14-$29. Entrées: $38–$43. Kids: $13.

OVERVIEW This upscale gourmet French restaurant replaced Bistro de Paris above Les Chefs de France in December 2012. Couples looking for the most intimate experience inside Epcot should look no further, but the formal atmosphere is not particularly kid friendly. In fact, the restaurant only recently introduced a kids' menu that includes just roasted chicken breast or filet mignon served with mashed potatoes. The very French staff may struggle to communicate in English, but they are among the most attentive property wide. Food impresses in quality and presentation and is not much more expensive than the pricier entrees downstairs.

Nine Dragons

China

CUISINE Chinese. **HOURS** 12pm–park close. **DDP** Yes. **DISCOUNTS** 20% TiW; 10% AP Lunch Monday-Friday only; 20% DVC.

PRICES Lunch/Dinner Appetizers: $4–$12. Entrées: $13–$27. Kids: $8–$10.

OVERVIEW Featuring a beautiful glass mural of two dragons chasing a glowing pearl, rosewood wall panels, and Chinese lantern lighting, Nine Dragons is not your typical neighborhood dive. The menu offers familiar favorites like Kung Pao Chicken ($16) and Honey-Sesame Chicken ($17) along with traditional dishes like the Fragrant Five-Spiced Fish ($22). Kids can get in on the action with interesting items like Pot Stickers, Sweet-and-Sour Chicken, and Ginger Ice Cream. Portions are huge and the kitchen consistently executes food that is less expensive than other restaurants. Service is friendly but tends to be abrupt. While Nine Dragons suffers from a poor reputation, we think it's improved handily in recent memory and don't have any qualms about recommending it, particularly as a last-minute walk-up.

Restaurant Marrakesh

Morocco, in the very back of the pavilion

CUISINE Moroccan/Mediterranean. **HOURS** 11:30am–park close. **DDP** Yes. **DISCOUNTS** 20% TiW; 10% AP Lunch Monday–Friday only; 20% DVC.

PRICES Lunch/Dinner Appetizers: $6–$17. Lunch Entrées $15–$28. Dinner Entrées $21–$45. Kids: $8–$10.

OVERVIEW This hard-to-find restaurant in the back of the Morocco Pavilion is unique and under-rated. Themed to an ornate Moroccan palace, stained-glass chandeliers provide the only light for the visiting band and belly dancer that perform throughout the day. Lunch is a better value with the same entrees as dinner at reduced prices, including a three-course chicken kebab lunch under $20. Kids' entrees may disappoint, offering only chicken tenders, a hamburger, or Moroccan-style Pasta. Consider letting adventuresome kids sample some items from one of the adult feast samplers. Rarely busy, this is the easiest walk-up at Epcot and the easiest reservation to snag same-day.

Rose & Crown Dining Room

United Kingdom

CUISINE British. **HOURS** 12pm–park close. **DDP** Yes. **DISCOUNTS** 20% TiW.

PRICES Lunch/Dinner Appetizers: $6–$12. Entrées: $15–$31. Kids: $9–$11.

OVERVIEW Situated along World Showcase Lagoon, Rose & Crown provides the only guaranteed IllumiNations viewing from a restaurant. Views are best outside on the patio, but guests seated inside the family-friendly pub, heavy on wooden furniture, will be invited outside shortly before the show. Food quality has fallen in recent years as chefs seem to push out a new menu every couple months. Stick with long-standing favorites like Bangers & Mash, Fish & Chips, and Shepherd's Pie. Kids choose from a menu that includes steak and fish & chips.

Rose & Crown Pub

United Kingdom

CUISINE Mostly beer. **HOURS** 12pm–park close. **DDP** No. **DISCOUNTS** 20% TiW.

PRICES Limited food menu with prices ranging from $4–$13.

OVERVIEW Frosted windows protect the privacy of those imbibing inside this cozy pub, which is virtually always hopping. The entrance is separate from the restaurant and reservations are not accepted here. Draft beer includes Bass, Bodington's, Guinness, Stella, and Harp. Scotch flights, mixed drinks like the Pimm's Cup and Welsh Dragon, and wine.

San Angel Inn

Mexico, inside the pyramid

CUISINE Mexican. **HOURS** 11:30am–park close. **DDP** Yes. **DISCOUNTS** 20% TiW; 10% AP Lunch Monday–Friday only; 10% DVC.

PRICES Lunch/Dinner Appetizers: $8–$13. Lunch Entrées: $18–$27. Dinner Entrées: $24–$29. Kids: $9–$10.

OVERVIEW San Angel Inn sits inside the Mesoamerican pyramid, and is themed as a Mexican village square at twilight. The evening theming makes the restaurant dark, to the point where reading the menu is nearly impossible without the help of tabletop candles. Like La Hacienda outside, the limited menu focuses on grilled meats rather than burritos and enchiladas. Unfortunately, tables are so close together that diners a table over might as well be on your reservation, eliminating any sense of intimacy. A good family choice as parents will find the setting romantic, and kids will find it fun. Request a table on the water for a delightful view of the Gran Fiesta Tour boats gliding by below. Kids' menu items include beef or chicken tacos, cheese quesadillas, and grilled chicken or tilapia.

Spice Road Table

Morocco, along the Lagoon

CUISINE Moroccan/Mediterranean. **HOURS** 11am–park close. **DDP** No. **DISCOUNTS** None, but expected to accept TiW in the future.

PRICES Small Plates: $7–$12. Samplers: $16. Kids: $8.

OVERVIEW This water-side eatery is the newest arrival on the Epcot culinary landscape, offering small-plate Mediterranean specialties like lamb sliders, fried calamari, and harissa chicken rolls. Additional emphasis is placed on mixed drinks, Moroccan wine, and Mediterranean beer. Spice Road does not take reservations and walk-ups are nearly always available without a wait. Unfortunately, small plates do not translate to good values here, and two or three $8 plates of bland food in limited quantities are unlikely to satisfy most appetites. Kids can pick from a Beef Slider or Chicken Kebab for $8 each. The view of IllumiNations is mostly blocked by islands and trees. Stop by for drinks and snacks, but crafting a filling meal here will be more expensive than Restaurant Marrakesh in the back of the pavilion.

Teppan Edo

Japan, above Mitsukoshi Department Store

CUISINE Japanese steakhouse. **HOURS** 12pm–park close. **DDP** Yes. **DISCOUNTS** No TiW. 10% AP Lunch Monday–Friday.

PRICES Lunch/Dinner Appetizers: $4–$10. Sushi: $10–$16. Entrées: $18–$32. Kids: $9–$14.

OVERVIEW This Japanese steakhouse seats guests around eight-person hibachi grills in one of six contemporary, windowless dining rooms. Parties with fewer than eight will most likely be seated with other parties. Food is prepared at each grill by Japanese chefs who interact with guests and put on a small show while cooking. Steak, chicken, shrimp, swordfish, vegetables, and other entrees are consistently under-seasoned, but the accompanying dips aid flavor. All meals arrive alongside rice and yakisoba. Kids are usually enamored by the friendly chefs as meals are created before their eyes. Service is sweet and attentive. We would rate this restaurant higher if it weren't so similar to the Benihana chain.

Tokyo Dining

Japan, above Mitsukoshi Department Store

CUISINE Japanese, mostly tempura and sushi. **HOURS** 12pm–park close. **DDP** Yes. **DISCOUNTS** 20% TiW; 10% AP Lunch Monday–Friday; 10% DVC Lunch.

PRICES Lunch/Dinner Appetizers: $3–$12. Individual Sushi: $10–$16. Sushi Samplers: $13–$28. Entrées: $17–$30. Kids: $11–$12.

OVERVIEW Tokyo Dining is a sleek, traditional Japanese restaurant with floor-to-ceiling windows looking out at World Showcase Lagoon on one side. It is much quieter and calmer than sister restaurant Teppan Edo, and, without the hibachi grills, is a more traditional dining experience. The menu focuses on sushi and tempura, with over two dozen selections. Kids enjoy their choice of teriyaki chicken or tempura chicken or shrimp. Service is among the friendliest anywhere. Go for dinner when the menu is the same as lunch.

Tutto Italia

Italy, on the left

CUISINE Italian. **HOURS** 11:30am–park close. **DDP** Yes. **DISCOUNTS** 20% TiW; 10% AP Lunch Monday–Friday only; 15% DVC.

PRICES Lunch/Dinner Appetizers: $9–$30. Lunch Entrées: $17–$30. Dinner Entrées: $23–$30. Kids: $10+.

OVERVIEW Featuring murals of ancient Rome amid shimmering chandeliers, Tutto Italia evokes Old World charm inside this traditional, formal Italian restaurant. Your omnipresent server will cater to your every need as you peruse a menu that's heavy on pasta, prosciutto, and lean protein. Lunch is a much less expensive proposition than dinner, with most sandwiches and entrees under $20. Unlike most restaurants that offer "Kids Complete Meals" for $9–$12, Italia offers only a la carte options with $6 appetizers, $10 entrees (pizza, spaghetti, mozzarella sticks, chicken tenders), and $6 desserts. The venue is not particularly unique, but service is splendid with high-quality food and a keen eye for detail.

Via Napoli

Italy, in the back

CUISINE Pizza (predominantly). **HOURS** 11:30am–park close. **DDP** Yes. **DISCOUNTS** 20% TiW; 10% AP Lunch Monday-Friday; 15% DVC Lunch.

PRICES Lunch/Dinner Appetizers: $8–$26. Salad Entrées: $18–$24. Pasta Entrées: $21–$30. Pizzas: $17–$41. Kids: $10+.

OVERVIEW Themed to a rustic Neapolitan pizzeria, Via Napoli takes its pizza, which is cooked at 900 degrees in one of three wood-fired ovens, very seriously. So seriously that they import their flour and tomatoes from Italy and source water from a secret spring in Pennsylvania that has the same unique properties as water from the homeland. Prices may seem high at first glance, but a $41 specialty mezzo metro pizza is plenty to feed four to five hungry adults, bringing per-person costs lower than most other Disney restaurants. Napoli is loud and service is frequently impersonal, but stick to the big pizzas and you'll leave satisfied for not much more money than quick service.

DINING AT DISNEY'S HOLLYWOOD STUDIOS

Disney's Hollywood Studios runs the food quality gamut more than any of the other theme parks. Our recommendations are Sci-Fi Dine-In Theater and 50's Prime Time Café, both of which offer richly themed atmospheres and relatively inexpensive fare. Dave prefers the comfort food favorites at 50's Prime Time, while Josh gives the nod to Sci-Fi, with its fun mockup of a dine-in theater and inexpensive sandwich and hamburger fare. Much more expensive—and with much finer food—is Hollywood Brown Derby, a signature restaurant (two credits on the Dining Plan) where the servers wear tuxedos and the fancy entrees average $33. Mama Melrose serves relatively inexpensive basic Italian favorites alongside flatbread pizzas that are higher quality than nearby Pizza Planet for only a couple dollars more. Hollywood & Vine is a fun character buffet for breakfast and lunch with kids still at the Disney Junior age, but dinner is too expensive when considering the low quality food and lack of characters.

Quick service fare has improved at the Studios, but is still lacking compared to the other parks. Best are Studio Catering Co. and Starring Rolls, both of which serve above-average sandwich fare. Starring Rolls sandwiches are served cold, while many of Studio Catering Co.'s are freshly pressed and served warm. Sunset Ranch Market offers the widest selection of food, including barbecue, pizza, hamburgers, and turkey legs, but seating is all outside and the multiple storefronts that make up the market necessitate standing in more than one line if you'd like to order different kinds of food.

We're less enthusiastic about most of the other options. Toy Story Pizza Planet serves up standard Disney pizza in a loud atmosphere, but the setting does not resemble Pizza Planet from the movie, making it disappointing for guests expecting more. Backlot Express is your spot for typical Disney burgers and chicken nuggets, in addition to hot dog and sandwich offerings. It's richly themed with a lot of covered outdoor seating, but the food is decidedly below average. Finally, ABC Commissary offers the most air-conditioned seating and a newly improved menu featuring an Asian salad with chicken and a couscous, quinoa, and argula salad with salmon, but the menu remains limited with just six entrée choices. Overall, we recommend Studio Catering Co., Starring Rolls, and Sunset Ranch Market first, with Backlot Express and ABC Commissary as air-conditioned backups for simpler food.

50'S Prime Time Café

Echo Lake, near Hollywood & Vine

CUISINE American comfort food. **HOURS** 11am–park close. **DDP** Yes. **DISCOUNTS** 20% TiW.

PRICES Lunch/Dinner Appetizers: $6–$11. Entrees: $14–$22. Kids: $9.

OVERVIEW This nostalgic throwback to a simpler time features a number of period piece knick-knacks as well as televisions that show clips from various 1950s era shows. Themed to Mom's kitchen, your servers will take up responsibility for raising you right and dole out punishment as required. The kids are sure to get a kick out of your server chastising Dad for wearing his Mickey Ears to the table. A good sense of humor is required to enjoy the fried chicken, pot roast, meatloaf, and Mom's other comfort foods. Fried chicken, the fresh fish, and the chicken pot pie are your best bets. Request a table with a TV.

Hollywood Brown Derby

End of Hollywood Boulevard, on the right

CUISINE Contemporary American fine dining. **HOURS** 11:30am–park close. **DDP** 2 credits. **DISCOUNTS** 20% TiW.

PRICES Lunch/Dinner Appetizers: $9–$16. Entrees: $29–$43. Kids: $6–$14.

OVERVIEW Serving up the best food at Hollywood Studios, this signature restaurant focuses on Filets of Beef and Blue Lump Crab Spring Rolls rather than burgers and chicken nuggets. This replica of the original Brown Derby retains much of the glitz and glamour of the 1930s original, with white linen tablecloths, tuxedo-clad servers, and an exquisite eye for detail. That is, if it weren't for all the guests wearing cargo shorts, WDW t-shirts, and Goofy hats. Kids are unlikely to connect with the restaurant, but they are more than welcome, with a kids' menu that includes hot dogs, fish sticks, grilled black grouper, and penne pasta.

Hollywood & Vine

Character meal (breakfast and lunch, only), at Echo Lake near 50's Prime Time Café

CUISINE American. **DDP** Yes.

HOURS AND PRICES *Breakfast* (8am–10:55am): $30 adults, $17 kids. *Lunch* (11am–2:25pm): $35 adults, $19 kids. *Dinner* (3:30pm–30 minutes before park close, no characters): $40 adults, $21 kids. *Pricing may vary depending on season.*

OVERVIEW Featuring Doc McStuffins, Sofia the First, Jake from *Jake and the Neverland Pirates*, and Handy Manny for Play 'n Dine breakfast and lunch, this character meal is squarely aimed at kids who are invited to join the characters for singing, dancing, and parading throughout the meal. Food is best at breakfast, which includes all the usual suspects like Mickey waffles, bacon, and made-to-order omelets. Lunch and dinner bring specialties like Pastrami Rubbed Porkloin, Beer Braised Boneless Beef Short Ribs, and Lobster & Shrimp Mac n' Cheese that all sound better than they taste. Visit this extremely loud buffet only for breakfast or lunch with kids excited about meeting the characters, as food quality is average at best. The expensive, characterless dinner should be skipped.

Mama Melrose's Ristorante Italiano

Streets of America, across from the exit to Muppet Vision 3D

CUISINE Americanized Italian. **HOURS** 12pm–park close. **DDP** Yes. **DIS-COUNTS** 20% TiW.

PRICES Lunch/Dinner Appetizers: $6–$11. Entrees: $13–$30; Kids: $9.

OVERVIEW Mama Melrose herself (not really) serves up Americanized Italian food in this backlot warehouse that's been repurposed (not really) into an eclectic neighborhood eatery. Mama does pizzas ($15 or less), spaghetti ($19), and Chicken alla Parmigiana ($19) better than the more expensive steaks ($30) and Pork Osso Bucco ($22). With one menu served all day, Mama is best at dinner. While not as richly themed as Sci-Fi or 50's, Mama's checked curtains, overhead Christmas lights, and old-time photographs of Disney characters create a fun and casual atmosphere. Kids' menu includes cheese pizzas, chicken parmesan, spaghetti, and grilled chicken.

Sci-Fi Dine-In Theater

Streets of America, near ABC Commissary

CUISINE American. **HOURS** 12pm–park close. **DDP** Yes. **DISCOUNTS** 20% TiW.

PRICES Lunch/Dinner Appetizers: $6–$11. Entrees: $13–$30. Kids: $9.

OVERVIEW Diners sit inside classic car-shaped booths at this indoor "drive-in theater" while old black-and-white movie clips, trailers, and commercials play on a large movie screen ahead. Above, the ceiling is lit up like the night sky, complete with twinkling stars. The menu offers several sandwiches and burgers under $16 all day, making this a great value out-of-pocket at dinner. The more expensive steak ($30) and chicken pasta ($24) don't offer as much value. The restaurant is dark, but kids usually love the carhop shtick and campy clips on screen. Kids' meal choices include grilled salmon, cheeseburgers, popcorn chicken, and pasta.

DINING AT MAGIC KINGDOM

Three of the most popular restaurants in all of Walt Disney World are found within Magic Kingdom. Overwhelmingly the most popular is the enchanting Be Our Guest Restaurant. Not only does it serve upscale, French-inspired fare at (relatively) reasonable prices, but it's also the first (and only) place at the Magic Kingdom to order wine or beer with dinner. Be Our Guest is a quick service for lunch, but lines typically form long before it opens at 10:30am, and waits just to order hit 30–90 minutes from 10:45am–2pm. If staying at a Disney-owned resort, you may receive a letter at check-in or email during your visit inviting you to participate in FastPass+ at Be Our Guest for lunch. This does not count against any FastPass+ limits and allows lucky users to bypass the standby line and immediately enter Beast's Castle. Take advantage of it if it's available because it will significantly cut down on the wait. Otherwise, get in line at 2pm to reduce the wait as much as possible and still have the ability to tour in low crowds earlier in the morning. Both the lunch and dinner kids' menus are best suited to more adventurous eaters.

Magic Kingdom is also home to two of the most popular character meals: Crystal Palace and Cinderella's Royal Table. The Crystal Palace buffet features Winnie the Pooh, Tigger, Piglet, and Eeyore in a Victorian solarium setting. Royal Table is located inside Cinderella Castle and includes a picture with Cinderella, in addition to four princesses meeting diners tableside. Both are excellent overall experiences for the target audience, but neither is likely to impress on food quality alone.

Tony's Town Square and Liberty Tree Tavern are better for cash lunch, when food is significantly less expensive. Tony's offers pizzas and a meatball sandwich for just a few more dollars than quick service. Liberty Tree offers an a la carte menu at lunch with all entrees under $20. Liberty Tree's family-style dinner is similar food but costs upwards of $36/person. Plaza Restaurant is your least expensive table service dinner option, with sandwiches that cost around $14 in a laidback atmosphere.

The character meals are excellent if you can swing the cost and have members of the group that want to meet the characters. Otherwise, for table service lunch with cash, we like Tony's Town Square and Liberty Tree Tavern. Dinner is best at Be Our Guest and Plaza Restaurant. You'll find more details on each of these table service restaurants in the reviews that follow.

With only a few exceptions, Magic Kingdom quick service is mostly burgers, hot dogs, and chicken nuggets. Josh's recommendation is Columbia Harbour House, where you'll find grilled salmon, lobster rolls, fried shrimp platters, a tuna fish or hummus and broccoli slaw sandwich, and great soups and fresh salads. The second floor seating area is usually quiet because there's no elevator access for strollers and the view of the Rapunzel area is more scenic than most. We also like Pinocchio Village Haus in Fantasyland, which serves interesting flatbread pizzas, salads, and an Italian sub sandwich.

Cosmic Ray's in Tomorrowland offers a lot of options with plenty of air-conditioned seating, but food quality is just average. Ray's also serves a different menu at each of its three "bays", resulting in guests having to wait in multiple lines if they'd like to order different items. Reducing the potential value of the Quick Service Dining Plan, the popular rib entrees are only available after 4pm. Pecos Bill in Frontierland offers just six entrees at lunch. Both are fine (Pecos Bill's remains Dave's recommendation for burgers) but they're busy most of the day and food can be below average. Casey's Corner, serving up a few variations of the usual hot dog, is the last major quick service. About $10 buys you a chicken/beef dog with your choice of chili/cheese or barbecue pork/coleslaw with fries or apple slices. A polish sausage topped with onions and mustard is available, in addition to a plain hot dog. While filling, they are pricey for a low quality, non-kosher dog.

Several quick service outlets are seasonal, based on expected crowds, or operate with limited hours. Tortuga Tavern, with its burrito and nacho fare usually served in Adventureland from 11am–3pm, is worth checking out for lunch. Sleepy Hollow Refreshments in Liberty Square serves excellent, economically priced waffle sandwiches with spicy chicken or ham, prosciutto, and swiss from 11am–5pm. The others, including Diamond Horseshoe, Friar's Nook, and Tomorrowland Terrace, are best skipped.

Overall, we suggest Columbia Harbour House, Be Our Guest, and Pecos Bills for quick service lunch. However, Be Our Guest can be such a time commitment to experience that it may best be skipped by those without FastPass+.

Be Our Guest Restaurant

Fantasyland, near Belle's Village

CUISINE French/American. **HOURS** 4pm–park close. **DDP** Yes. **DISCOUNTS** 20% TiW.

PRICES Dinner Appetizers: $5–$16. Entrées: $17–$33. Kids: $9-$11.

OVERVIEW Set inside Beast's enchanted castle, Be Our Guest is Disney's (arguably) most lavishly themed restaurant and currently the hardest reservation to snag. With three elaborately themed rooms, you may find yourself in the dark and mysterious West Wing, the expansive two-story Grand Ballroom, or the bright Rose Gallery complete with a spinning Belle and Beast music box. The menu is French-inspired and includes items like Thyme-scented Pork Rack Chops, Pan-seared Salmon on Leek Fondue, and Herb-crusted Lamb Rack with a Stone-ground Mustard Demi-glace, all under $30 each. The kids' menu may be too refined for the picky eater and includes Grilled Cheese and Tomato Soup, Beast Casserole, Grilled Steak, Chicken Brochette, and Grilled Fish of the Day. Food and service are better than any other Magic Kingdom restaurant, and it's worth going out of your way to book at 180 days if possible.

Cinderella's Royal Table

Princess character meal, in Cinderella Castle with check-in at rear of castle

CUISINE American. **DISCOUNTS** 20% TiW.

HOURS AND PRICES *Breakfast* (8am–10:40am): $58 adults, $35 kids. *Lunch* (11:45am–2:40pm): $60 adults, $38 kids. *Dinner* (3:50pm–9:40pm): $72 adults, $42 kids.

OVERVIEW By far the most popular character meal, dining here is ordinarily the only way for guests to see the inside of Cinderella Castle. The pricey affair begins in the Grand Hall waiting area and continues through a personal meet and greet with Cinderella on the ground floor. Continue up the red-carpeted spiraling staircase and enter the banquet hall fit for kings and queens. Four princesses greet tableside–usually Ariel, Aurora, Jasmine, and Snow White, and a picture package with Cinderella is included. Diners select items from a set menu featuring upscale fare. Breakfast choices include the standard plate of bacon, eggs, and sausage, or the more lavish Lobster and Crab Crêpes, or Grilled Beef Tenderloin. Lunch brings items like Braised Short Rib and Gnocchi with Roasted Vegetables. Dinner offers similar items along with Beef Tenderloin. Food quality and service are decent, but you're paying for the magical atmosphere, princess interaction, and photos. For cash, breakfast is the best and cheapest meal; on the DDP, all meals are two credits. Lunch is the easiest reservation to snag.

The Crystal Palace

Character meal, at end of Main Street on the left, past Casey's Corner

CUISINE American. **DDP** Yes. **DISCOUNTS** 20% TiW.

HOURS AND PRICES *Breakfast* (8am–10:45am): $26 adults, $16 kids. *Lunch* (11:30am–2:45pm): $28 adults, $15 kids. *Dinner* (3pm–park close): $38 adults, $19 kids.

OVERVIEW Join Winnie the Pooh, Tigger, Eeyore, and Piglet at this all-you-care-to-enjoy buffet. The bright, airy restaurant is inspired by Victorian greenhouses of the late 1800s, complete with high ceilings, character topiaries, and plenty of natural sunlight. Character interaction is above average, as is the food, which includes items like Spit-roasted Carved meats, Spice Boiled Shrimp, 20+ salads, and over a dozen desserts. Crystal Palace is often the most over-booked restaurant on property. Even with a reservation, plan to wait 15–30 minutes for your table. For guests paying cash, an early lunch is the best choice–cheaper than dinner, shorter waits, and no rush to get through the meal.

Liberty Tree Tavern

Liberty Square, near Diamond Horseshoe

CUISINE American. **DDP** Yes. **DISCOUNTS** 20% TiW.

HOURS AND PRICES *Table service Lunch* (11:30am–3pm): Appetizers: $6–$15. Entrees: $12–$20. Kids: $9. *Family-style Dinner* (4pm–park close): $36 adults, $18 kids.

OVERVIEW Lunch is the usual table service gig with an a la carte menu, while dinner is served family style. Liberty Tree is a Colonial-themed tavern, featuring candelabra chandeliers, brick fireplaces, and rooms filled with artifacts from some of America's most famous patriots. Lunch is significantly less expensive, with entrees plenty large enough to fill up the biggest appetites, all under $20. Guests choosing to pay about $40/ adult for the Thanksgiving-inspired dinner will receive a wider variety of foods, in addition to dessert and non-alcoholic beverages. We prefer a late lunch at this well-air-conditioned, moderately priced restaurant where the turkey, pot roast, and salad are similar to dinner. Other lunch options include pasta, sandwiches, and a burger. Kids choose from turkey, pasta with marinara, macaroni and cheese, and flatbread pizza.

The Plaza Restaurant

End of Main Street, on the right

CUISINE American. **HOURS** 11am–park close. **DDP** Yes. **DISCOUNTS** 20% TiW.

PRICES Lunch/ Dinner Entrees: $12–$18. Kids: $9.

OVERVIEW Continuing the Main Street theme, The Plaza features Art Nouveau touches inside a turn-of-the-century ice cream parlor. By far the least expensive theme park sit-down-restaurant, Plaza is an excellent choice for cash guests on a budget, particularly at dinner, when sandwiches are all under $15 and no item is over $20. Kids' options include a cheese sandwich, burger, chicken strips, turkey sandwich, and PB&J. Food and service are great for the money, but we are not talking highfalutin' dining at this casual eatery.

Tony's Town Square Restaurant

Entry Plaza, on the right

CUISINE Americanized Italian. **HOURS** 11:30am–park close. **DDP** Yes. **DISCOUNTS** 20% TiW.

PRICES Lunch/Dinner Appetizers: $6–$11. Lunch Entrees: $14–$21. Dinner Entrees: $18–$30. Kids: $9.

OVERVIEW Modeled after Tony's from *Lady and the Tramp*, guests have an opportunity to relive the romance at this casual family trattoria that serves Olive-Garden-quality Italian food in a relaxing atmosphere. Lunch is the better choice with items like pizzas (all under $17), Meatball Sliders ($14), and Shrimp Scampi ($18) all good quality at reasonable prices. At dinner, less expensive pizzas and sandwiches are replaced by New York Strip Steak ($30), Braised Short Rib ($25), and that sort of thing, though less expensive pastas are also available. Quality on the higher-end items doesn't justify the prices. Kids' choices include spaghetti, pizzas, and pasta. Service is conspicuously fast, with most meals complete within an hour.

DINING AT DOWNTOWN DISNEY

The Downtown Disney shopping and entertainment complex (DTD, currently seeing massive construction and soon to be renamed Disney Springs) includes more than a dozen third-party-operated table service restaurants and quick services, most on the Dining Plan and reservable on My Disney Experience. Some have additional capacity that can be reserved directly over the phone or via OPENTABLE.COM. More will come as part of the current Disney Springs expansion. In addition to restaurants, you'll find in DTD many stores, some Disney and others of the variety you'd find at the local mall. There's also the AMC movie theater, Splitsville upscale bowling alley, DisneyQuest interactive arcade, and a Cirque du Soleil show called La Nouba.

DTD is currently broken up into three sections: the West Side, Pleasure Island, and Marketplace.

The West Side. The West Side is dominated by the Cirque du Soleil, DisneyQuest, Splitsville, and AMC buildings, with a sprinkling of retail and several restaurants and quick services.

West Side quick service options are diverse, though relatively limited. Bongos Cuban Café includes a small takeout window offering mostly sandwiches with a few traditional Cuban entrees from the kitchen available to-go. With drab outdoor seating as the only option, most guests will bypass it for something more comfortable. House of Blues opened a barbecue joint in late 2013 to mixed reviews—seating is also outside, but live music permeates the area beginning daily around 4pm. One of two Wolfgang Puck Express locations is attached to the restaurant across from the movie theater. The pizza is excellent, but the menu is far less diverse than the Express location in the Marketplace and seating is again all outdoors. A new Starbucks concept expected to serve sandwiches and similar fare in a Panera-like casual atmosphere will open in summer 2014. Finally, Disney is getting into the food truck game with an area dedicated to food trucks opening between Bongos and Wolfgang Puck sometime in summer 2014. The trucks will serve a variety of Disney favorites from around the globe, in addition to unique offerings.

On the table service front, Splitsville often has last-minute availability and is an easy walk-up when other restaurants are quoting 45+ minute waits without a reservation, as they often are after 6pm. Its pizza, burgers, and sushi are surprisingly good. House of Blues is economically priced and extremely casual for a nice, no-fuss lunch or dinner. It may be busier if a popular act is scheduled to perform in the club next door. Bongos Cuban Café's menu favors quantity over quality, where you'll find over 50 entrée choices. Grab a mojito from the outdoor bar and look for dinner elsewhere. We don't have a lot of nice things to say about the Wolfgang Puck Café or the Grand Café above it. Food, service, and ambiance are better elsewhere.

Pleasure Island. Much of Pleasure Island has either been closed or will be demolished in 2014. Remaining are a handful of restaurants: Planet Hollywood, Paradiso 37, Portobello, Fulton's, and Raglan Road. The clubs that once dotted the landscape closed years ago.

Even so, Pleasure Island is still home to several great restaurants, particularly for lunch when prices are far more reasonable. The island's quick service is Cookes of Dublin. We like Cookes' Irish food a lot for lunch and early dinners, but it gets backed up in the evenings and there's rarely anywhere to sit. For lunch, our favorite is Fulton's Crab House, which is located in a riverboat on the water. The lunch menu replicates the famous dinner menu's focus on fish and seafood, but the lobster is found in a sandwich for $16 instead of on a plate for $50+. Lunch at next-door Portobello is also a good value—the same great Italian food as at dinner for about half the price, but in a forgettable atmosphere. Raglan Road Irish Pub is best at dinner. While prices are a couple dollars higher here and there, the live music and dancing are worth the extra cost. The only two stragglers are Planet Hollywood and Paradiso 37. Paradiso is great for appetizers and margaritas, but the south-of-the-border entrees are overpriced and the atmosphere is lackluster considering the other options. The worst restaurant on just about every front is Planet Hollywood—loud, garish, and expensive.

The Marketplace. The Marketplace section is predominantly retail with a few restaurants and quick services mixed in. Shoppers looking for Disney items should pay special attention to World of Disney, Tren-D, Once Upon A Toy, The Art of Disney, and the Marketplace Co-Op. You'll find just about every imaginable theme park item in one of these stores.

The Marketplace is home to our favorite DTD quick services: Earl of Sandwich and Wolfgang Puck Express. Earl of Sandwich serves excellent hot sandwiches for less than seven dollars each, in addition to great tasting sides and desserts. Lines can appear long, but service is surprisingly fast. Wolfgang Puck Express is more expensive than most quick services, but its food is table service quality and a server will deliver your meal and take care of drink refills and other needs. Ghirardelli Ice Cream and Chocolate Shop is one of the best places on property to indulge. Decadent sundaes are $9–$10 and, for those looking to be able to walk out after without assistance, best shared.

Two kid favorites operated by the same parent company are located in the Marketplace: Rainforest Café and T-Rex. Rainforest is best known for providing dining in a tropical setting complete with Animatronic animals that rival some of Disney's best. T-Rex is similar, but with a dinosaur theme. We give the nod to T-Rex, partly because it's more likely to be new to a visitor (there are only two locations worldwide) but also because the food and drinks are slightly more inspired. Rainforest, however, is fun and less intimidating for some youngsters than T-Rex.

A visit to Downtown Disney is not an essential part of a first vacation, particularly with all the other things to do at Disney World. Ongoing construction walls and machinery detract from the experience and make travel more difficult. If you do go, plan a single afternoon or evening in DTD perusing the shops and grabbing a meal. Crowds are considerably lower in the afternoon. If you arrive after 5pm, don't expect to eat without very long waits unless you have secured a dinner reservation

DTD is served by buses to and from the Disney resort hotels (but not to and from the parks). These buses are slow and can have many stops, so allow more time than you'd think. DTD is also served by slow, low-capacity boats from the Port Orleans resorts, Old Key West, and Saratoga Springs, and there's a walking path from Saratoga Springs, which is sometimes closed due to construction.

We can't advise driving on evenings or weekends. Parking is free but always a challenge at DTD, and has become much worse since the Disney Springs construction project absorbed much parking lot capacity. Save driving until after the first parking garage component of the project opens in 2015. If you must drive, you'll find more parking in the lots near the West Side than at those near the Marketplace.

Bongos

West Side, across from Splitsville

CUISINE Cuban. **HOURS** 11am–11pm or Midnight. **DDP** Yes. **DISCOUNTS** 20% TiW.

PRICES Lunch/Dinner Appetizers: $3–$23. Lunch Entrées: $8–$40. Dinner Entrées: $15–$40. Kids: $8–$10.

OVERVIEW Enter this two-story 1950s-era Havana nightclub and dine on one of over 50 Cuban specialties, including Cuban Style Skirt Steak, Shrimp Cuban Criolla, and Bongos Famous Fried Shredded Beef. Or pull up a seat at one of three bars, including one housed inside of a 75-foot tall pineapple sculpture, and select from a cocktail list including everything from Bongos Original Mojito to a 45-ounce Cuban Rum Runner. Kids are welcome all day, but it's a loud and boisterous crowd on weekends and late nights when live music is prevalent and dancing encouraged. Service is spotty, but food is prepared well and drinks are excellent.

Fulton's Crab House

Old Pleasure Island, between Portobello and T-Rex

CUISINE Seafood and Steak. **HOURS** 11am–Midnight. **DDP** 2 credits. **DISCOUNTS** 20% TiW; 20% AP Lunch; 10% AP Dinner; 20% DVC dinner; 10% DVC lunch.

PRICES Lunch/Dinner Appetizers: $8–$20. Lunch Entrées: $11–$24. Dinner Entrées: $27–$59. Kids: $8–$14.

OVERVIEW Set inside of a majestic full-size replica of a riverboat anchored in Lake Buena Vista Lagoon, Fulton's imports fresh seafood daily. This is the most upscale Downtown Disney restaurant for dinner where a lobster costs $50 and steaks start at $43. Visit for lunch when a soup/sandwich combo is under $15 and Fish and Chips cost $13 and you'll be able to enjoy the same atmosphere for a lot less money. Kids' entrees include filet mignon, snow crab legs, shrimp pasta, chicken fingers, and burgers. The high prices aren't justified for dinner, but this is a venue worth checking out.

Crossroads at House of Blues

West Side, across from DisneyQuest

CUISINE Southern American. **HOURS** 11am–11pm on weekdays, 1am on weekends. **DDP** Yes. **DISCOUNTS** 20% TiW. 20% AP Lunch; 10% AP Dinner; 20% DVC.

PRICES Lunch/Dinner Appetizers: $6–$16. Entrées: $12–$29. Kids: $7–$9. Sunday Gospel Brunch: $41 adults, $21 kids.

OVERVIEW Celebrity Chef Aaron Sanchez took over the menu in July 2011, "incorporating flavors from around the world" in the process. The menu still favors southern favorites like jambalaya, voodoo shrimp, and buttermilk fried chicken, but you'll find inexpensive flatbread pizzas, sandwiches, and pastas, too. Heavy on edgy religious artwork that may appeal to some more than others, Blues is supposed to be themed to a shack on the side of a road down in the New Orleans bayou. Free live music inside the restaurant on weekends after 10pm. Calmer and kid friendly until then.

Paradiso 37

Old Pleasure Island, between Portobello and West Side

CUISINE North/South American. **HOURS** 11am–Midnight on weekdays, 1am on weekends. **DDP** Yes. **DISCOUNTS** 20% TiW. 15% AP; 20% DVC.

PRICES Lunch/Dinner Appetizers: $4–$17. Entrées: $14–$27. Kids: $8.

OVERVIEW The appetizers and margaritas are better than the entrées at this waterfront restaurant that focuses on cuisine of the Americas. Much busier after 6pm when the live music starts outside, Paradiso is best experienced without kids, who are unlikely to be impressed by the Latin flair or tequila tower stacked with 37 varieties. Walk-up tables are usually available, as are seats at one of the three bars.

Planet Hollywood

West Side, across from entrance to AMC Fork-and-Screen Theater

CUISINE American. **HOURS** 11am–1am. **DDP** Yes. **DISCOUNTS** 20% TiW. 10% AP; 10% DVC.

PRICES Lunch/Dinner Appetizers: $9–$25. Entrées: $14–$30. Kids: $8.

OVERVIEW One of very few remaining restaurants in this dwindling franchise, it should come to the surprise of no one other than Sylvester Stallone and Arnold Schwarzenegger that lousy, overpriced food in a deafeningly loud restaurant is not the key to long-term success. Yes, a few pieces of memorabilia are neat, but that won't make up for everything else wrong here. Diners that must visit should stick to burgers, salads, and beer, and be certain they have nowhere else to be. Advil not included.

Portobello

Old Pleasure Island, between Fulton's and Paradiso 37

CUISINE Italian. **HOURS** 11am–11pm. **DDP** Yes. **DISCOUNTS** 20% TiW. 20% AP Lunch; 10% AP Dinner; 20% DVC Lunch; 10% DVC Dinner.

PRICES Lunch/Dinner Appetizers: $6–$16. Lunch Entrées: $9–$17. Dinner Entrées: $10–$29. Kids: $5–$11.

OVERVIEW With virtually no name recognition, a rather mundane dining atmosphere, and a menu that doesn't do much to draw in guests, this Italian restaurant is the least popular in Downtown Disney. It's a great value before 4pm for lunch, when virtually the same menu as dinner is offered for half the price, but meals here are not particularly memorable. Visit when other restaurants are full and your party doesn't have a reservation elsewhere, or for lunch when it's cool enough for the patio and seating overlooking the water is available. Pizzas come in under $15 and are a great value for lunch or dinner.

Raglan Road

Old Pleasure Island, near Fulton's and Portobello

CUISINE Irish. **HOURS** 11am–1am. **DDP** Yes. **DISCOUNTS** 20% TiW; 10% DVC.

PRICES Lunch/Dinner Appetizers: $6–$27. Lunch Entrées: $10–$25. Dinner Entrées: $15–$29. Kids: $8–$14.

OVERVIEW The restaurant features a live band playing Irish songs, popular ballads, and pub classics alongside traditional Irish jigs beginning at 6pm nightly (except for Sunday, when the live band plays only during brunch). Each of the four bars, some over 130 years old, were imported directly from Ireland. Celebrity Chef Kevin Dundon oversees the menu, which includes favorites like Shepherd's Pie, Guinness & Onion Bangers on Mash, and Roasted Chicken all under $20 for lunch or dinner. Add Guinness, Smithwick's, and a dozen more beers on draft, and you have yourself an authentically Irish good time. Kids' entrees at this family-friendly, highly-recommended restaurant include steak, shepherd's pie, burgers, and macaroni-and-cheese. Nearly everything, from the food to the service to the beer, is excellent. A cult favorite among Disney World guidebook authors.

Rainforest Café

Marketplace, near Earl of Sandwich

CUISINE American. **HOURS** 11am–11pm or 12am. **DDP** Yes. **DISCOUNTS** No TiW; DVC: 10% on entrees; AP: 10%.

PRICES Lunch/Dinner Appetizers: $7–$19. Entrées: $13–$26. Kids: $6–$7.

OVERVIEW See the Animal Kingdom table service reviews for background info on this raucous chain restaurant. The Downtown Disney location is extremely popular with kids and online reservations are hard to come by because only part of the inventory is released to Disney. Call the restaurant directly at 407-827-8500 to book, or visit before 4pm when walk-ups don't require 60+ minute waits. The Lava Lounge next door offers the same menu without any of the restaurant's antics. The water view at the lounge is pleasant for couples, but most families will want to eat inside where the action is.

Splitsville Luxury Lanes

West Side, across from Bongos

CUISINE American, Sushi, Pizza. **HOURS** 11:30am–11pm or later. **DDP** Yes. **DISCOUNTS** 20% TiW.

PRICES Lunch/Dinner Appetizers: $6–$15. Entrées: $12–$25. Kids: $7.

OVERVIEW The food at Splitsville is not quite as luxurious as the bowling setup (your've never read a sentence like that before, we bet), but it does offer a bevy of options, including a dozen freshly made sushi rolls, a half-dozen pizzas, a dozen sandwiches and salads, rice bowls, and more. The pricier entrées are best skipped in favor of sushi and pizza, which are executed quite well. The nicest part of dining in this 50,000 square foot complex loosely themed to 1960s kitsch is the lack of a wait for a table when Downtown Disney is crawling with people. Eat outside to get away from the bowling noise and stick to beer—the cocktails are overpriced and watered down.

T-Rex Café

Marketplace, near the Lego Store

CUISINE American. **HOURS** 11am–11pm or 12am. **DDP** Yes. **DISCOUNTS** No TiW; DVC: 10% on entrees for up to 3 guests; AP: 10%.

PRICES Lunch/Dinner Appetizers: $7–$17. Entrées: $14–$33. Kids: $7–$8.

OVERVIEW Operated by the same parent company as Rainforest Café, T-Rex replaces Rainforest's drizzle with thundering meteor showers and singing birds with a massive undulating octopus and life-sized Animatronic dinosaurs. The T-Rex menu offers a staggering number of items, mostly of decent quality and universally in large amounts. Stick with the lower-priced fare or chance a regrettable $30 steak. Younger kids may be scared of the dinosaurs, noise, fire, and occasional darkness, but most kids between the ages of six and twelve love the atmosphere. With apprehensive kids, consider a walk through the restaurant before committing to a meal, or request a table near the entrance. Call the restaurant directly at 407-828-8739 to book because few slots are offered to Disney Reservations.

Wolfgang Puck Grand Café

West Side, across from DisneyQuest

CUISINE American. **HOURS** 11:30am–11pm. **DDP** Yes. **DISCOUNTS** 20% TiW; 20% AP Lunch; 10% AP Dinner; 20% DVC Lunch; 10% DVC Dinner.

PRICES Lunch/Dinner Appetizers: $8–$15. Entrées: $13–$30. Kids: $7–$9.

OVERVIEW Wolfgang Puck has nothing to do with this restaurant that bears his name, which is now operated by the same company that runs Portobello and Fulton's. The restaurant is reminiscent of "The Max" from *Saved by the*

Bell and the menu features an assortment of fresh pizzas, salads, pastas, sushi, and traditional entrees like steak and chicken. Kids are unlikely to connect with the art-deco style, though their menu includes spaghetti, cheese pizza, chicken tenders, and sushi. Wolfgang Puck Express next door serves pizzas that come out of the same oven for less money, and is a better choice.

Dining Reviews: The Disney Resorts

Disney's resorts offer the majority of the best restaurants on property, whether we're discussing five-star dining at Victoria & Albert's at the Grand Floridian or the rootin' tootin' good time that is hollering along to Hoop-Dee-Doo Revue at Fort Wilderness. We provide reviews of all these meals in the material that follows.

Unfortunately, resort-to-resort travel is often inconvenient because Disney does not offer resort-to-resort buses. Guests relying on Disney transportation from the values and moderates in particular will need to wait for a bus to a theme park or Downtown Disney, then wait for a bus for the resort they're headed to, and then take the time to ride the bus over to the resort and find the restaurant. Disney recommends allowing 90 minutes each way for such travel. And they're not wrong. Travel is particularly taxing for early morning breakfasts when buses run less frequently (check with your concierge for the schedule) and for late night dinners when the theme parks may already be closed, limiting transfer options.

There are some alternatives. Taxis are usually stationed outside the resort or bell services will be glad to call, but they add $25-$60 roundtrip to the cost of the meal. Guests already renting cars have it easiest and can drive directly to the resort with the help of signs and GPS.

We have some tips on reducing the hassle using Disney transportation.

- Guests staying at the monorail resorts—Contemporary, Polynesian, and Grand Floridian—are connected by the resort monorail and visiting any of the resorts from any other will only take about 15 minutes each way.
- Guests staying at the Contemporary, Wilderness Lodge, or Fort Wilderness are connected by boat and visiting any of the resorts from any other will only take about 15-30 minutes each way.
- Guests staying at the Epcot resorts—Beach Club, Yacht Club, BoardWalk Inn, Swan, and Dolphin—are all within a 15-minute walk from each other and watercraft transportation is also available between the resorts.

- If you find yourself at Magic Kingdom, you can take the resort monorail to any of the monorail resorts, or watercraft to Fort Wilderness or Wilderness Lodge.
- If you find yourself at Epcot, you can exit the park via the International Gateway in between the United Kingdom and France Pavilions and either walk or take the boat to any of the Epcot resorts.

Particularly for first-time visitors relying on Disney transportation away from the monorail or Epcot area, our strong advice is eat where you otherwise plan to be in order to reduce the time commitment of transferring from one place to another. If you simply can't resist a breakfast with Mickey at the Contemporary or a romantic dinner at the Grand Floridian, that's fine, too. But take a cab and consider it the low cost of doing business versus the high cost of your time.

DINING AT DISNEY'S ANIMAL KINGDOM LODGE

Boma Flavors of Africa

Take the elevator to the first floor

CUISINE African-inspired. **DDP** Yes. **DISCOUNTS** 20% TiW; 10% AP; 10% DVC.

HOURS AND PRICES *Breakfast* (7:30am–11:00am): $23 adults, $12 kids. *Dinner* (4:30pm-9:30pm): $41 adults, $19 kids.

OVERVIEW Featuring a robust dinner menu of over 50 African-inspired specialties, Boma is a favorite of many for its wide selection and high quality, unique options. Best are the soups and roasted meats, but just about everything from the seasonal salads to the zebra dome desserts are excellent. Kids enjoy the full buffet in addition to items like macaroni-and-cheese, mashed potatoes, pasta, and baked chicken legs. Breakfast is more pedestrian with the usual selection of French toast, Mickey waffles, bacon, sausage, and the like. The only downside is that very few tables in the African-marketplace-themed dining room have views of the savannas outside.

Jiko - The Cooking Place

Take the elevator to the first floor

CUISINE African. **HOURS** 5:30pm–10pm. **DDP** 2 credits. **DISCOUNTS** 20% TiW; 10% AP; 10% DVC; 10% Disney Visa.

PRICES Appetizers: $9–$17. Dinner Entrées: $28–$45. Kids: $8–$16.

OVERVIEW Jiko isn't afraid to use a liberal amount of exotic spices on many of its constantly changing menu items. Flatbreads, like the KG's

Peri-Peri Roasted Chicken with Lime Chakalaka, Lamb Chopper Cheese, and Pickled Sweet Bell Peppers are excellent. Filet mignon, scallops, and short ribs are menu mainstays. Kids have a wide range of options from macaroni-and-cheese or cheese pizza to pan-seared scallops and grilled steak. The main dining room, themed to the opening scenes from *The Lion King*, is elegant and reserved. This is one of the best date-night restaurants on property. Request a window table deep inside the restaurant to get away from the lobby noise.

Sanaa

In the Kidani Village wing (at Kidani, take the elevator to the first floor)

CUISINE African/Indian. **HOURS** Lunch from 11:30am-3pm; Dinner from 5pm–9:30pm. **DDP** Yes. **DISCOUNTS** 20% TiW; 10% AP; 10% DVC; 10% Disney Visa lunch only.

PRICES Lunch/Dinner Appetizers: $6–$15. Lunch Entrées: $12–$22. Dinner Entrées: $15–$30. Kids: $9.

OVERVIEW Sanaa features expansive savanna views in a fun, low-key dining room themed to an African spice market. The Indian Bread Service with nine accompaniments is not to be missed. Excellent Tandoori options reliably come in under $20, in addition to slightly more expensive chicken and steak. Kids' options are a little out there and include items like Tandoori Chicken Pot Pie and Fish of the Day served with Pearl Pasta, Green Beans, Carrots, and Sliced Apples. The lounge is open until midnight. Request a window table.

DINING AT DISNEY'S BEACH CLUB RESORT

Beaches and Cream Soda Shop

Behind Stormalong Bay

CUISINE American burgers, sandwiches, and ice cream. **HOURS** 11am–11pm. **DDP** Yes. **DISCOUNTS** 20% TiW.

PRICES Lunch/Dinner Entrées: $8–$15. Kids: $9.

OVERVIEW Themed to a boardwalk-style ice cream shop, Disney's smallest table service restaurant offers inexpensive burger and sandwich fare in a fun, bright setting. The restaurant began accepting reservations for the first time in late 2013, cutting down waits from as much as two hours to just a few minutes. The $24 Kitchen Sink Dessert, featuring eight scoops of ice cream and an entire bottle of whipped cream, is a favorite tradition of many returning visitors. An ice-cream to-go window is also available.

Cape May Café

Character meal (breakfast only); inside the lobby to the left of check-in

CUISINE American character breakfast with Minnie, Goofy, Donald in beach outfits. Dinner buffet is heavy on seafood. **DDP** Yes. **DISCOUNTS** 20% TiW.

HOURS AND PRICES *Breakfast* (7:30am–11:00am): $30 adults, $16 kids. *Dinner* (4:30pm–9:30pm): $40 adults, $20 kids.

OVERVIEW Like the rest of the resort, Cape May Café is themed to a comfortable beachside setting with inviting pastel colors. Breakfast is a character affair with the usual suspects like waffles and pancakes, in addition to elevated offerings like smoked salmon, creamy cheddar grits, and sliced capicola. Dinner is more expensive and characterless, with an emphasis on seafood paella, peel-and-eat shrimp, snow crab legs, salmon, clams, and mussels, in addition to salads and roasted meats. Kid options include chicken nuggets and macaroni. Both meals are above average, though the lack of Mickey at breakfast is disappointing.

DINING AT DISNEY'S BOARDWALK

Big River Grille and Brewing Works

On the end, near Jellyrolls

CUISINE American. **HOURS** 11am–11pm. **DDP** Yes. **DISCOUNTS** 20% TiW.

PRICES Lunch/Dinner Appetizers: $5–$13. Entrées: $10–$26. Kids: $8.

OVERVIEW Big River is the only working brewpub on property, offering five beers brewed on-site, in addition to a robust menu featuring less expensive sandwich fare along with more expensive steaks and ribs. The less expensive burgers and sandwiches are more reliable than the more expensive items. Beer is unique and decent, but not up to snuff compared to some of the better bottled craft brews available at other restaurants. Diners can sit inside the family-friendly restaurant or outside on the boardwalk overlooking Crescent Lake. Most sports and beer fans will want to take a look at ESPN Club a few hundred feet away. The restaurant otherwise has very little kid appeal, though its menu includes similar burgers and sandwiches.

ESPN Club

Closest to Epcot

CUISINE American. **HOURS** 11:30am–11:30pm. **DDP** Yes. **DISCOUNTS** 20% TiW.

PRICES Lunch/Dinner Appetizers: $7–$14. Entrées: $13–$21. Kids: $9–$11.

OVERVIEW With around 100 video monitors showing just about every televised sporting event imaginable, ESPN is heaven for anyone looking to catch a game while on vacation. Food and drinks are better and more varied than you might expect, including appetizers like the very good lobster bites and tuna tartare. Entrees are almost entirely burgers and sandwiches that are relatively inexpensive at $12–$15. ESPN Club is extremely popular during major sporting events and all day Saturday and Sunday during football season. Arrive early or take advantage of the $50 reserved seats, which includes $50 toward food and drink.

Flying Fish

Nearest entrance to the BoardWalk Inn

CUISINE Seafood. **HOURS** 5:30pm–10pm. **DDP** 2 credits. **DISCOUNTS** 20% TiW; 10% AP; 10% DVC; 10% Disney Visa.

PRICES Dinner Appetizers: $11–$18. Entrées: $27–$47. Kids: $6–$15.

OVERVIEW Reliably serving the best food in the BoardWalk area, Flying Fish is an upscale restaurant with a playful boardwalk theme. Specialties include the excellent Potato-wrapped Red Snapper and Char-crusted Angus New York Strip Steak which can be ordered together as part of an entrée duo. Seafood and salads featuring Florida produce are otherwise highlighted at this restaurant with a more discerning eye for detail than most. Kids' choices include fish sticks, grilled cheese, and steak skewers. While expensive, the fresh, high ingredient quality and seasonal menu changes keep locals and vacationers alike returning time and time again.

Kouzzina by Cat Cora

Near Flying Fish

CUISINE Greek/Mediterranean. **HOURS** Breakfast 7:30am–11am; Dinner 5pm–10pm. **DDP** Yes. **DISCOUNTS** 20% TiW; 10% AP; 10% DVC; 10% Disney Visa.

PRICES Breakfast Appetizers: $7–$9. Entrées: $9–$15. Kids: $6. Dinner Appetizers: $8–$18; Entrées: $20–$35. Kids: $9.

OVERVIEW Greek for kitchen, "Kouzzina" blends celebrity Iron Chef Cat Cora's contemporary flair with traditional family recipes. Relying heavily on ouzo, orzo, and olive oil, the Mediterranean-influenced menu is virtually all meat. Best are the Fisherman's Stew, full of scallops, seasonal fish, shellfish, fennel, and ouzo butter, and the Kouzzina Trio: tasting-size portions of Greek-style lasagna, char-grilled lamb burger, and cinnamon-stewed chicken with orzo. Pair either with Cora's excellent Coranation wine flight. Kids can go American or Greek with their choice of hot dog, macaroni-and-cheese, Greek lasagna, or seasonal fish. Kouzzina's breakfast is one of the best on property, marrying traditional favorites like poached eggs with feta cheese and Kalamata olive toast. Kouzzina is expected to close at the end of September 2014.

DINING AT DISNEY'S CARIBBEAN BEACH RESORT

Shutters

Old Port Royale, on the far end of the food court

CUISINE American with a Caribbean twist. **HOURS** 5pm–10pm. **DDP** Yes. **DISCOUNTS** 20% TiW; 10% AP; 10% Disney Visa.

PRICES Dinner Appetizers: $6–$11. Entrées: $17–$32. Kids: $9–$11.

OVERVIEW While not a destination restaurant by any stretch of the imagination, Shutters has improved significantly recently with the arrival of a fantastic chef from the Disney Cruise Line. A pastel-pink dining room lined with sea-green shutters invites guests inside the restaurant that offers a menu heavy on steak, pork, and chicken. The Caesar Salad with Cornbread Croutons and Barbecue Pork Brisket are best alongside one of the unique rum flights. Kids may enjoy chicken nuggets, pasta, fish, cheese pizza, or grilled chicken or steak.

DINING AT DISNEY'S CONTEMPORARY RESORT

California Grill

Check in on 2nd floor, ride designated elevator to the restaurant on the 15th floor

CUISINE American, Sushi. **HOURS** 5pm–10pm. **DDP** 2 credits. **DISCOUNTS** 20% TiW.

PRICES Appetizers: $12–$20. Sushi: $23–$29. Dinner Entrées: $32–$50. Kids: $9–$18.

OVERVIEW Best known for its wide angle views of Magic Kingdom from the 15th floor of the Contemporary, California Grill underwent renovations throughout much of 2013. The restaurant retains its emphasis on $50 steaks, in addition to many of the same excellent, albeit pricey, sushi dishes. Schedule a meal about an hour before Wishes begins. Guests may watch the show from their table or head outside to the balcony. It's first come, first served at the large bar and lounge area in the middle of the restaurant, making it perfect for drinks and appetizers closer to when the restaurant opens. Check on the second floor for availability. California Grill is great for a date night, but kids are more common than at other signature restaurants due to the excellent fireworks view. Kids may choose between cheese pizza, pasta, chicken, or grilled beef tenderloin.

Chef Mickey's

Character meal, 4th floor Concourse

CUISINE American. Character meal with Mickey, Minnie, Goofy, Donald, and Pluto in chef gear. **DDP** Yes. **DISCOUNTS** 20% TiW.

HOURS AND PRICES *Breakfast* (7:30am–11:00am): $35 adults, $19 kids. *Dinner* (5pm–9:30pm): $45 adults, $21 kids.

OVERVIEW Consistently the most popular and most expensive single-credit character meal on property, this is the only place you'll find Mickey, Minnie, Donald, Goofy, and Pluto greeting diners tableside. Meals are a crowded, raucous affair with the monorail whizzing by just one floor up, but kids don't seem to mind and parents are happy to take pictures of the Fab Five without having to wait an hour in the sun. Breakfast is the stronger and less expensive meal with all of the usual suspects, in addition to Pixie-Dusted Challah French Toast, Minnie's Breakfast Pizza, and Pluto's Cheese Blintz. Dinner food quality is below average, but there's a wide variety of roasted meats, soups, and salads, in addition to an all-you-can-eat ice cream bar. Visit only if the characters are important.

The Wave of American Flavors

First floor on the left, past the check-in area

CUISINE American. **HOURS** Breakfast 7:30am–11am; Lunch 12pm–2pm; Dinner 5pm–9:30pm. **DDP** Yes. **DISCOUNTS** 20% TiW; 10% AP; 10% DVC; 10% Disney Visa.

PRICES Breakfast Entrées: $9–$13. Breakfast Buffet: $20 adult, $12 kid. Lunch/Dinner Appetizers: $7–$19. Lunch Entrées: $14–$20. Dinner Entrées: $17–$33. Kids: $9–$11.

OVERVIEW With more emphasis on healthy food and fresh, locally sourced ingredients than almost any other restaurant on property, The Wave offers an innovative menu for all three meals. The breakfast buffet is excellent, with a wide array of fresh fruit, made-to-order omelets, a smoked salmon bar, and all the traditional accompaniments like pancakes, sausage, and waffles. Less hungry patrons can order a la carte for not much more than the counter-service Contempo Café upstairs. Lunch focuses mostly on sandwiches, burgers, and salads under $20. Only a few tables are usually occupied unless convention goers take over the space. Dinner brings signature quality fare at one-credit prices, including items like the Dry-Rubbed Flat Iron Steak with Citrus Aïoli, Potato Leek Gratin, and locally-sourced Spring Vegetables for $24, and Lobster Ravioli, Florida Clams, and Royal Red Caribbean Shrimp on a bed of Fennel with a creamy Tomato Ragú for $29. Same-day reservations are usually easy to secure.

DINING AT DISNEY'S CORONADO SPRINGS RESORT

Maya Grill

Inside the main building, down the hall to the right of Pepper Market

CUISINE Mexican. **HOURS** 5pm–10pm. **DDP** Yes. **DISCOUNTS** 20% TiW.
PRICES Appetizers: $7–$11. Dinner Entrées: $17–$30. Kids: $7–$10.

OVERVIEW Because of its high prices, Maya Grill's clientele is mostly DDP users and conventioneers on an expense account, but guests who find themselves unexpectedly back at the resort may find value in the $25 Chimichanga Platter or $30 Filet Mignon. Operated by the same company as the so-so restaurants in Epcot's Mexico Pavilion, Maya Grill focuses on Tex-Mex and grilled meats instead of the nuanced, regional favorites that Epcot San Angel Inn and La Hacienda are known for. Kids are unlikely to connect with the restaurant's loosely themed Mayan motifs of fire, sun, and water, but their menu includes some interesting options like the Quesadilla, Beef or Chicken Tacos, and Grilled Fish, in addition to Chicken Nuggets and Mac 'n Cheese.

DINING AT DISNEY'S FORT WILDERNESS RESORT AND CAMPGROUND

Hoop-Dee-Doo Musical Revue

Dinner show at Pioneer Hall, near the boat dock

CUISINE Fried chicken, ribs, and all the fixins. Includes unlimited beer and wine for those 21 and older. **HOURS** Usually three shows daily: 4pm, 6:15pm, and 8:30pm. **DDP** 2 credits. **DISCOUNTS** 20% TiW for final show only.

PRICES Hoop Dee Doo offers tables in three price categories. Category 1, which we recommend, is $66-$70 for adults, and $34-$36 for kids. Category 2 and 3 tables ($7/$11 less for adults and $5/$6 less for kids) are distant from the main stage.

OVERVIEW Run more than 35,000 times over the last 40-or-so years, Hoop-Dee-Doo is as much of a Walt Disney World institution as chicken nuggets and Peter Pan's Flight. While expensive at first blush, your admission includes all-you-care-to-eat fried chicken, ribs, corn, salad, baked beans, corn bread, and strawberry shortcake, in addition to unlimited soft drinks, sangria, house wine, and beer. And, of course, the two-hour, kid-friendly Western musical remains the star of the show. Expect a lot of banjos, sing-a-longs, and audience participation in what ends up being a hokey, joke-filled experience where nobody takes themselves seriously. Take the boat from Magic Kingdom if possible for an easy walk to Pioneer Hall. Those arriving via Disney bus will need to transfer to the internal shuttle for transportation to the show, which can take an extra 20 minutes.

Mickey's Backyard Barbecue

Dinner show and character meal, near Pioneer Hall on the stables side

CUISINE Fried chicken, ribs, hot dogs, hamburgers, and the like. Includes unlimited beer and wine for those 21 and over. **HOURS** Open seasonally during the warmer months, typically from early April until early November. Shows are usually scheduled at 6:30pm on Thursdays and Saturdays, with the possibility that additional days will be available from June through August. **DDP** 2 credits. **DISCOUNTS** None.

PRICES $60 adults, $36 kids.

OVERVIEW Mickey's Backyard Barbecue takes place in a roofed but otherwise open-air (thus not air-conditioned) space. The show features a country band, line dancing, and interactions with Mickey, Minnie, Chip, Dale, and Goofy. Most guests will get more entertainment for their money from Hoop-Dee-Doo, and any number of other meals provide better (and less expensive) chances to meet Mickey and friends. Line-dancers and families with young, excitable kids enjoy the experience most. Take the boat from Magic Kingdom if possible for an easy walk to the Barbecue. Those arriving via Disney bus will need to transfer to the internal shuttle for transportation to the show, which can take an extra 20 minutes.

Trail's End

Pioneer Hall, near the boat dock

CUISINE American/BBQ. **HOURS** Breakfast 7:30am–11:25am; Lunch 11:30am–2pm; Dinner 4:30pm–9:30pm. **DDP** Yes. **DISCOUNTS** 20% TiW; 10% AP; 10% DVC; 10% Disney Visa.

PRICES Breakfast Buffet: $19 adult, $12 kid. Lunch Appetizers: $3–$10. Entrées: $12–$16. Dinner Buffet: $26 adult, $15 kid.

OVERVIEW Consistently the cheapest Disney World buffet at breakfast and dinner, with an inexpensive a la carte lunch served in between, Trail's End serves up country cooking in Disney's most casual sit-down restaurant. Breakfast is satisfying with a spread of the usual Mickey waffles, pancakes, pastries, bacon, sausage, etc., in addition to unique items like Pulled Pork Eggs Benedict and Brisket Mash. Lunch is a nice selection of southern favorites like Shrimp and Grits and Pulled Pork Sandwiches, in addition to burgers and sandwiches that cost only a dollar or two more than quick service. The dinner buffet consists of much of the same food as the much more expensive family-style dinner at Whispering Canyon at Wilderness Lodge. Enjoy all-you-care-to-eat peel and eat shrimp, pulled pork, baked beans, chili, brisket, and more. While not necessarily a destination restaurant, Trail's End is a fantastic, economical choice for those staying at the campground.

DINING AT DISNEY'S GRAND FLORIDIAN RESORT & SPA

1900 Park Fare

Character meal, just inside the first-floor entrance on the left

CUISINE American. Character meal with Mary Poppins, Mad Hatter, Alice, Winnie the Pooh, and Tigger for breakfast. Dinner has Cinderella, Prince Charming, Lady Tremaine, Anastasia, and Drizella. All characters may not appear. **DDP** Yes. **DISCOUNTS** 20% TiW.

HOURS AND PRICES *Breakfast Buffet* (8am–11:15am): $25 adults, $13 kids. *Dinner* (4:30pm–8:30pm): $40 adults, $20 kids.

OVERVIEW 1900 Park Fare's Victorian theme is carried out subtly throughout the restaurant with carousel animals placed around the massive dining room. A calliope, or steam organ, is the focal point, hanging high above the buffet area. The restaurant is otherwise nondescript for the most part—loud, and without windows. Food is quite good for a buffet. Breakfast includes specialties like Lobster Benedict, Smoked Salmon Lox, and Hickory-smoked Ham, in addition to the usual. Dinner brings a large selection of salads and roasted meats, as well as Spice-crusted Salmon, sushi, and Roasted Root Vegetable Gratin. Don't forget the Strawberry Soup. The five very different characters present at each meal otherwise steal the show, as they visit every table taking pictures and mingling with guests.

Citricos

Second floor of the main building, near Mizner's

CUISINE American/Mediterranean. **HOURS** 5:30pm–10pm. **DDP** 2 credits. **DISCOUNTS** 20% TiW; 10% AP; 10% DVC; 10% Disney Visa.

PRICES Appetizers: $9–$16. Dinner Entrées: $29-$53. Kids: $8–$17.

OVERVIEW Citricos is Grand Floridian's best signature restaurant, serving inspired steak and seafood with a Mediterranean twist. Old World furnishings and mosaic-tiled floors invite guests into a restaurant that is just fancy enough that everyone feels welcome, yet an air of glamour and prestige permeates throughout. Shrimp, pork, and veal are done best here with seasonal changes that bring out the freshest flavors. Kids can choose from basics like cheese pizza and macaroni-and-cheese, or go big with Grilled Berkshire Pork Tenderloin or Grilled Steak. Views out the expansive windows are pleasant, but don't provide much of a theme park or Wishes view.

Grand Floridian Café

First floor, all the way back on the left

CUISINE American. **HOURS** Breakfast 7am–11am; Lunch 11:30am–2pm;

Dinner 5pm–9pm. **DDP** Yes. **DISCOUNTS** 20% TiW; 10% AP; 10% DVC; 10% Disney Visa.

PRICES Breakfast Entrées: $9–$18. Lunch/Dinner Appetizers: $6–$13. Lunch Entrées: $12–$27. Dinner Entrées: $19–$30. Kids: $9.

OVERVIEW It's usually easy to secure reservations at Grand Floridian's least expensive and most casual restaurant, subtly themed to the Victorian era with charming views of the rose gardens outside. Unlike the signature restaurants, nobody will bat an eye if you arrive with fanny packs still on waists and Mickey ears still on heads. Breakfast is best, with upscale items like Lobster Eggs Benedict and Citrus Pancakes stealing the show. Lunch is a relatively inexpensive affair with sandwiches, salads, and burgers all coming in under $20. Still, upscale touches remain, with butter-poached lobster topping the burger and roasted garlic aioli, balsamic onions, spinach, and fennel salad adorning the chicken sandwich. Don't miss the gigantic Grand Sandwich. Dinner isn't great, with just six or seven entrees on the menu, but the Shrimp & Grits, Grilled Pork Chop, and Chicken Breast all arrive under $22 with large portions and fresh ingredients. Kids are unlikely to be impressed by the ambiance, but they can get in on the action with salmon, cheese pizza, chicken, and meaty mac 'n cheese.

Narcoossee's

Located outside, near the boat dock

CUISINE Steak and Seafood. **HOURS** 5:30pm–10pm. **DDP** 2 credits. **DISCOUNTS** 20% TiW.

PRICES Appetizers: $11–$19. Dinner Entrées: $31–$72. Kids: $7–$15.

OVERVIEW Disney's most expensive signature restaurant is not its best in food quality, service, or ambiance. The windows and waterfront veranda do provide decent, albeit off-centered views of Magic Kingdom and Wishes, but it's far less impressive than California Grill's 15th floor observation deck. Food is generally on point, but the menu is far less innovative than Citricos, and it's hard to justify a $70+ filet mignon/lobster tail combo when the beef isn't even certified Choice. The atmosphere is otherwise bland at what Disney describes as an "elegant waterfront retreat" with basic wood furniture and standard wood floors. Book about an hour before Wishes begins and request a window table at check-in, or consider other options.

Victoria and Albert's

Second floor of the main building, near Citricos

CUISINE Fine Dining; **HOURS** Two seatings nightly: first from 5pm–6:05pm and second from 8:30pm–9:20pm. **DDP** No. **DISCOUNTS** 20% TiW through July 31, 2014, only.

PRICES $135/person seven–course Prix Fixe menu.

OVERVIEW Victoria & Albert's, boasting the AAA Five Diamond Award every year since 2000, is unlike any other restaurant on property. With a seven-course menu that starts at $135 per person, it's also the most expensive. The restaurant does not serve children under the age of ten in the main dining room and there is a strict dress code: men must wear dinner jackets with dress pants or slacks and shoes. Ties are optional. Women may wear a cocktail dress, nice dress, dressy pant suit, or a skirt with a blouse. The 18-table restaurant is otherwise equal parts intimate and opulent, with reliably impeccable service from the inviting staff. Menus change daily, but Chef Hunnel reliably offers Australian Kobe-style beef tenderloin, Holland white asparagus, braised oxtail, Imperial osetra caviar, and other fine ingredients. Desserts, overseen by the venerable Erich Herbitschek, are excellent. While expensive, Victoria & Albert's may be the best value on property. Strongly consider the $65 wine pairings with seven healthy pours of fine wines perfectly paired to each selection. V&A's is not for everyone, but it doesn't get any better than this for those celebrating something special.

DINING AT DISNEY'S OLD KEY WEST RESORT

Olivia's

Next to the gift shop, across the way from check-in

CUISINE American. **HOURS** Breakfast 7:30am–10:30am; Lunch 11:30am–4:55pm; Dinner 5pm–10pm. **DDP** Yes. **DISCOUNTS** 20% TiW; 10% AP; 10% DVC; 10% Disney Visa.

PRICES Breakfast Entrées: $10–$16. Lunch/Dinner Appetizers: $6–$13. Entrées: $12–$30. Kids: $9.

OVERVIEW Nautically themed with wooden fish and pictures of past guests adorning the walls, Olivia's is one of the friendliest restaurants on property. Breakfast is excellent with specialties like Crab Cake Eggs Benedict and the Conch Republic Omelet with Shrimp, Avocado, and Pepper Jack Cheese. Standard fare includes pancake, waffle, and egg platters. Lunch and dinner both feature inexpensive burger and sandwich fare, in addition to more expensive steak, scallops, and prime rib. Order at least one Conch Fritters. Kids enjoy this colorful, boisterous restaurant with their menu of pasta, salmon, pizza, chicken, hamburgers, and grilled fish. While not a destination restaurant for first time-visitors, anyone staying here should plan at least one meal back at the resort. Outdoor patio seating is available.

DINING AT DISNEY'S POLYNESIAN RESORT

'Ohana

Character meal (breakfast only), on second floor of main building

CUISINE Character breakfast with Mickey, Pluto, Lilo, and Stitch. Dinner (served family style) is heavy on meat. **DDP** Yes. **DISCOUNTS** 20% TiW.

HOURS AND PRICES *Breakfast* (7:30am–11:00am): $25 adults, $14 kids. *Dinner* (5pm–10pm): $40 adults, $20 kids.

OVERVIEW Characters stop by for the Polynesian-themed breakfast served family-style. Scrambled eggs, Mickey waffles, fried potatoes, pork sausage, bacon, and biscuits will all be delivered in copious quantities throughout the meal. It's a limited selection compared to buffets, but it does the trick and the characters are friendly. Dinner starts with pineapple-coconut bread and salad and continues with honey-coriander chicken wings and potstickers. Skewers with char-sui pork loin, marinated sirloin steak, and spicy grilled peel-n-eat shrimp follow with stir-fried vegetables and lo mein as accompaniments. The restaurant is incredibly loud, particularly at dinner when staff leads kids in games and parades throughout the meal. Very few tables have window views of Magic Kingdom. (Protip: It's 'Ohana. Not O'hana. Or O'hana's. Just, 'Ohana. It means "family".)

Kona Café

Second floor of main building

CUISINE American, Pan-Asian. **HOURS** Breakfast: 7:30am–11:15am; Lunch: 12pm–2:45pm; Dinner; 5pm–10pm. **DDP** Yes. **DISCOUNTS** 20% TiW.

PRICES Breakfast Entrées: $9–$15. Lunch/Dinner Appetizers: $6–$15. Lunch Entrées: $12–$18. Dinner Entrées: $18–$30. Kids: $9.

OVERVIEW Kona is too many people's "best kept secret" to really count as a secret anymore, but the restaurant remains one of Disney's hidden gems, particularly for its relatively inexpensive, high-quality lunch. Although most famous for its Tonga Toast (banana-stuffed sourdough French toast rolled in cinnamon sugar and served with a strawberry compote), the Macadamia-Pineapple Pancakes with macadamia nut butter and pineapple sauce might be even better. Lunch is sandwiches, Pan-Asian noodle bowls, tacos, and satisfying plated lunches featuring grilled steak or chicken for under $16 each. Dinner remains reasonably priced with many entrees under $25 and more of an emphasis on steak, ahi tuna, chicken, and the like. Excellent sushi is served inside the restaurant and next door at the Sushi Bar after 5pm. Just off the main lobby, Kona is extremely loud and not particularly private for dinner, but it's a casual affair and guests can fill up for about half as much as 'Ohana next door.

Spirit of Aloha

Dinner show, in dedicated space on the Grand Floridian side

CUISINE American/Polynesian. **HOURS** Usually two shows Tuesday-Saturday at 5:15pm and 8pm. **DDP** 2 credits. **DISCOUNTS** 20% TiW, for final show only.

PRICES The Spirit of Aloha show offers tables in three price categories. Category 1, which we recommend, is $70-$74 for adults, and $36-$40 for kids. Category 2 and 3 tables ($7/$11 less for adults and $5/$6 less for kids) are distant from the main stage.

OVERVIEW Food is okay at this Polynesian luau and dinner show, which follows the story of a young woman returning home after spending time as a city girl on the mainland. All-you-care-to-enjoy Island pulled pork, BBQ ribs, roasted chicken, and Polynesian rice are served family-style alongside fresh salad with honey-lime vinaigrette, seasonal vegetables, and pineapple-coconut bread. Complimentary beer and wine are served, though it may be difficult to flag down a server for a refill. Kids receive chicken nuggets with tater tots, cheese pizza, and either grilled chicken or mahi mahi with rice and green beans. The show has its moments, with an outstanding fire-dancing and sword-eating finale, but at over two hours, it drags in places. With the amount of better entertainment already seen at the parks, the Luau is going to be superfluous for many, and, at $70/adult, is an expensive proposition.

DINING AT DISNEY'S PORT ORLEANS RIVERSIDE RESORT

Boatwright's

Inside the main building, near the quick service

CUISINE Cajun/American. **HOURS** 5pm–10pm. **DDP** Yes. **DISCOUNTS** 20% TiW; 10% AP; 10% Disney Visa.

PRICES Appetizers: $7–$12. Dinner Entrées: $16–$30. Kids: $9.

OVERVIEW Loosely themed to a shipyard warehouse with the skeletal hull of a fishing boat suspended overhead, Boatwright's is a casual restaurant just off the main lobby. The menu revolves around typical New Orleans favorites like Jambalaya, Crawfish Ètouffée, and Andouille-crusted Catfish with Dirty Rice, but the usual American steaks, prime rib, short ribs, and pork chop are also present. Unfortunately, most of the Cajun entrees are under-seasoned and bland. Boatwright's is excellent for guests who unexpectedly find themselves back at the resort, but do make sure you have reservations because waits can be surprisingly long, particularly on weekends in lousy weather.

DINING AT DISNEY'S SARATOGA SPRINGS RESORT & SPA

The Turf Club Bar & Grill

Inside the main building, beyond the quick service

CUISINE American. **HOURS** 5pm–10pm. **DDP** Yes. **DISCOUNTS** 20% TiW; 10% AP; 10% DVC; 10% Disney Visa.

PRICES Appetizers: $6–$11. Dinner Entrées: $17–$32. Kids: $9.

OVERVIEW Turf Club is themed to a turn-of-the-century, upstate New York racetrack clubhouse. Wood-paneled walls and dark wood furniture provide a gentlemanly ambiance with views of Lake Buena Vista Golf Club down below and Downtown Disney in the distance. It's not the most inviting restaurant, particularly with kids, but it's a great choice for couples staying at the resort who are looking for a more intimate experience, and riders will find the displayed horse tack delightful. Kids may enjoy the covered patio seating outside more. The menu leans toward steak, lamb, and pork. The Root Beer Brined Pork Chops and Grilled Lamb Chops with Honey-Mint Glaze are best. Start with the Turf Club Signature Grilled Romaine Salad and Buffalo Chicken Dip. Kids have the usual burger/nugget/pizza/fish/chicken/pasta options. The Saratoga Cocktail with Maker's Mark Bourbon and Mint Julep with Woodford Reserve are a nice departure from most cocktail menus heavy on flavored vodkas and light rum.

DINING AT DISNEY'S WILDERNESS LODGE

Artist Point

Back of main building

CUISINE American. **HOURS** 5:30pm–9:30pm. **DDP** 2 credits. **DISCOUNTS** 20% TiW; 10% AP; 10% DVC; 10% Disney Visa.

PRICES Appetizers: $10-$15. Dinner Entrées: $28–$49. Kids: $7–$14.

OVERVIEW Specialties of the Northwest are served as guests take in the large, open dining room inspired by national park lodges. Two-story high murals capture the heart and romance of the American frontier as iron lanterns provide the only light. Be sure to request a window table overlooking Bay Lake and Silver Creek Falls, or you risk a lousy view of a walkway or the lobby. The restaurant welcomes kids, but they are unlikely to be transfixed with the restaurant's subtle charm. The restaurant is best enjoyed as a romantic rendezvous. Best are the Smokey Portobello Soup appetizer and anything with buffalo strip or venison loin paired with one of the Northwest wine flights. Don't miss the Artist Point Cobbler for dessert.

Whispering Canyon Café

Just inside the main entrance, on the left

CUISINE American. **HOURS** Breakfast: 7:30am–11:15am; Lunch: 11:45am–2:30pm; Dinner: 5pm–10pm. **DDP** Yes. **DISCOUNTS** 20% TiW; 10% AP; 10% DVC; 10% Disney Visa.

PRICES Breakfast Entrées: $10–$17. Lunch/Dinner Appetizers: $6–$12. Lunch Entrées: $12–$22. Dinner Entrées: $18–$33. Kids: $9–$12.

OVERVIEW Whispering Canyon Café is like a Western-themed 50's Prime Time Café. While the antics have been toned down in recent years, guests requesting a bottle of ketchup will find that 25 bottles from around the restaurant appear. Don't be surprised if your drink refill comes in a gallon jug or a two-ounce miniature jar, depending on how generous your server is feeling. All-you-care-to-enjoy platters are the most popular here. Breakfast brings scrambled eggs, Western home fries, bacon, sausage, waffles, buttermilk biscuits, and sausage gravy. A la carte choices include the usual. Lunch and dinner platters include family-style mixed greens tossed in an apple-vinaigrette dressing and freshly baked cornbread. Start with three: smoked pork ribs, barbecue-pulled pork, herb-baked chicken, beef strip loin, market fish, or sausage, along with vegetables, mashed potatoes, cowboy-style baked beans, and corn on the cob. Bring your sense of humor to enjoy this loud, raucous restaurant, particularly at dinner.

DINING AT DISNEY'S YACHT CLUB RESORT

Captain's Grille

Off the main lobby

CUISINE American. **HOURS** Breakfast: 7:30am–11:25am; Lunch: 11:30am–2pm; Dinner: 5pm–9pm. **DDP** Yes. **DISCOUNTS** 20% TiW; 10% AP; 10% DVC; 10% Disney Visa.

PRICES Breakfast Entrées: $9–$14. Breakfast Buffet: $17/adults, $7 kids. Lunch/Dinner Appetizers: $4–$15. Lunch Entrées: $13–$20. Dinner Entrées: $18–$33. Kids: $9–$12.

OVERVIEW Serving seafood classics in a bland dining room, Captain's Grille had its menu and décor revamped in early 2014. New breakfast items include the $14 Butter-poached Lobster, Asparagus, Chive Cream, and Savory Hash Brown, in addition to the excellent breakfast buffet that includes fruit, pastries, eggs, bacon, sausage, smoked salmon, bread pudding, and more. It's an excellent value. Lunch is sandwich and burger fare, with the New England-style Lobster Roll on Butter-toasted Parker House Roll leading the way. Dinner brings more expensive items like the classic New York strip steak, snow crab legs with new potatoes and corn on the cob, and cabernet-braised short ribs. Kids may enjoy a burger, chicken nuggets, beef kebabs, baked fish, or shrimp skewers. Décor remains forgettable, but it's easy to secure a last-minute reservation, and food and service are excellent.

Yachtsman Steakhouse

Back of lobby

CUISINE American. **HOURS** 5pm–9:30pm. **DDP** 2 credits. **DISCOUNTS** 20% TiW.

PRICES Appetizers: $12–$19. Dinner Entrées: $30–$65. Kids: $8–$15.

OVERVIEW Yachtsman takes its meat more seriously than any other Disney restaurant on property. Steaks are aged, trimmed, and hand cut on site before being prepared on an oak-fired grill in the open kitchen. The traditional steakhouse setting is heavy on wood with elegant white linens topping every table. While all steaks come in over $40, their quality is higher than at any other signature restaurant on property. The restaurant is not the best with young kids in tow, as there's little about the restaurant that will keep them occupied, but they may choose from mac 'n cheese, baked fish, grilled chicken, pasta and meatballs, or a steak skewer. Consider the restaurant for an intimate meal or special occasion, particularly with someone who knows their meat.

Which Tickets To Buy and How Much to Budget

8

"What should we budget?" is the hardest simple question for this book to answer.

This is because smaller families, families whose kids are younger, families staying at a less expensive hotel, families going during a less expensive week, and families on shorter trips will pay less. Larger families, families where everyone is over nine, families staying at a more expensive hotel, families going during a more expensive week, and families on longer trips will pay more.

- A parent and one younger child, with three days of tickets and three nights in a value resort during one of the less expensive price seasons, could spend as little as $1,300 in Orlando.
- Add another parent and another younger child and this trip jumps to $2,100.
- Stretch the visit out to the 8 nights we recommend for "only visits" and the in-Orlando price exceeds $4,000.
- Stay this long in one of the more expensive deluxe resorts instead, and the price is more than $7,500.
- Shift to the most expensive times to visit at this deluxe resort and add $1,700 more.

(All the figures are before transportation costs and souvenirs.)

The good news is that budgeting for a specific trip is relatively straightforward, with most costs set and paid far in advance of arrival.

This chapter discusses the ins and outs of budgeting. More precisely, we'll walk you through how to establish what you can expect to pay for each component of your trip, whether it includes just one adult and one child on a tight budget over a few days, or a week-long extended family blow-out.

We open with a discussion of the one major budget issue we haven't discussed yet: theme park tickets with their various add-ons and related costs. The section that follows covers estimating your budget based on your dates, resort hotel, group, etc. Then we cover budgets for "only" trips, several ways to reduce costs, and even a few reasons to spend even more!

Disney World Tickets and Prices

Like most of our budgetary concerns thus far, deciding on the right theme park tickets for your group is simple at first blush and a bit more complicated once we delve into the specifics. Let's break it down.

The Magic Your Way base ticket is the name of the basic theme park admission ticket that Disney offers. The great majority of Disney World visitors will purchase a Magic Your Way ticket, although some guests return with Annual Passes (good for unlimited admissions throughout the year, sometimes with blackout dates) or have a promotional ticket of some kind. You may purchase a Magic Your Way ticket with one to ten days of theme park admissions. The tickets expire 14 days from their first use at Disney World (the day of first use plus 13 additional days), not from the date of purchase or the date of receipt in the mail.

COST OF MAGIC YOUR WAY BASE TICKETS

While the cost always goes up to add more days to your base ticket, the cost per day goes down as you add days.

On June 2, 2013, Disney began charging $5 more for a one-day ticket to Magic Kingdom than a one-day ticket to the other three major theme parks. Pricing for tickets of all lengths is indicated in the chart below, which includes 6.5% sales tax:

Number of Ticket Days	Adult Price	Price to Add Day	Child Price	Price to Add Day
1--Magic Kingdom	$105.44	n/a	$99.05	n/a
1--Any Park but Magic Kingdom	$101.11	n/a	$93.72	n/a
2	$200.22	$94.78	$186.38	$87.33
3	$291.81	$91.59	$271.58	$85.20
4	$313.11	$21.30	$291.81	$20.23
5	$323.76	$10.65	$302.46	$10.65
6	$334.41	$10.65	$313.11	$10.65
7	$345.06	$10.65	$323.76	$10.65
8	$355.71	$10.65	$334.41	$10.65
9	$366.36	$10.65	$345.06	$10.65
10	$377.01	$10.65	$355.71	$10.65

As you can see, the cost to add the fourth day is about $22 and each day after that is $10.65. Disney prices their tickets in this way so it is cost-effective to visit the parks for additional days, which means you will be spending more money on food, souvenirs, and hotel rooms, which is where the Walt Disney Company makes even more money than on admission. It also dissuades people from purchasing tickets to other theme parks. After all, the cost to add the 7th day to your Disney vacation is "only about $10", compared to $90+ for a one-day ticket to SeaWorld, Universal Studios, etc. Disney keeps its single-day tickets expensive in order to capitalize on those only spending one day at Disney World.

ADDING DAYS TO YOUR TICKET

The Magic Your Way ticket is the bare minimum ticket that can be purchased, but that doesn't necessarily mean you need "more ticket". There are a few rules for upgrading base tickets. First, all upgrades must be done within 14 days of the first use of the ticket. You may also add days to your ticket as needed at the same price as it would have cost had you originally added them. For example, if you're unsure whether you need six, seven, or eight days of admission, you can purchase a six-day ticket and add a seventh or eighth day if you decide that you need them, even after using the tickets. You would only pay the additional cost per day at the same rate had you originally purchased a seven-day ticket ($10.65 per day, as noted in the chart above). These upgrades must be made before the end of the last day on the ticket. For example, if you've purchased a five-day ticket and would like to add a sixth, you must add it before the end of your fifth day spent in the theme park. Disney uses this policy to cut down on ticket resellers that offer unsuspecting visitors money for their used tickets. The resellers used to take these used tickets to Disney, add extra days for the $10.65 per day cost, and then turn around and resell them as "new" one-day tickets for $50 or more. Reselling used tickets is illegal in Florida, and if you find yourself in the unfortunate situation of trying to use bogus tickets, you'll be refused admission to the parks. Stick with Disney directly or a trusted third party, not the various resellers with strip mall storefronts.

ADDING PARK HOPPERS

The Park Hopper ticket add-on allows the user to visit more than one theme park on the same day. For example, the Animal Kingdom might close at 5pm on the day you choose to visit. With the Park Hopper upgrade, you could exit the Animal Kingdom at any time and travel to and enter any of the other three theme parks to take advantage of evening Extra Magic Hours, a late dinner reservation, or anything else.

For both kids and adults using a one-day ticket, the cost of the hopper is $37.28 with tax. For two- or three-day tickets, the cost is $52.19. With a four- to ten-day ticket, the cost is a flat $63.90 per ticket with tax. On a six-day ticket, the cost for the upgrade comes out to $10.65 per day. Guests adding both Park Hopper and Water Park Fun & More (described next) at the same time receive a discount of about $35 versus adding them separately. The cost to add both upgrades is $91.59.

Many guests have what they think is the bright idea of bypassing the expensive Park Hopper upgrade and instead purchase more days of theme park admissions than they need with the idea that they will visit a second theme park on the same day and simply use a second day's admission. For example, a family might be visiting the parks on five days and purchase seven days of admission with the idea that on day five they'll visit Animal Kingdom in the morning and then use a sixth day of admission on the same day to visit Epcot at night. This will not work. Disney is wise to the fact that adding Park Hopper would be over $60 per ticket, while adding two additional days is only about $20. In our example, the Cast Member at Epcot would explain the benefits of upgrading to Park Hopper after the ticket was rejected at the scanner.

In most situations, we don't recommend spending the money on the Park Hopper upgrade, at least not until you experience Walt Disney World for the first time and realize how big it is, how much there is to do everywhere, and how long it takes to get from park to park. Remember, Disney will very rarely not take your money and they are more than happy to add the Park Hopper upgrade to your ticket should you deem the cost necessary, even after you've started using the ticket.

Remember that the regular base ticket allows unlimited re-entries to the same theme park on the same day. Should you take a recommended afternoon break, you can return to the same theme park later for dinner, additional attractions, and the night-time entertainment. It's true that Animal Kingdom routinely closes around 5 or 6pm, and it may seem like there's a lot of time after it closes to do *something*. Instead of pushing on to another theme park, consider making a dinner reservation and exploring a nearby resort. In Animal Kingdom's case, Animal Kingdom Lodge is just a few minutes away. It's a beautiful resort where anyone is free to use the observatories to check out the giraffes, zebras, and other animals on the savannas. The restaurants and quick service are all excellent as well.

Park Hopper does have its uses, particularly for guests staying at Epcot area resorts or guests visiting for a special event. Guests staying at a resort like the Beach or Yacht Clubs may wish to start their day at Magic Kingdom, take a break back at the resort, and then simply walk the five minutes to Epcot for drinks, dinner, rides, entertainment, or whatever else.

If you are considering the Park Hopper upgrade, calculate how much it's going to cost and then divide that by the number of times you plan to hop. That's the cost per hop and will give you a better idea if the real additional theme park time is worth the money.

ADDING WATER PARK FUN & MORE

The Water Park Fun & More add-on includes an allotment of entrances to the following "minor parks" in Disney World: Typhoon Lagoon water park, Blizzard Beach water park, Disney's Wide World of Sports Complex, DisneyQuest, one round of golf at 9-hole Oak Trail, Disney's Fantasia Gardens Mini Golf (before 4:00 pm), or Disney's Winter Summerland Mini Golf (before 4:00 pm). The number of entrances you will receive to the minor parks is based on the number of days your Magic Your Way Base Ticket is valid. The following chart illustrates this:

Magic Your Way Base Ticket Days:	Water Park Fun Admissions:
1	2
2	2
3	3
4	4
5	5
6	6
7	7
8	8
9	9
10	10

For example, if your ticket is good for five days, then you will receive five entrances to any of the minor parks. Note that guests with both one- and two-day theme park tickets receive two minor theme park admissions.

With tax, the cost to add the Water Park Fun & More upgrade is $63.90, regardless of how many days the ticket is valid for admission and regardless of whether it's a child or adult ticket. The cost is $91.59 with tax to add both Park Hopper and Water Park fun & More.

Water Park Fun & More is a great value if you plan to visit the water parks and/or DisneyQuest at least twice.

Here are the costs (with tax) of a one-day ticket to the minor parks that you can visit with the Water Park Fun & More upgrade:

- DisneyQuest: $47.93 Adult, $41.54 Child (age 3–9)
- Blizzard Beach or Typhoon Lagoon: $56.45 Adult, $47.93 Child (age 3–9)
- Disney's Wide World of Sports: $17.57 Adult, $12.25 Child (age 3–9)
- Round of Golf at Oak Trail: $40.49 Adult, $21.32 Junior (17 and under)
- Fantasia Gardens Mini Golf: $14.91 Adult, $12.78 Child (age 3–9)
- Winter Summerland Mini Golf: $14.91 Adult, $12.78 Child (age 3–9)

As you can see, the cost of a one-day ticket to DisneyQuest, Blizzard Beach, Typhoon Lagoon, or Oak Trail is just a little less expensive than adding the Water Park Fun & More upgrade. The upgrade becomes cost effective if you're planning to visit at least two of the more expensive minor parks. If you're unsure of whether you'll be visiting a second time, you can apply the cost of one day's admission to the water parks, DisneyQuest, golf, or one of the other minor parks toward the full cost of the upgrade so long as you present the receipt at the time of upgrade.

While the water parks and other minor attractions are a lot of fun, we don't usually recommend the add-on for a first visit because the major theme parks offer so much to see and do. For return trips or vacations lasting more than eight days, it is potentially a great value for those planning several visits to the minor parks.

Estimating Budgets

Now that we've determined the cost of theme park tickets, let's add them to the resort and dining costs discussed in Chapters 5 and 7, and consider the following variables:

- **DATES OF THE VISIT** Walt Disney World price seasons for hotel rooms vary tremendously over the year.

- **GROUP SIZE AND AGE STRUCTURE AT PLANNED CHECK-IN DATE** Kids less than three years old don't require theme park admission and aren't charged at buffets. Kids from three to nine are charged a little less than older folk for theme park tickets, and a lot less for kids' meals and kids' buffets. Kids ten and older as of the check-in date are charged the same as adults for theme park tickets and the Dining Plan. With the exception of the Disney Vacation Club rooms and the Fort Wilderness campground, Disney includes two guests age 18 or older in the room at the base price. Additional guests over the age of 18 will be charged $10–$25 per night extra, depending on the resort level.

- **TARGETED HOTEL** Walt Disney World hotel rooms are available for prices just south of $100 per night to well over $600 per night.

- **TRANSPORTATION COSTS** These vary greatly depending on mode and length of travel.

- **TIPS, SNACKS, SOUVENIRS, AND OTHER EXTRAS** Add about $25 per person, per night.

Now that we have an idea about when and for how long we want to visit, let's input our information and get an idea of how much it's all going to cost. Visit DISNEYWORLD.COM and input your check-in date, check-out date, and desired hotel, and then select Find Prices. Select Room-only, Package, or one of the special offers (if available), and then scroll down and select the room type. The next page lists tickets and the add-ons discussed previously in the chapter. Select the tickets and then click Dining Plan. Note the cost with and without the Plan. While we don't recommend the Dining Plan in most situations, it does give a general idea about what it will cost to eat one quick service and one table service meal per day, in addition to a snack or two. Don't worry if this number seems too high—we'll cover discounts and ways to save money shortly.

Budgeting an Only Visit

For a nine-day itinerary during the Fall 2014 price season, assuming a family of four with two adults, one child younger than ten and one older, budget if possible:

- $7,500+ if you are staying at a deluxe resort
- $5,200 if you are staying at a moderate
- $4,500 if you are staying at a value

Add to this budget the costs of getting the group to and from Orlando.

We suggest that a day or two shorter can also work for an "only" visit. For shorter visits, subtract about $400/day if you are staying at a value resort, $500/day at a moderate, and $850/day at a deluxe.

Saving Money on a Disney World Visit

The money-saving opportunities available depend greatly on when you go and where you stay:

- When you go matters because Disney changes seasonal pricing roughly 25 times over the course of the year. Staying in the same exact standard-view room at the Polynesian for eight nights during the most expensive time of the year can cost $2,100 more than it would cost during the cheapest period.

- Where you stay matters because Walt Disney World has resorts priced at many different levels. Staying eight nights at the Polynesian instead of Art of Animation during the lower cost season will cost almost $3,000 more.

- Combining these effects—staying eight nights at the Polynesian during the highest cost time of the year instead of at Art of Animation during the lowest cost time of the year—costs a whopping $5,100 more for the same family with the same theme park tickets!

So the takeaways for the first-time family visitor:

- On a tight budget, first consider sticking with one of Disney's less expensive on-property resorts like Art of Animation or Pop Century.

- Think carefully about what is really getting in the way of going during one of the less expensive seasons. Is it possible to pull the kids out of school to visit when crowds and prices are much lower?

Because Disney controls the entire supply of theme park tickets, discounts from reputable sources are slim. Check UNDERCOVERTOURIST. COM for some of the best discounts on multi-day tickets.

Fortunately, major savings may be available on other aspects of your vacation:

- Keep an eye out for deals available to the general public—typically room rate discounts, but sometimes a version of the Dining Plan for free—especially in September. Find them at YOURFIRSTVISIT. NET/DEALS or at Disney World's Special Offer web page as they are announced. These discounts are usually available to Disney Visa card holders a few days before they become available to everyone else. Visit DISNEYREWARDS.COM for more information.

- Use special discounts that you qualify for, the most valuable of which is the Armed Forces Salute. See MILITARYDISNEYTIPS.

COM for more. There may also be discounts for Florida residents, Annual Passholders, international guests, and others.

- Access Disney Vacation Club rooms for a lot less by renting points from owners who won't be using them—this is a particular boon for large families, who have the most difficulty finding Disney-owned accommodations at reasonable prices. Visit DVCREQUEST.COM for pricing and options.

- Consider staying offsite, especially with large groups. As noted in Chapter 5, there are some takeaways on the convenience side of things, but it may be the most viable option for some groups, and the savings can be substantial. It's hard to find reasonably priced Disney-owned options on-site for groups larger than four people, and even more difficult for groups larger than five. You'll find lots of ideas at YOURFIRSTVISIT.NET/LARGE-FAMILIES, but the least expensive way to stay will be offsite.

For groups that will fit into a four person standard Little Mermaid room at Disney's value resort Art of Animation, the chart below illustrates what it will cost two adults, one kid older than ten, and one aged from three to nine, to stay for various trip lengths during the Fall 2014 price season.

Designing to a Target Budget

Art of Animation Nights	1	2	3	4
Base Ticket Days	2	3	4	5
Hotel Cost	$ 155	$ 310	$ 442	$ 574
Dining Plan and other Basic Food	$ 375	$ 607	$ 839	$ 1,071
Park Tickets	$ 787	$ 1,147	$ 1,231	$ 1,274
Extras, Souvenirs, etc.	$ 200	$ 233	$ 311	$ 389
TOTAL--NO EXTRAS	$ 1,317	$ 2,064	$ 2,512	$ 2,919
TOTAL--WITH EXTRAS	$ 1,517	$ 2,297	$ 2,823	$ 3,308

Art of Animation Nights	5	6	7	8
Base Ticket Days	6	7	8	9
Hotel Cost	$ 706	$ 838	$ 970	$ 1,125
Dining Plan and other Basic Food	$ 1,304	$ 1,536	$ 1,768	$ 2,000
Park Tickets	$ 1,316	$ 1,359	$ 1,402	$ 1,444
Extras, Souvenirs, etc.	$ 467	$ 544	$ 622	$ 700
TOTAL--NO EXTRAS	$ 3,326	$ 3,733	$ 4,140	$ 4,569
TOTAL--WITH EXTRAS	$ 3,792	$ 4,277	$ 4,762	$ 5,269

Standard 4-person "Little Mermaid" rooms
Assumes Friday arrival, fall 2014 price season
Assumes family of 4 with one child younger than 10

Spending Even More at Walt Disney World

There's almost no limit to what could be spent on a first visit to Walt Disney World, with a fat enough wallet and sufficient desire to thin it. For example, how about a couple of newly-published authors as really expensive tour guides?

For a fuller list, see "The Comfortable Guide to Walt Disney World" on YOURFIRSTVISIT.NET/COMFORTABLE. But a shorter list of extra spending that may significantly increase comfort levels on a first visit includes the following:

- **RENTING A CAR** Disney's Magical Express (discussed in Chapter 9) will transport your group back and forth from the airport, but it requires that guests return to their resort for pickup no later than three hours before the flight is scheduled to leave. With a car, you can potentially leave for the airport directly from the theme park. On property, Disney's transportation system will get you from your Disney hotel to the parks, but a rental car reduces waits, increases flexibility, and offers a more comfortable, private ride. Transport to all the parks but the Magic Kingdom is faster by car than by Disney bus: it's the only simple way to get from most resort hotels—especially values and moderates—to another for dining, etc.; it's the only easy way to get to the non-Disney parks; and it makes shopping, off-site dining, and other activities much easier.

- **STAYING A FEW DAYS LONGER** Adding two or three days to a trip—and planning on relaxing those days—can make your vacation much more comfortable. A Disney World trip is like a backpacking expedition—lots of walking, lots of energy used, lots of early mornings. A few more days off can make a world of difference.

- **GETTING A MULTI-SPACE ROOM** Even the happiest families can tire of staying together in a single room. Several Disney lodging options—mostly at the expensive deluxe resorts—give you more space. Consider (in order of increasing prices) deluxe rooms at the Wilderness Lodge, one and two bedroom villas at the Disney Vacation Club resorts, and suites at all the deluxe resorts. Much lower priced—but still expensive—multi-room options are Family Suites at All-Star Music and at Art of Animation, and the Cabins at Fort Wilderness. Many—but not all—of these options include full kitchens as well.

None of these are inexpensive...but they might make a real difference to comfort!

Pricing out a Walt Disney World vacation is daunting. The good news is that once you've arrived, most everything is already taken care of and you can let loose and enjoy your trip. In fact, if you've added the Dining Plan, the only additional costs most guests encounter in Orlando is souvenirs (and there will be souvenirs), tips, and a few treats. With the ability to save a substantial amount of money on resort costs and a few dollars on tickets, it's easy to design around just about any budget.

How to Set Everything Up and Get Everything Done

There are three key dates to consider:

- Restaurant reservations open for booking 180 days before a potential dining date
- For those staying at a Disney-owned resort, FastPass+ reservations can be booked beginning 60 days before their arrival date
- For everyone else, FastPass+ reservations can be booked beginning 30 days before planned use

Building a To-Do List is keyed to these three dates because booking as early as possibly will result in the widest selection of experiences being available.

The first section of this chapter outlines how to sign up for and use Disney's new My Disney Experience mobile app and website. From there, we'll walk through customizing MagicBands and setting up FastPass+.

Tailored to-do lists are available for each of the sample itineraries available at YOURFIRSTVISIT.NET/ITINERARIES. For guests building custom itineraries, the second section of this chapter discusses putting together a to-do list to make sure everything is booked as easily and conveniently as possible.

My Disney Experience, FastPass+, and MagicBands

MY DISNEY EXPERIENCE

If you don't already have a My Disney Experience (MDE) account, sign up for one by visiting DISNEYWORLD.COM and clicking the "sign in or create account" button on the top right of the screen. An account is required to make dining and FastPass+ reservations, in addition to customizing MagicBands and keeping track of each component of your vacation online.

If you already have an account and booked a trip through the website while logged in, you should already see these reservations upon signing in. If not, link them manually by clicking "My Reservations and Tickets" under the My Disney Experience dropdown menu (located in the top right under the search box) and input the confirmation numbers and ticket IDs.

If people on the reservation are missing, click from the same MDE dropdown menu, "My Family and Friends". Once the new screen opens, click the little "Add a Guest" button at the upper right. Type the names of the missing people, and, if applicable, their ticket IDs. If you have trouble, try tech support—at (407) 939-5277—and have the ticket and reservation numbers of the missing elements at hand.

BOOKING FASTPASS+ AHEAD OF YOUR ARRIVAL

At press time, FastPass+ can be booked in advance by everyone with a valid "Magic Your Way" ticket or annual pass. Guests staying in Disney-owned resorts can begin booking FastPass+ 60 days before their arrival date. Guests staying elsewhere can book up to 30 days before planned use. FastPass+ strategy is covered in depth back in Chapter 6.

Booking FastPass+ as soon as eligible is advantageous because the most attractions and times will be available. Each FastPass+ experience has a limited number of slots. Fewer and fewer experiences will be available as a specific visit date approaches because more and more people have gone online and secured their choices.

Two notes related to timing and changes:

- Parades and firework shows may not to be offered for FastPass+ until much closer to the visit date. Typically, an entire month of availability opens a few days before a given month. For example, Festival of Fantasy might become available for August 1–31 on July 27, giving people visiting early in August just a few days lead time. Don't panic if a parade or night-time spectacular isn't available at the 30- or 60-day mark. Typically, when an experience is sold out, it will say "Standby Available". When an experience is not yet available for booking, it will simply not be listed.

- Tiering (more on this shortly) is currently in place at Epcot and Disney's Hollywood Studios, with the possibility that it might arrive at Animal Kingdom and Magic Kingdom in the future. If it does, previously booked FastPass+ experiences will not be canceled, but future changes to them may be limited.

Read Chapter 6, if you haven't already, and decide which FastPass+ experiences and times you'd like to book. Beginning at midnight exactly 60 days out, you can sign into your MDE account on DISNEYWORLD.COM and complete the following steps:

- From the My Disney Experience drop down, pick FastPass+.
- On the next screen, select the date you'd like to book.
- Not all members of the group are required to select the same FastPass+ experiences. Some groups with younger and older children may want to book two separate sets of FastPass+ experiences because the little ones want to ride Winnie the Pooh and Tomorrowland Speedway with Dad while the older kids prefer Space Mountain and Big Thunder Mountain with Mom. On the next screen, select the members of the party for whom you'd like to reserve the same experiences and times. This may be the entire group or just a few people. Simply repeat the FastPass+ booking process for each group if booking two or more separate groups.
- Then pick the park. One of two types of screens opens here, depending on whether or not the park is tiered. In the tiered parks, the FastPass+ rides are split into two groups. In the first group (Tier One) pick only one ride from among those offered, and in the second group (Tier Two), pick only two. At the non-tiered parks, pick any three experiences from the options listed.
- Then click Next ("Next" gets clicked a lot in this process) to be offered four different options, labeled A, B, C, and Best Match. Not all options may include all of your selections. Pick the one that includes all of your selections but ends earliest in the day. This is usually Option A, and it will make it easier to change times to the afternoon later because it reduces overlapping experiences. Save it.
- As we learned in Chapter 6, booking FastPass+ times in the afternoon or early evening is advantageous because lines and crowds will have peaked and FastPass+ will save us the most time. There's no reason to use most FastPass+ experiences in the early morning when standby waits are short. We originally selected morning times so we have the entire afternoon free to change the times without any worry that My Disney Experience will say that times are unavailable because we already have an experience booked in that slot. Unless it's your departure day or you have afternoon/evening plans elsewhere, we'll change the times so they're convenient later in the day. Click the box that says Make Changes on the confirmation screen. (If you're modifying selections at

a later date, click the My Disney Experience dropdown menu and choose My Itinerary and then Modify FastPass+.)

- Click the party members to make the change for, then click Change the Time, and move the FastPass+ around based on your desired timing. Because FastPass+ can't be double-booked at any time that overlaps, a couple of changes may have to be made to a single ride—first to move it out of the way of another FastPass+, then to move it back to a time newly vacated. You'll be offered the most desirable times if you initially book your experiences first thing in the morning or at the very end of the night.

- Then, if needed, move on to the rest of the party for that day. When done with the day, move on to the next day.

Times and experiences may be changed as often as wished (limited, though, to what is available at the time you change them), up through the last hour the theme park is open on the day you're visiting. If you run into problems, try tech support at (407) 939-5277.

MAGICBANDS

For those staying at a Disney-owned resort, MagicBands play many roles on a trip. Most importantly, they are room keys, park tickets, the link to using your Dining Plan credits, the link to FastPass+, and, if charging privileges are enabled, a means to charge back to the room.

They contain no personal data—rather, all they have encoded within them is a unique numeric identifier which Disney uses to link up databases in its own systems behind the scenes.

MagicBands are waterproof and hypoallergenic, and don't even need to be worn on a wrist—you can stick them in a pocket or purse and just wave them about when needed. Many need to take them off and wave them about anyway since not all the readers work perfectly when they are on a wrist, especially hotel room locks.

The color and names printed on the MagicBands can be customized online at DISNEYWORLD.COM after booking. Disney will email you when you can begin this customization. To do so, log in to your MDE account at DISNEYWORLD.COM and select MagicBands and Cards from the My Disney Experience dropdown menu we've visited several times thus far. First confirm the shipping address, then select MagicBands one by one for the people in your party. For each MagicBand, pick a color and customize the name, which is limited to nine characters including spaces. So "easyWDW" fits, but not "yourfirstvisit.net". Colors can be the same among your group, so long as the names are different. Well, names can be the same, too...but why would you do that? Haven't we already helped you cause enough confusion?

MagicBands will be shipped directly to the U.S. address of your choice if they're customized at least 10 days (at press time) before the arrival date. MagicBands customized closer to the check-in date will be available at check-in at the resort. Disney does not ship MagicBands internationally, which means all visitors without a U.S. address will pick up their MagicBands at check-in. If you fail to customize the MagicBands at all, grey MagicBands with or without the names listed on the reservation will be waiting at the resort at check-in.

Those not staying at a Disney-owned resort can purchase MagicBands on site, with current pricing at $12.95 each. The MagicBands of such visitors are linked at the time of purchase to a theme park ticket, and the MagicBand can then be used for FastPass+. Note that a MagicBand is not required to use FastPass+ (a ticket, of course, is required) and off-site guests can simply scan their ticket instead of a Band. There are no charging privileges for off-site guests, so you'll need to keep cash or a credit card handy.

Disney World To-Do List

Tailored To-Do lists are available for each of the itineraries located at YOURFIRSTVISIT.NET/ITINERARIES. For more general guidelines, see below:

A. *More Than 181 Days Before Your Planned Arrival Date*

1. Double-check budget (Chapter 8), dates (Chapter 4), intended hotel (Chapter 5), intended dates in each park (Chapter 6), intended dining venues (Chapter 7), and transportation choices and their availability for the planned dates.

2. Make transportation arrangements as necessary, including any flight or rental car reservations.

3. Create your My Disney Experience account and add your group members to it.

4. If staying at a Disney-owned hotel, book your hotel and purchase your tickets. Call 407-939-7675 to book by phone (optimal, because this allows you to tell the reservationist which area at a resort you want to be in, if you have a preference) or go to DISNEYWORLD.COM/PLAN to use Disney's online system. At the same time, you'll have the opportunity to sign up for

Disney's Magical Express service that transports Disney-owned hotel guests from Orlando International (but not Sanford) Airport directly to their hotel. Don't worry if you don't have your flight details set. You can come back to this page later or call 866-599-0951 to set it up. Disney hotel reservations can be made over the phone up to 500 days before an arrival date. Online, the system may only show reservations available through the end of the calendar year, particularly if you try to book for the next year more than six months in advance. Call Disney reservations at 407-939-7675 if your dates aren't available online but you are within 500 days of your arrival date.

5. If not staying at a Disney resort, buy your tickets from within your My Disney Experience account—this increases the chance that they will be properly linked. Alternatively, purchase tickets from an authorized reseller and link them manually.

B. *Exactly 6am EST, Exactly 180 Days Before Arrival Date*

Log on to DisneyWorld.com/dining by at least 5:50am EST, and have your highest priority reservation all set up on the page. Keep refreshing, as you will be let in as soon as Disney's system decides it is 6am. Make as many of the following hardest-to-get reservations that are on your itinerary, in the order listed:

- Be Our Guest Restaurant [Magic Kingdom]
- Cinderella's Royal Table [Magic Kingdom]
- Chef Mickey's [Contemporary Resort]
- 'Ohana [Polynesian Resort]
- Akershus Royal Banquet Hall [Epcot]
- 1900 Park Fare Dinner [Grand Floridian Resort]
- California Grill [Contemporary Resort]
- Crystal Palace [Magic Kingdom]
- T-Rex [Downtown Disney]
- Hoop-Dee-Doo Revue [Fort Wilderness Campground and Resort]

For other restaurants, booking at 6am 180+ days in advance isn't necessary, but doing so will guarantee a desired day and time.

If you have trouble online, call (407) WDW-DINE (939-3463) to book reservations offline, beginning at 7am EST on the same date.

C. 60 Days Before Arrival Date (If Staying at Disney-Owned Resort)

1. Beginning (if you choose) at midnight, go to your My Disney Experience account and set up your FastPass+ selections

2. Do online resort check in, requesting any special location or amenity preferences

3. Customize MagicBands

D. 30 Days Before First Park Visit (If Not Staying at Disney-Owned Resort)

Beginning (if you choose) at midnight, go to your My Disney Experience account and set up your FastPass+.

E. Notes on Packing, Etc., Before You Leave

1. If you have them, bring your MagicBands in your carry-ons or wear them on your wrists.

2. If you use Disney's Magical Express, you do not need to collect your bags at the Orlando airport unless you choose to, arrive late in the evening/at night (between 10 pm and 5 am), or are an international traveler. Disney will obtain them for you (without the bags ever going to baggage claim) and deliver them directly to your room. Your bags will likely arrive at your hotel hours after you do. Plan to pack an appropriate change of clothes for Orlando weather, medications, etc., in a carry-on. Follow the instructions in the Magical Express packet you will receive in the mail regarding both tagging your bags pre-departure and where to go at the Orlando airport to find the bus to your resort. Magical Express check-in is located on the B side of Level 1. If you arrive on the A side or pick up your luggage yourself on the A side, you will need to walk over to the B side. Note that this is only possible on Level 3. There is no way to walk from the A side to the B side on any other level.

3. Bring copies/printouts of your room reservation, confirmation numbers, and any tickets for special events you may have received in the mail.

4. When you arrive at the hotel, if you used Online Check-in, look for the special Online Check-in line, and get into it.

We're almost there! Setting up dining and FastPass+ reservations can be stressful and frustrating, but you're armed with the best possible strategy. Once the reservations are booked, there's little to worry about.

Where to Go Next

Congratulations! You either skipped to the end of the book to find out if the princess really does end up with the prince, or have now read so much great Disney World information that there's really no need to actually go on the vacation. And this book isn't even billed as a money saver. Oh, you still want to go, and you want to be kept up to date on any changes? We weren't expecting that, but we might still be able to help.

First of all, bookmark YOURFIRSTVISIT.NET/EASY-GUIDE-2014-CHANGES and EASYWDW.COM/EASY-GUIDE for anything in the book that's changed since the publication date. As FastPass+ continues its rollout, there are bound to be some details that change in the coming months – not to mention potential price increases, character switch-eroos, and whatnot. The latest scoop will always be at those links.

From there, easyWDW.com is your best chance to see what's going on inside the theme parks as it happens. With weekly visits, thousands of pictures, up-to-date info on operating schedule changes, crowd calendars, and ideal touring strategies, there's no other website in the world like it. If you'd like to join other WDW fans and have an opportunity to ask Josh questions about your trip directly, sign up for the forums at WWW.EASYWDW.COM/FORUMS.

Pay close attention to yourfirstvisit.net for new material aimed squarely at first-timers who both may never return and also don't necessarily want to spend a lot of time planning. Advice there for such visitors is very specific, but always comes with next best options ranked in order for those who can't, or won't, follow Dave's specific advice. The site is particularly helpful for choosing among hotels. Read it, and EASYWDW.COM, too, and your life will be fulfilled.

We sincerely hope this book helped you plan a special trip full of the best that Walt Disney World offers. Get out there and put everything you learned into action. And after you've left Disney World and come back home—leave us comments at YOURFIRSTVISIT.NET/EASY-GUIDE-2014-CHANGES and EASYWDW.COM/EASY-GUIDE to let us know how it went!

Acknowledgments

Dave would like to thank those who helped with this book and the years of work that led up to it:

- This book would not have been possible without the encouragement and skills of Bob McLain and Theme Park Press.
- And it wouldn't have been too good without my co-author Josh Humphrey. The best Disney World thinker of his generation, Josh has made this book more than twice as good as it would have been without him, thanks to his capability and stubbornness.
- Gratitude to my family—Amy, Ted, and Alex—who once again let a Walt Disney World project divert my time and attention.
- Many thanks to a list of people whose support over the years made the work that led to this book possible: Steve Bell, Joe Black, Tom Bricker, Lee Cockerell, Mary Conor DeFazio, Beth Pickel Doda, Faith Dority, Mike Ellis, Kristen Hoetzel-Go, Jackie Hutnik, Allison Jones, Linda Stevens Jones, Kathleen Kelly, Karen Landry, Kuleen Lashly, Sarah Harvey Mitchell, Julie Neal, Steve Seifert, Len Testa, Carl Trent, and Jodi Whisenhunt.
- Last, but not least, thanks to the readers of YOURFIRSTVISIT.NET—coming up on ten million of them—you all inspire me every day.

Josh would like to thank:

- My mom and dad for smiling as their (favorite) son crossed the country to try and chase down yet another dream.
- The lovely Miss Lisa Taylor for her love and generosity through all of this nonsense. And for taking me where I need to go.
- Dave Shute for bringing me this posh book deal, in addition to providing the foundation and structure for everything in it.
- Everyone that's ever recommended easyWDW to a friend, colleague, family member, or fellow DISboards member. Your continued support is what drives everything I do. Thank you.

About the Authors

Dave by day is a strategist and problem solver for clients ranging from the Fortune 500 to local not-for-profits. At night and on weekends he writes yourfirstvisit.net, and, lately, Disney World guidebooks. All the time he's a husband, dad, son, and brother. He has a BA from the University of Chicago, and both an MA in English Literature and MBA from the University of Virginia, where he also completed the majority of work for a PhD in English Literature. He spent almost a decade as a strategy consultant at McKinsey & Co., Inc., and since then has largely operated as an independent strategy consultant. He founded yourfirstvisit.net more than six years ago—the first Disney World site aimed squarely at first-time visitors who may never return. He visits Disney World eight times a year, and later in 2014 he will stay in his hundredth different Disney World hotel room.

Josh grew up in Seattle, Washington, the only known city to adequately prepare a person for Orlando's wet summers. He was fascinated by Disney theme parks long before his first visit to Disneyland at age eight. He started easyWDW.com in the spring of 2010 as an outlet to help visitors maximize their theme park experience with practical, hands-on advice. He lives just 15 minutes from Magic Kingdom's gates and records more than a hundred theme park visits every year, each with the express intent of uncovering ways to better enjoy everything the parks offer. In his spare time, he enjoys dressing his Duffy the Disney Bear in fabulous outfits, taking his dog to the park, and the occasional single malt scotch.

About the Publisher

Theme Park Press is the largest independent publisher of Disney and Disney-related pop culture books in the world.

Established in November 2012 by Bob McLain, Theme Park Press has released best-selling print and digital books about such topics as Disney films and animation, the Disney theme parks, Disney historical and cultural studies, park touring guides, autobiographies, fiction, and more.

For more information, and a list of forthcoming titles, please visit:

ThemeParkPress.com

More Books from Theme Park Press

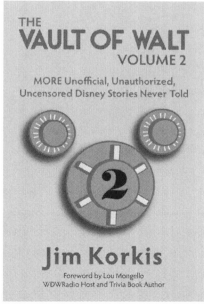

To see all our books, visit ThemeParkPress.com